# HIMALAYAN BATTLEGROUND

*Sino-Indian Rivalry in Ladakh*

# *HIMALAYAN BATTLEGROUND*

Sino–Indian Rivalry in Ladakh

*by*

Margaret W. Fisher

Leo E. Rose

*and*

Robert A. Huttenback



FREDERICK A. PRAEGER, *Publisher*

New York · London

FREDERICK A. PRAEGER, PUBLISHER
64 UNIVERSITY PLACE, NEW YORK 3, N.Y., U.S.A.
49 GREAT ORMOND STREET, LONDON W.C.1, ENGLAND

Published in the United States of America in 1963 by
Frederick A. Praeger, Inc., Publisher


Library of Congress Catalog Card Number: 63-11121

Printed in the United States of America

# PREFACE

The outbreak of hostilities in the fall of 1962 at the eastern and western extremities of the far-flung Sino-Indian border was an event of outstanding significance, the widespread ramifications of which—one can safely assume—have not yet reached an end. The potential threat to world peace arising from this conflict could ultimately involve the vital interests of both Western alliances and the Communist bloc. The bloc has itself been severely strained by these developments, and certain areas of opposition between Chinese and Russian interests have been thrown into sharp relief. The long unacknowledged competition between India and China for leadership of the Afro-Asian world has been dramatically forced into the open.

Certain tensions between China and India, growing out of their diametrically opposed foreign policy aims, were indeed always discernible, but only in recent years have these differences been taken as irreconcilable. India has achieved considerable success in her efforts to reduce world tensions by reversing the trend toward polarization of nations between the Communist bloc and the West—by increasing the area of "nonalignment." The Chinese Communists, who early took the position of "leaning to one side" and scoffed at "nonalignment" as fraudulent, have appeared increasingly bent on creating and exacerbating world tensions and on sharpening the polarization process. And "leaning to one side" has not brought China the rewards, even from the Soviet Union, that "nonalignment" has brought India. Furthermore, Chinese internal failures have been in recent years rather more conspicuous than the vaunted successes supposedly obtained during its "great leap forward." China's boasts began to have a hollow ring in Asia just at the time when Indian progress gained world-wide commendation. The Chinese attacks on India may have had as one purpose to impede further Indian progress by forcing the diversion of significant Indian resources to defense. However, among the various reasons that impelled the Chinese to strike out at India, there must surely be numbered a severely wounded pride for which, furthermore, no balm has been offered within the Communist bloc.

Despite the long-range importance of these Himalayan developments, the background to the Sino-Indian conflict has received insufficient attention in the world press and scholarly journals alike. Confusion is widespread concerning the border terrain itself, as well as the nature of the issues involved. A Western observer tends to find combat over possession of these admittedly remote and bleak areas somewhat incomprehensible.

In this study, we intend to explore the history of the key Ladakh area, emphasizing the strategic factors that have caused this region to be fought over since the dawn of history. In Chapters X and XI, we shall give extended attention to conflicting Indian and Chinese claims and counterclaims, in part to clarify the points at issue in a complex and confusing dispute, and in part to show in some detail how the Chinese Communists approach negotiation and what tactics they employ. In Ladakh, for example, after seizing a corridor between Tibet and Sinkiang by stealth, they have since attempted to gain a "negotiated" Indian surrender of further strategic territory. Indeed, they have tried to force India into a position that denies her any effective use of the Himalayan bastion in her own defense. To that end, the Chinese have employed a dual strategy directed on one level against India, but designed so as to operate on another level to confuse or deceive the rest of the world. For this purpose, they have made clever tactical use of deceptive propaganda of various kinds, including spurious documentation and the frequent reiteration of allegations that had already been refuted beyond any attempt at rebuttal.

Our major effort has been to place this entire conflict in broad perspective, and to explore and illuminate complex interregional relationships, focusing on the Ladakh area, which—whatever the future may hold—is initially the area of greatest importance in a conflict of yet unknown dimensions.

The sources that we used include—in addition to documents published by Great Britain, China, and India—the relevant archival material in the India Office Library, London, and in the National Archives of India, New Delhi.

For the early history of Ladakh, the main source is the Ladakhi chronicles. These manuscripts have been thoroughly studied and made available in English translation. The attempts made by Chinese representatives during the 1960 border talks to disparage these chronicles as utterly worthless were unwarranted. Study of these chronicles was begun by Tibetanists of German origin in the nineteenth century and later carried on by an eminent Italian scholar. These studies were undertaken long before any dispute arose as to the borders of Ladakh, and the scholars in question—A. H. Francke, Karl Marx, and Luciano Petech—were animated solely by a desire to achieve as accurate an understanding as possible of the early history of Ladakh.

The documentary material in Chinese we examined includes a rare, privately printed book (*Hsi-Tsang Tsou-shu* [*Tibetan Memorials and Reports*]) to which we should like to call special attention. This book is a compilation by Meng Pao, Imperial Resident at Lhasa from 1839 to 1844, of the documents that either originated with him or passed through his hands during his tenure. He arranged these state papers in six volumes according to their subject matter, and they were privately printed in Peking, presumably in 1851 or soon thereafter. Because of the destruction by fire in 1850 of all the archives of the Board of Colonial Affairs at Peking, this collection is the only known source for certain state papers dealing with Tibet, Nepal, Ladakh, etc., from 1839 to 1844. Volume I deals with the Dogra-Tibetan War of 1841–42, and has never, so far as we know, been utilized before in English. Because of the rarity and importance of these documents, English translations of the more important reports and memorials concerning the Dogra War are given in the Appendix.

These documents are interesting in several ways. For one thing, they refute Chou En-lai's contention that the Central Government of China knew nothing of what was going on during 1841–42.* For the Emperor not only received and commented on reports from the front, but was so pleased with them that he distributed decorations to those concerned with a lavish hand. The documents are also of interest because they show some of the steps in the process by which official Chinese historians—by skillful omission and juxtaposition, leading the reader to make incorrect inferences without being aware that he has done so—have reinterpreted history to China's advantage. Techniques of this sort were undoubtedly essential to survival under the Empire, when unpleasant truths had to be kept from the Emperor at all costs. The end results of this process have often been noted, but the opportunity to observe steps in the process is less frequently available.

It is a pleasure to make the following acknowledgments:

To the Ford Foundation, from whose generosity all three of the authors greatly benefited.

To the Institute of International Studies, University of California,

* "Letter [of Chou En-lai] of September 8, 1959," in *Notes . . . Exchanged Between the Governments of India and China* ([Government of India] Ministry of External Affairs, White Paper No. II [New Delhi: 1959], p. 28).

Berkeley, under whose ultimate sponsorship the program of research that resulted in this volume was conducted.

To the Center for South Asia Studies, of the Institute of International Studies, with which all three authors have been associated.

To all the members of the staff of the India Office Library and of the National Archives of India, and especially to Mr. V. C. Joshi, Associate Director of the National Archives of India, whose assistance greatly facilitated the task of the authors.

To Mr. Hugh E. Richardson, the well-known British expert on Tibet and Tibetan history, for his kindness in reading an early draft of the manuscript and making many valuable suggestions.

To Professor Turrell V. Wylie, Professor of Tibetan Language and Civilization, University of Washington, for guidance in the standardization of Tibetan and Ladakhi names.

To the Indian Press Digests Project Research Assistants who participated in this study—Leonard Rubin, Bernard Freiwald, and Russell W. Volckmann.

To our cartographer, Alan S. Fisher.

To Mrs. Corinne D. Bennett, whose help in the preparation of the manuscript was invaluable, going far beyond the routine aspects of such a task.

And, finally, to all the many friends and associates whose contributions are difficult to enumerate or acknowledge here, but whose interest played an important role in sustaining the authors throughout the work on this study.

MARGARET W. FISHER
LEO E. ROSE
ROBERT A. HUTTENBACK

*Institute of International Studies*
*Berkeley, California*
*December 20, 1962*

# CONTENTS

# *MAPS*

# HIMALAYAN BATTLEGROUND

*Sino-Indian Rivalry in Ladakh*

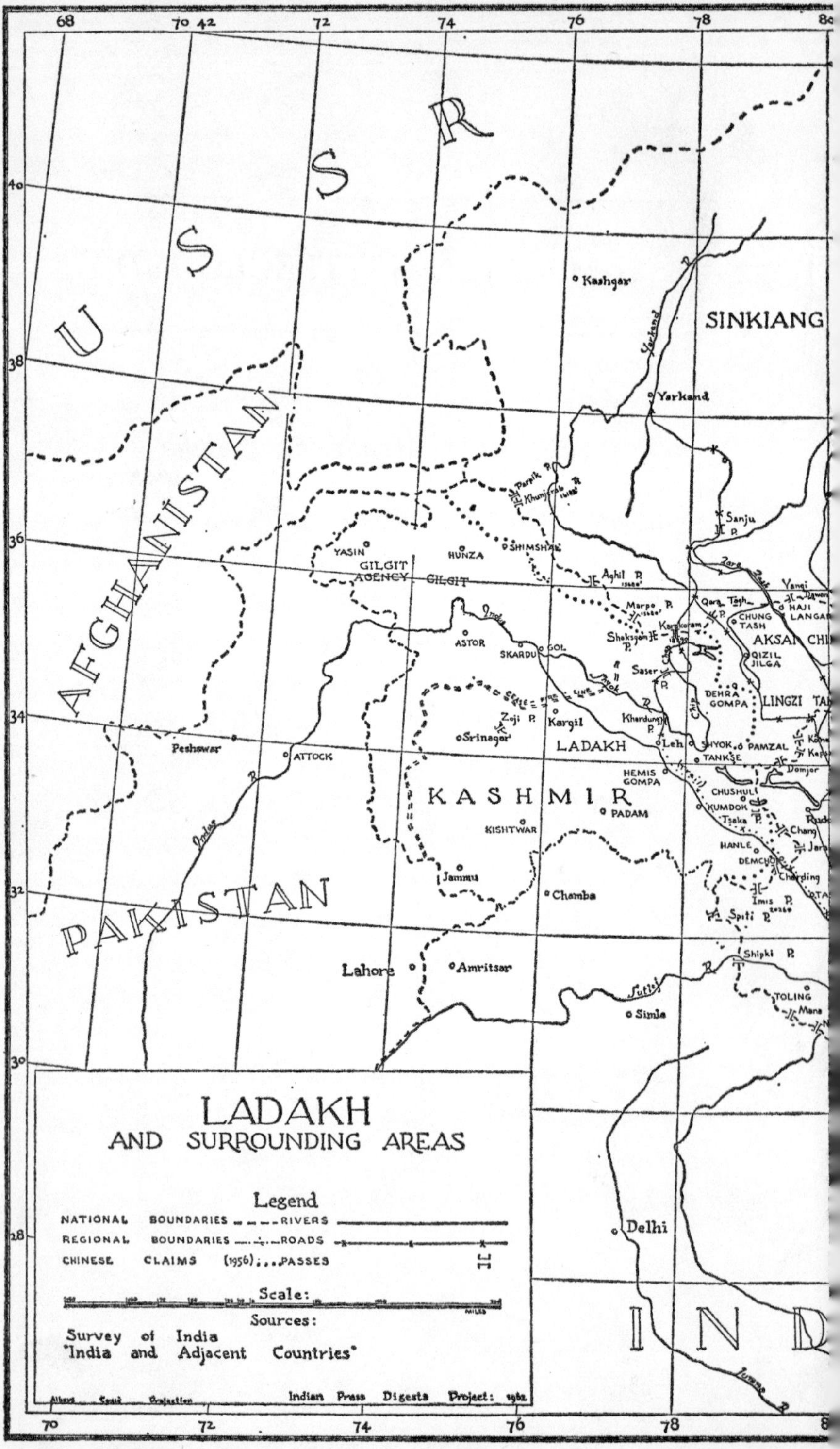
LADAKH
AND SURROUNDING AREAS
Legend
NATIONAL BOUNDARIES
RIVERS
REGIONAL BOUNDARIES
ROADS
CHINESE CLAIMS (1956)
PASSES
Scale:
MILES
Sources:
Survey of India
"India and Adjacent Countries"
Albers Equal Projection
Indian Press Digests Project: 1962
U S S R
AFGHANISTAN
PAKISTAN
SINKIANG
AKSAI CHI
LINGZI TA
KASHMIR
LADAKH
IND
Kashgar
Yarkand
Sanju P.
Parpik P.
Khunjerab P.
YASIN
GILGIT AGENCY
GILGIT
HUNZA
SHIMSHAL
Aghil P.
Marpo P.
Karakoram
Saser P.
Sheksgam P.
Qara Tagh
CHUNG TASH
HAJI LANGAR
Yangi
QIZIL JILGA
DEHRA GOMPA
ASTOR
SKARDU
GOL
Indus
Shyok
Chip Chap
Kargil
Zoji P.
Srinagar
Khardung P.
Leh
SHYOK
PAMZAL
TANKSE
HEMIS GOMPA
CHUSHUL
KUMDOK
Tsaka P.
Chang
HANLE
DEMCHOK
Charding
Imis P.
Spiti P.
Shipki P.
TOLING
Mana
Peshawar
ATTOCK
Indus R.
PADAM
KISHTWAR
Jammu
Chamba
Lahore
Amritsar
Sutlej
Simla
Delhi
Jumna R.

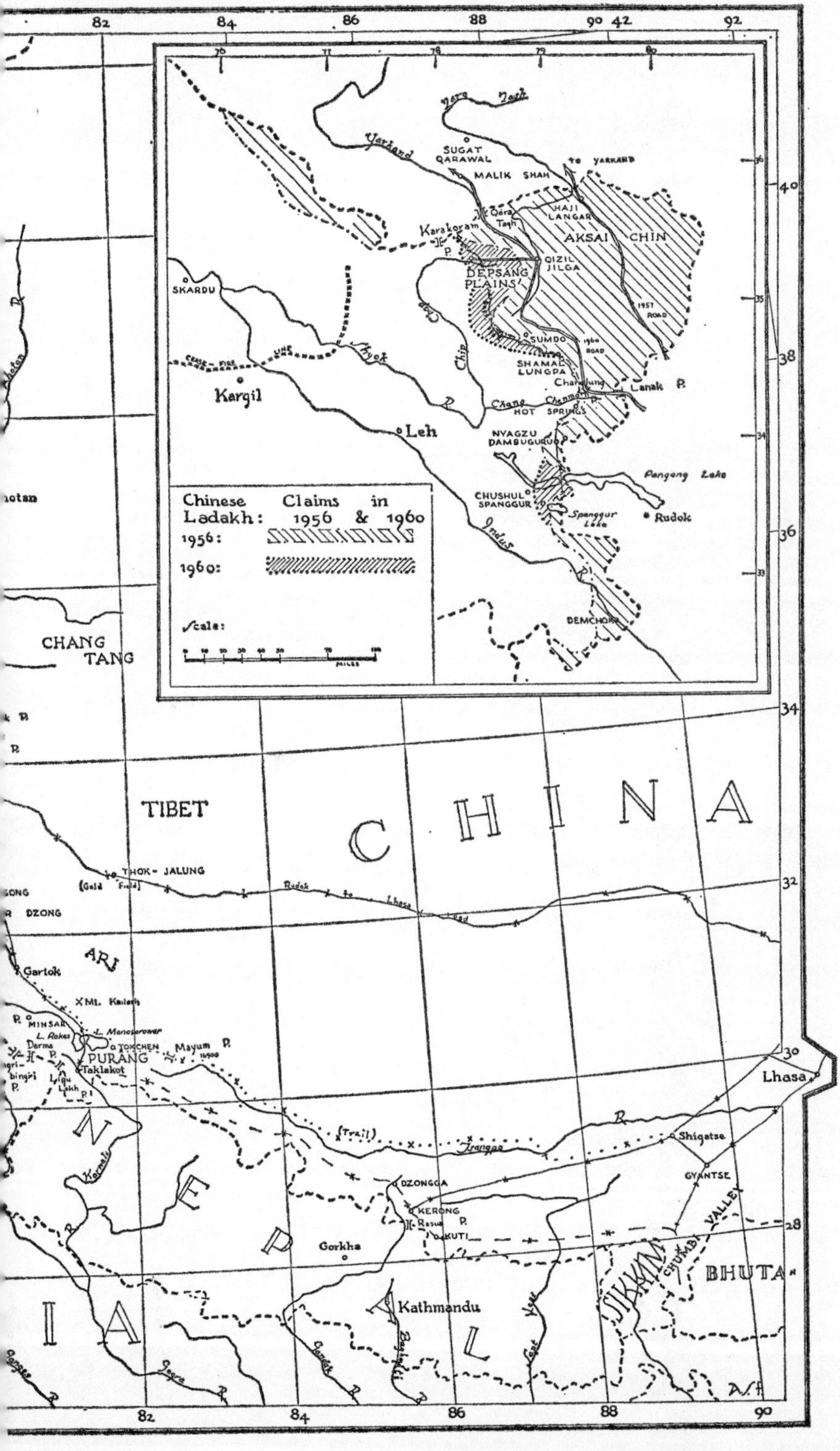

Chinese Claims in Ladakh: 1956 & 1960
1956:
1960:
Scale:
MILES
Yarkand
SUGAT QARAWAL
TO YARKAND
MALIK SHAH
HAJI LANGAR
AKSAI CHIN
Qara Tagh
Karakoram P.
QIZIL JILGA
DEPSANG PLAINS
SKARDU
CEASE-FIRE LINE
Shyok
Chip Chap
1957 ROAD
SUMDO
1960 ROAD
SHAMAL LUNGPA
Lanak P.
Kargil
Chang Chenmo
HOT SPRINGS
Leh
NYAGZU
DAMBUGURU
Pangong Lake
CHUSHUL
SPANGGUR
Spanggur Lake
Rudok
Indus
DEMCHOK
CHANG TANG
TIBET
CHINA
THOK-JALUNG
(Gold Field)
Rudok to Lhasa Road
DZONG
ARI
Gartok
Mt. Kailas
MINSAR
L. Rakas
L. Manasarowar
TOKCHEN
Mayum P.
PURANG
Taklakot
NEPAL
INDIA
Karnali
(Trail)
Tsangpo
DZONGGA
KERONG
Rasua P.
KUTI
Gorkha
Kathmandu
Lhasa
Shigatse
GYANTSE
CHUMBI VALLEY
SIKKIM
BHUTAN

# I

## *THE SETTING*

Prior to the Tibetan uprising against their Chinese Communist overlords, Ladakh received only infrequent mention in the world press. Indeed, it is unlikely that many persons in the Western world could then have located Ladakh with any precision, or even, perhaps, have stated with any confidence the nationality of the Ladakhis. Certainly very few would have credited a prediction that armed clashes and the threat of full-scale war between India and China would arise over possession of the high alkaline plain known as the Aksai Chin ("white stone" desert) where the frontiers of Tibet, Sinkiang, and Ladakh march together. The Aksai Chin is beyond doubt among the world's bleakest stretches, a land where—as Nehru put it—no people live and no blade of grass grows. Yet the armed clashes have taken place, and there is no certainty that the conflict can be resolved through negotiation.

As threats of war are replaced by the grim realities of armed combat, questions continue to be raised as to the true nature of the dispute. Is it—as it sometimes appears—largely a matter of touchy national honor in which neither side can withdraw from a strong public stand without serious loss of face? Are the issues themselves as narrow and legalistic as most of the arguments so heatedly hurled back and forth between the hostile governments? The answer to both questions can only be: assuredly not. National honor and the minutiae of legal interpretation have their roles in this dispute, but basically the issues hinge on considerations affecting national security and the broad economic and political interests of India and China, and also involving long-term interests of neighboring states, among them the Soviet Union. The answers are to be found in the strategic realities and potentialities of Central Asian topography on the one hand, and its mineral resources on the other. (Prominent among the latter are the known oil resources of Sinkiang and the gold and uranium deposits in western Tibet.)

Central Asia has a long history as the center of chronic turbulence from which violent explosions have periodically erupted and spread disaster—either directly or by chain reaction—over enormous distances. Over the centuries, China was the principal sufferer, but northern India, despite the Himalayan wall, did not entirely escape. That cities as far removed as Rome and Moscow also felt the sting of conquest has never been forgotten. During the last few centuries, however, the process was for the most part reversed. Pressure from the more developed civilizations succeeded in diminishing the area and scope of this former reservoir of turbulence. Three expanding empires—Chinese, Indian, and Russian—drew ever closer together as they gradually subdued the turbulence on their respective frontiers through conquest, subsidy, or intimidation. By common consent, however, autonomous territories were left—until recently—to act as buffers between the major powers, to reduce mutual fears, and to minimize the danger of accidental embroilment over frontier incidents.

Today, China, Russia, and India confront one another in Central Asia under greatly changed circumstances. That these three ancient empires have, in the last half century, acquired characteristics vastly different from their predecessors is a matter that preoccupies many of the world's chancelleries and need not be labored here. Certain consequences of these changes, however, may well be stressed.

One has been the near elimination of the old buffer system. With the tightening of China's control over Sinkiang and its conquest of Tibet, only Mongolia—bolstered now with U.N. membership—intervenes in the vast stretches between Communist China and the Soviet Union. In the Himalaya, only Nepal—also a U.N. member—and the semi-independent states of Bhutan and Sikkim cut into the long and impressive frontier between China and India. Chinese activity in Tibet put pressure on these Himalayan states which, in various subtle ways, verged on intimidation. In their efforts to absorb Tibet, the Chinese Communists followed policies that transformed a peaceful, harmless, neighboring country into a fresh area of turbulence. In attempting to crush the Tibetan revolt while at the same time denying its existence, the Chinese used methods that brought China and India into sharp conflict. Mutual fears and tensions were exacerbated, and the threat that border incidents might provoke open warfare was dangerously increased.

The question of Peking's ultimate designs must remain as yet in the realm of controversy. Perhaps the Chinese are primarily engaged in pursuing opportunistic policies intended to reap all possible advantages short of war. It is at least equally plausible, however, that they are carefully laying the groundwork for a more sinister long-range plan, and that their current activities in Ladakh and elsewhere are designed to advance a number of objectives simultaneously. Whatever may yet unfold, one conclusion can be drawn with relative certainty. The road that the Chinese first "built" * in 1956–57 across Ladakh was important to the maintenance of their control over Tibet. Without such a supply route, the officially unacknowledged Khampa revolt in eastern Tibet might have reached dangerous proportions.

What were the topographical problems faced by Peking in 1956? Access to Tibet is easiest from the south and west. The direct routes from China proper run through exceptionally difficult terrain where ambushes can be easily prepared. In the homeland of the sturdy Khampas, banditry was endemic and guerrilla bands can even now find virtually ideal conditions. To quell a revolt in Kham by moving into Tibet directly from the east would have been a major task attended by political as well as military risks, since all Tibet would have risen against such a move. The Chinese chose to deny all rumors of trouble in Kham and find another way to supply their garrisons in Tibet. The relatively easy southern routes would not do, for they run through Bhutan, Sikkim, Nepal, and India, and are not only some distance from China but also subject to customs control posts, where inconvenient questions would be raised. The major trade route from the northwest, passing through Leh, not only is subject to Indian customs control, but is reached from Sinkiang over the difficult Karakoram Pass, which can be relied on for only a few months of the year. But the almost forgotten bypass route through the Aksai Chin—long abandoned by traders and other travelers because of the dreaded summer heat and absence of water—is a serviceable winter route, as two invasions occurring in the early winter months have demonstrated—one in the early eighteenth century by the Dsungars when they took Lhasa from the rear, and the other in 1950 by the Chinese Communists themselves. The Chinese quietly set about improving this route, and it soon gained the status of a major road, connecting Yarkand and Khotan with Rudok, Gartok, and finally Taklakot, a trade and agri-

* As Nehru pointed out to the Indian Parliament on August 31, 1959, roads in these areas "are of a peculiar type. The only thing you have to do to build a road is to even the ground a little and remove the stones and shrubs." (Jawaharlal Nehru, *India's Foreign Policy, Selected Speeches, September, 1946–April, 1961* [Delhi: (Government of India) Ministry of Information and Broadcasting, Publications Divisions, 1961], p. 333.)

cultural center of long recognized strategic interest just north of the point where the borders of Tibet, Nepal, and India meet.*

It is instructive to note in passing that the old east-west "grand route" between the Kashmir valley and Lhasa, a caravan route that also served to link the trading centers of the Indus valley with the settlements along the Tsangpo (or Brahmaputra) River, was soon relegated to minor importance, as evidenced by Chinese maps showing it as no more than a "minor road or trail."† That new major east-west roads have avoided the normal route along the Tsangpo is highly suggestive. It would appear from the maps that Chinese road building in Tibet has been designed primarily for military purposes and secondarily for the exploitation of the gold and uranium deposits in western Tibet.

With regard to the problem facing the Chinese during 1956–57, it seems clear that the Aksai Chin route was essential to Chinese plans for the exploitation of a sullen Tibet. Indeed, in the event of any serious weakening of the Peking Government, this area might well prove to be the key to the Chinese hold on Tibet.

What does Chinese possession of this area mean to India? Quite apart from the loss of territory, and the proof that China's intentions are actively hostile, the same factors that make the area strategic for China could not but affect Indian security adversely. It has been asked how the Chinese could complete a road across Indian territory without the knowledge of the Indian Government. A number of factors combined to make this possible: The work involved in improving the route was minimal; and the choking off of trade between Sinkiang and Ladakh removed the possibility that Indian traders might readily observe the development of new traffic patterns beyond the Karakoram Pass. If a permanent Indian trade agency had been at Gartok (in West Tibet)—as provided by the 1954 Sino-Indian treaty—news of this road would undoubtedly have reached India earlier, but the Chinese, using one pretext after another, had contrived to reduce the agency's period of operations to a few weeks in the year.

It was not that the unexpectedly comprehensive character of the

* Later, a second route through the Aksai Chin was made, slicing off considerably more territory. Furthermore, the Chinese have stated their intention to extend their railroad along this same route from Khotan to Taklakot.

† This designation is shown on Plate 3, "China, Railroads and Selected Roads, May, 1959," [United States] Central Intelligence Agency, *China: Provisional Atlas of Communist Administrative Units* (Washington: [U.S.] Department of Commerce, Office of Technical Services, 1959). This famous old caravan route started from Srinagar, led over the Zoji Pass to Leh and thence to the sacred lakes area, the Tsangpo valley, Shigatse, and Lhasa. From the Tibetan capital, several routes branched off to Peking and other Chinese cities.

Chinese occupation of Tibet had failed to arouse Indian apprehensions. Prudence had dictated reticence while New Delhi strove to salvage as much as possible of the former Indian position in Tibet, but it is clear that the Government of India was from the first aware that a "dead" frontier had suddenly become very much alive. Nevertheless, a compromise was necessary in the allocation of India's sparse resources between the demands of frontier defenses and India's no less complex and conceivably much more pressing developmental problems. The decision was to place major emphasis on economic development, to cultivate amicable relations with Peking, and to move quietly to strengthen the more strategic areas of the border. This assessment in 1950–51 of India's most pressing defense needs missed the significance of the relatively unpublicized Chinese entry into West Tibet, and focused on the better understood problems of the northeastern frontier area, the strategic importance of which had been highlighted during World War II. Moreover, it was in respect to the boundaries of the latter that the major discrepancies appeared between published Chinese and Indian maps. Some attention was also given to the middle section of the Himalayan border—i.e., that portion west of Nepal and east of Ladakh where important passes between India and the sacred lakes region of West Tibet had been traveled over in the past by traders and pilgrims.

The vital importance of Kashmir to the defense of India had long been recognized, but in 1950 and for several years thereafter, it was Kashmir's border with Pakistan that received the most attention. The barren wastes fronting on Sinkiang—rarely visited once the caravan trade ceased—might well have been considered just that portion of the long Indian frontier for which natural defenses were most adequate, and such an assessment would have been corroborated by earlier British experience. For intensive exploration in the nineteenth century had convinced the British rulers of India that the Karakoram Pass was far too difficult to permit passage of an armed force of dangerous proportions, but that no better route between Chinese Turkestan (Sinkiang) and Ladakh existed. Leh, situated on the upper Indus where this north-south route crossed the major east-west Central Asian trade route, grew in importance, both as a trade center and listening post.

Leh, however, had been bypassed before and was to be bypassed again. If the lessons of earlier Ladakhi history had been well and truly learned, the Government of India might have kept a closer watch on the Aksai Chin. But it was not immediately understood in New Delhi that the reasoning that relegated Ladakh to a position of lesser strategic importance had been based in part on technological considerations that had radically changed. If the Tibetans had been in control of their homeland, these considerations could have safely been ignored, but a unified and dynamic China controlled Sinkiang and Tibet, and modern technological developments made it possible to use the arid wastes of northeastern Ladakh to link together into an all-weather communications system routes that previously could be traversed only seasonally, and even then with difficulty. From earlier Central Asian history, the following conclusions can be drawn: West Tibet* and Ladakh together form a natural geographic unit reaching from the Mayum Pass to the Zoji Pass; this area—if joined together under the control of an aggressive power based south of the Himalaya—could, under conditions of conventional warfare, provide a vital and perhaps decisive key to Central Asia. Under present conditions, with Sinkiang and all of Tibet in Chinese possession, the addition of the Aksai Chin area of Ladakh could outflank Leh and offer strategic possibilities that—to put it at its mildest—no Government of India could conceivably ignore.

A study of Ladakh's history during a millennium and a half demonstrates that the present struggle over this desolate area is part of an old, established pattern. Indeed, the similarity between current developments and those of centuries past is strikingly evident—further proof that strategic considerations, including those dictated by topography, have long dominated politics in this area. For these reasons, an analysis of the role Ladakh has played in Central Asian, Indian, and Chinese affairs will follow, in order to place the present dispute in its proper historical perspective.

* West Tibet (Mnga-ris in Tibetan) is often referred to as Ari, Nari, or Ngari in English, and as Ari and Ali in official Chinese documents written in English.

# II

## *LADAKH'S ROLE IN CENTRAL ASIA:* A.D. *600–900*

The early history of Ladakh is shrouded in mystery. The myths and legends with which the Ladakhi chronicles commence bear a distinct resemblance to those of both Central Asia and India, leading one to suspect that they may be in large part examples of borrowed history. Not until the establishment in the first half of the tenth century of a Ladakhi dynasty of Tibetan origin can we consider that these chronicles are dealing with historical events, and such accounts as we do have of the dynasty's almost 600-year rule are by and large sparse and uncommunicative. The chronicles expand in scope and content only with the rise of the Namgyal (Rnam-rgyal) dynasty in the latter half of the fifteenth century.

Nevertheless, a careful reading of the earlier chronicles, taken together with the brief and tantalizingly obscure references to Ladakh found in Tibetan, Mongolian, Chinese, and Kashmiri sources, yields at least an outline of major developments in Ladakh and the surrounding territories. On this basis—tentative though it must remain—it is possible to speculate on the role of Ladakh in the complex system of power politics from the seventh to the tenth centuries. We shall accordingly venture to carry our analysis of the main trends affecting Ladakhi history back to this remote period.

In Central Asia, China, and for a time in India also, the seventh century witnessed the culmination of integrative drives, begun in the previous century, to weld together new empires from the petty chiefdoms that had emerged from the ruins of old empires. The short-lived Sui dynasty (581–618) reunited most of China proper under a centralized administration, providing a sound foundation for the even more vigorous T'ang dynasty (618–907), which soon embarked on a series of campaigns to consolidate the northwest frontier of China. In 630, the Turks of eastern Turkestan were completely routed by a Chinese army, and during the next two decades, the petty states of western as well as eastern Turkestan offered their submission to the T'ang emperors.

The struggle to dominate Central Asia was not, however, restricted to China and Turkestan (modern Sinkiang), but directly involved Tibet, Kashmir, Baltistan, Ladakh, and to a lesser extent, northern India and Nepal. In Tibet, a dynastic line, whose influence prior to the seventh century had been mainly restricted to a small area south of the Tsangpo River, began a rapid expansion of its domains. The most famous of its kings, Song-tsen-gam-po (Srong-btsan-sgam-po), made Tibet the dominant military power of the area for a time, and was able to demand and receive a royal princess in marriage from both Nepal and China. With the founding of his capital at Lhasa (*c.* 640), a new route was briefly opened connecting China with India by way of Lhasa and Nepal.*

In Kashmir, the Karkota Naga dynasty was founded more or less contemporaneously.† Harsha Vardhana of Kanauj (606–48), brought much of northern India briefly under his sway. The two middle decades of the seventh century were marked by comparatively extensive contacts between northern India, Nepal, Tibet, Kashmir, and China. There is much that is still unknown about the interrelations of these kingdoms, but a catalytic role—whatever its exact nature—can certainly be claimed for Tibet.

A new facet was added to these complexities with the advance of the Islamic Arabian empire into Central Asia late in the seventh century and with the fall of Sind to the Arabs in 712. Kashmir was at that time an important Buddhist center and one of the primary channels through which Buddhism had been transplanted to Central Asia and China. For the main line of communication from India to China ran at that time through the Kashmir valley, Baltistan, Nubra (a northern district of Ladakh), and across the Karakoram and Sugat passes into Turkestan, and thence to China. It can be presumed that Buddhism

* This route, which many centuries later became of major importance, was closed after a scant two decades by the intermittent warfare that then marked Tibet's relations with China.

† The date when this dynasty was founded still remains doubtful. U. N. Mukerjee accepts 625. ("Chronology of the Karkota Nāga Dynasty of Kashmir, the Ancient Land of the Nāgas," *Uttara Bharati*, IV, No. 2 [March, 1958], 49–53.) G. L. Kaul sets the date at 602. (*Kashmir Through the Ages, 5,000 B.C. to 1954 A.D., a Historical Survey* [Srinagar, Kashmir: Chronicle Publishing House, 1954], p. 31.)

had, by that time, already left an imprint upon Ladakh, or at least upon the small settlements that may have sprung up along the major communication routes.

West Tibet (i.e., the territory west of the Mayum Pass, called Zan Zun in Tibetan chronicles of that date) was in the first half of the seventh century independent of the Tibetan kingdom whose capital was Lhasa. Under the Lig dynasty,* Zan Zun's dominance included territory south of the Himalayan crest and extended at least to the Kunlun range and possibly to Khotan. It cannot be stated with assurance that Ladakh constituted a province within this empire, but Tucci, noting both the location of the capital of the Lig dynasty near Tsaparang, not far from the Ladakh border, and the major trade route connecting West Tibet with Turkestan through Ladakh, is inclined to doubt that Ladakh could have remained outside it.[1]

The bitter struggle between Tibet and China was resumed in 660, and lasted for nearly three centuries in all, involving at one time or another most of the neighboring states. There were three principal areas in which the contest was waged: Szechuan, lying directly east of Tibet; Tsinghai (Koko Nor) and Kansu in the northeast; and Turkestan (the "Four Garrisons," i.e., Kashgar, Khotan, Kucha, and Karashahr) to the north and northwest. It was the war over Turkestan that involved Kashmir, Baltistan, Ladakh, and West Tibet. If Chinese dominance of Turkestan was to be challenged successfully, a first requisite was to control West Tibet and the passages into Turkestan. West Tibet was accordingly brought under Tibetan hegemony at some point during Song-tsen-gam-po's reign. After several years of fluctuating Tibetan fortunes, the territory of the "Four Garrisons" was conquered in 670 and held for more than twenty years before a Chinese expeditionary force—taking advantage of dissension within Tibet—recovered Turkestan for the T'ang empire.

Soon thereafter, Baltistan and Ladakh became the chief arena of the struggle between Tibet and China to control the passes into Turkestan, a struggle into which Kashmir was actively drawn. And the conflict became even wider with increasing Arab pressure against the domains of both China and Kashmir, which brought the two kingdoms together in an alliance of sorts against the advancing Arabs on the one hand and the Tibetans on the other. Chinese records state

* This dynasty appears to have been Indian or Turki rather than Tibetan in origin, and there is ground for believing that culturally and linguistically the area remained more closely tied to India and Turkestan than to Tibet, even as late as the tenth century. (L. Petech, "A Study on the Chronicles of Ladakh, Indian Tibet," *Indian Historical Quarterly*, XV, No. 4, Supplement [December, 1939], 39–189.)

that during 713–14 three Indian embassies visited the Chinese court to ask for aid against both Arabs and Tibetans.[2] It is known that at least one of these embassies was sent by King "Tchen-ko-lo-pi-li" of Kashmir, who has been identified as Chandrapida Vajraditya.[3] Already one can discern the pattern of alliances that characterized much of eighth-century politics in this vast area: China, Kashmir, and other Indian states versus the Arabs and the Tibetans—the latter finding allies from time to time among the powerful Shan kings of Yunnan and the local Turki rulers in Turkestan.

There were relatively few periods in the eighth century that were free of active hostilities. Much of the combat centered on the Baltistan-Turkestan area—roughly that where today Indian troops face Pakistani troops across a cease-fire line, and not far from where Indian and Chinese military forces are engaged in a grim struggle in which, once again, control of crucial Central Asian access routes is at stake.

In 722, a Chinese force (said to number 4,000 soldiers) coming to the aid of Baltistan was able to prevent Tibetan domination of the passes into Turkestan. Ten years later, the great Kashmiri monarch Lalitaditya Muktapida not only turned back a Tibetan invasion of Baltistan, but also advanced into the northwest area of the Tibetan empire. But in 737, the Tibetans launched yet another invasion of Baltistan, aimed, it appears, at the exclusion of Kashmiri influence from the crucial pass areas. This time China was able to extend aid to Kashmir and Baltistan only indirectly, by a diversion in Koko Nor, in northeastern Tibet. This maneuver's lack of success is attested by a note in the Chinese annals not long after, which states that the King of Baltistan was "in alliance" with the Tibetans.

Once again the fortunes of war shifted, and in 747, a large Chinese force—presumably acting in conjunction with the Kashmiris*—successfully crossed the passes and re-established T'ang influence in Baltistan. Chinese garrisons were placed as far west as Gilgit in an effort to counter an Arab advance. But the Chinese success was only temporary, for in 751, the Arabs inflicted a serious defeat on them, forcing them to withdraw from the Gilgit garrison and to surrender much of western Turkestan to the Abbasid caliphate.[4] This Chinese disaster enabled the Tibetan King Tri-de-tsuk-tsen (Khri-lde-gtsug-btsan) to bring Baltistan once again under his control. His successor, Tri-song-de-tsen

* At some point between the Tibetan invasion of Baltistan in 737 and this expedition, the Chinese annals record the visit of a Kashmiri embassy to the court of China (U. N. Mukerjee, *op. cit.*, p. 50). We can presume that this mission was directly connected with the deteriorating situation in Baltistan, and may have been successful in effecting a Kashmiri-Chinese alliance leading to the expedition of 747 and the expulsion of the Tibetans from Baltistan.

(Khri-srong-lde-btsan, 755–97), carried the Tibetan empire to what was to be its maximum expansion—conquering Turkestan, most of Kansu, and a large portion of Szechuan from the sorely beset T'ang emperors. In 763, Tibetan forces even captured Ch'ang-an, the western capital of China, and held it for 15 days before they were forced to retreat. The Kashmiri empire, King Lalitaditya's remarkable achievement, did not long survive that monarch's death in 760, and the Tibetan empire became the dominant power throughout Central Asia, capable of applying almost continuous pressure against the hill states south of the Himalaya.[5]

The precise fate of Ladakh during this period of turmoil is not clearly delineated in the chronicles of Tibet, China, Kashmir, or even Ladakh itself. The silence on this matter is scarcely surprising, however. Ladakh's geographical position leaves no room for doubt that its ancient caravan routes must have often served as a path first for conquest and then for retreat of the opposing armies as they alternated between victory and defeat. Ladakh could do little but bow to its successive conquerors, and its relatively passive role as an artery rather than as a military objective in itself doubtless diminished its importance in the chronicles.

Ladakh's main allegiance may well have been to Tibet from the first period of Tibetan expansion in the late sixth century on. The Ladakhi chronicles appear to support this conclusion, since they in fact consist, for that period, of the annals of the Lhasa kings. This evidence cannot be considered conclusive, since the pride with which later Ladakhi dynasties insisted that they were descended from the Lhasa kings may have influenced the content of the chronicles as they have come down to us, but there is no real reason to doubt Ladakh's subordination to Tibet during most of this time. It certainly must have become a part of the Tibetan empire no later than the conquest of Baltistan in the middle of the eighth century. Yet Tibetan rule may well have been nominal in Ladakh, since this sparsely settled area appears to have retained the cultural imprint characteristic of the mountainous region stretching from Gilgit through Baltistan and Ladakh to the sub-Himalayan hill states.

Tibetan power reached new heights when a series of decisive victories over the Chinese between 760 and 780 culminated in a peace treaty in 783, the terms of which were very favorable to Tibet. However, this settlement proved no more enduring than those that had preceded it. Within five years, hostilities commenced anew on a grand scale. The early period of the war was marked by consistent Tibetan successes, notably in Turkestan, where the Tibetan empire was extended to the area around modern Urumchi. But developments became unfavorable for Tibet after 790, primarily because of the collapse of its alliances with the Arabs to the west and with the Shans to the east. For the Shan Kings of Yunnan, the first fruit of the alliance had been the expansion of their domain at the expense of the T'ang emperors. But by 790, they were competing not with the Chinese but with the Tibetans for control of the upper Yangtze valley, with the result that they found it expedient to conclude a peace agreement with China in 791 and turn against their erstwhile ally. A powerful Tibetan force sent to punish the Shans for this betrayal was virtually exterminated.[6] This defeat had a disastrous effect on the Tibetan position, endangering the lines of communication between Lhasa and the forces on the frontier.

Tibet's successes in Turkestan had a parallel effect on its alliance with the Caliphate. The substitution of Tibetan for Chinese rule in eastern Turkestan meant that henceforth it was Lhasa that stood in the way of Arab expansion eastward and of the conversion of the Turki tribes to Islam. The Caliph of Bagdad, Harun al-Rashid, abandoned the alliance with Lhasa in 798 and sent an envoy to the Chinese court to arrange a joint attack on Turkestan.* Tibet was able to withstand, with only minor setbacks, the first shock of the challenge posed by this Arab-Chinese coalition, in part because Arab attention was diverted by a renewal of hostilities with Byzantium in 803. It was not until 808 that Harun al-Rashid was ready to conduct a campaign in the area bordering on Tibetan-held eastern Turkestan; his death during the campaign and the subsequent dissension over his succession forced another postponement of Arab expansion in Central Asia. But the Tibetan empire was never able to regain its lost momentum. From this date to the final downfall of the dynasty, Tibetan efforts were focused not on further conquests but on the effort to retain the fruits of past conquests. As the Ladakhi chronicles put it, in a terse summary of the events of Mu-tri-tsen-po's reign (Mu-khri-btsan-po, *ca.* 798–804): "Although in (some) parts of both countries of Rgya (China and India) not all those who had bowed before his father bowed before him, he endured it with patience."[7]

The Chinese, for their part, were unable to profit from the weak-

* Interestingly enough, this was also the time of the "great debate" in Tibet between two Buddhist teachers representing "Indian" and "Chinese" Buddhism. The famous "Council of Lhasa" ended with the victory of Pandit Kamalshila and "Indian" Buddhism. (See Paul Demiéville, *Le Concile de Lhasa*, [*Bibliothèque de l'Institut des Hautes Etudes Chinoises*, VII] I (1952), 177, 183.) This event had considerable effect on the future development of Buddhism in Tibet, and the period really marks the introduction of Buddhist monachist institutions in Tibet. Could political factors have played a significant role in the outcome of this debate, and was the war with China instrumental in the defeat of "Chinese" Buddhism?

ened Tibetan position. After years of rather desultory warfare, during which other neighboring powers wrested concessions from both Tibet and China, a peace settlement between them was concluded in 822.* Perhaps because of the basic incapacity of each side to renew the struggle, the peace was successfully maintained for some time. The integration that had characterized the earlier period gave way to a process of decay, in the course of which much of the territory over which the Chinese and Tibetan empires had fought so bitterly reverted to local rulers or fell to other conquerors. Within Tibet, internal disorders ensued, intensified by religious strife and bringing swift dissolution of the greater Tibetan empire. Turkestan fell to the Uighurs; West Tibet and Ladakh broke up into petty principalities over which Lhasa exercised no effective authority.

From these chaotic conditions, there emerged in Ladakh in the early years of the tenth century a new émigré type of dynasty proud of its royal Tibetan origins. A paradoxical result was that Ladakh's political separation from Tibet was accentuated at the same time that its cultural, religious, and social structure was "Tibetanized." Interestingly enough, in a parallel development south of the Himalayas, similar émigré dynasties of Hindu origin, in flight from Islamic persecution, were established in the mountain fastnesses of Kumaon and Nepal. The eventual result here, too—although the process took much longer—was an accentuation of Nepal's political separation from India together with the "Sanskritization" of its cultural, religious, and social life. Thus, the cultural homogeneity that had earlier characterized a surprisingly extended mountain area gave way to new and divergent patterns, with political as well as cultural consequences that have yet to run their full course.

* The terms of this agreement were carved in Tibetan and Chinese on the famous stone pillar at Lhasa. For an English version, see H. E. Richardson, *A Short History of Tibet* (New York: Dutton, 1962), pp. 244–45.

# III

## *LADAKH'S EMERGENCE AS AN INDEPENDENT STATE*

By the end of the ninth century, central Tibet was involved in what seemed to be endlessly protracted hostilities. Around 900, Kyi-de Nyi-ma-gön (Skyid-lde Nyi-ma-gon), a descendant of one branch of the old Tibetan dynasty, was forced to flee across the Mayum Pass into West Tibet. According to the Ladakhi chronicles, only a hundred followers accompanied the refugee prince into exile, and his livelihood depended on the good will of the local rulers in West Tibet. Nevertheless, within a comparatively short period, Kyi-de Nyi-ma-gön was master not only of West Tibet, but also of Ladakh to the west, and of Zanskar, Spiti, and Lahul south of the Himalaya. The factors behind this remarkable improvement in his fortunes are not made clear in the chronicles, but the statement that the King of Purang (the district between the Mayum Pass and the Kailash range) invited Kyi-de Nyi-ma-gön to his country and offered him a wife may prove an important clue. Francke speculates that the wife was the King's only daughter and heir, and that after his death Kyi-de Nyi-ma-gön succeeded to his throne. With Purang as a base and with the prestige still associated with the name of the ancient Tibetan dynasty, he probably found it relatively easy to expand his domain in the chaotic political situation then prevailing.

The extensive kingdom conquered by Kyi-de Nyi-ma-gön did not long survive intact, for around 930, presumably on his death, it was divided among his three sons. There is some disagreement in the various sources concerning the actual distribution of territory. The Ladakhi chronicles state that the eldest son, Pal-gyi-gön (Dpal-gyi-mgon), received Ladakh and the Rudok area; the second son, Tra-shi-gön (Bkra-shis-mgon), Guge and Purang; while the third son, De-tsuk-gön (Lde-gtsug-mgon), was given Zanskar, Spiti and Lahul.[1] The central Tibetan annals, however, assert that the eldest son received Ladakh, the second son Guge and Zanskar, and the third son Purang.[2] Probably the Ladakhi chronicles should be followed here. Certainly their concern with these events was more immediate. Furthermore, as Petech has pointed out, there is no evidence of an independent Purang state in this period, whereas the Zanskar chronicles assert that De-tsuk-gön, "the younger brother, became King of Pa-dam (Dpal-ldum) in Zanskar."*

The Ladakhi chronicles define the boundaries only of the territory bestowed on the eldest son. According to the chronicles, Pal-gyi-gön received:

> Mar-yul of Mnah-ris, the inhabitants using the black bows; Ru-thogs of the east and the gold mine of Hgog; nearer this way Lde-mchog-dkar-po; at the frontier Ra-ba-dmar-po; Wam-le, to the top of the pass of the Yi-mig rock; to the west to the foot of the Kashmir pass, from the cavernous stone upward hither, to the north to the gold mine of Hgog; all the places belonging to Rgya.[3]

Most of these place names are readily identified today. Mar-yul (literally "lower land") is the common Tibetan name for the Leh district in Ladakh. Mnah-ris (Mnga-ris), although now restricted to West Tibet, then referred to the entire territory between the Zoji and Mayum passes.[4] Ru-thogs is Rudok, the Tibetan district north of Gartok that borders on Ladakh. Lde-mchog-dkar-po is Demchok, a village now in dispute between China and India. Wam-le is Hanle, slightly northwest of Demchok and also in dispute. Yi-mig is the Imis Pass south of Hanle, and on Indian, but not Chinese maps, the present boundary between Ladakh and Tibet. The Kashmir pass is the Zoji Pass, the dividing line between Ladakh and Kashmir even today. Rgya is a frontier town between Ladakh and Rupshu, the latter an upland district situated between Ladakh, Lahul, and Spiti, apparently the boundary between the domains of the first and third sons. The only place names that elude identification are Ra-ba-dmar-po† and Hgog.‡

* L. Petech, "A Study on the Chronicles of Ladakh, Indian Tibet," *Indian Historical Quarterly*, XV, No. 4 [Supplement, December, 1939], 94. Francke thought that the second brother, Tra-shi-pön, died without issue, and that the third brother inherited Guge and Purang and added them to his dominions. A. H. Francke, "Antiquities of Indian Tibet" (Registrar of the Vassal-kings of Bzan-la in Zansdkar), *Archaeological Survey of India*, II, 164.

† Ra-ba-dmar-po has been tentatively identified as Rabma, a place halfway between Rudok and Spanggur and somewhat east of the frontier presently claimed by India. (Z. Ahmad, "The Ancient Frontier of Ladakh," *The World Today*, XVI [July, 1960], 314–15.)

‡ Francke advances two theories to identify Hgog. He notes that Thog (Thok

The verification of these place names and their identification with well-known landmarks is not solely a matter of academic or historical interest, for the question of Ladakh's "traditional boundaries" has assumed some significance in the present border dispute between India and China. It should be noted that in most instances the Indian idea of the Ladakh-Tibet boundary, from the Lanak Pass in the north to the Imis Pass in the south, conforms essentially with that defined in the ancient Ladakhi chronicles, as far as the main identification points are concerned. The one possible exception is Ra-ba-dmar-po, and in this case, the deviation appears to be in the favor of Tibet rather than Ladakh. It is reasonable to presume that references made to the "traditional and customary boundary" in later documents and manuscripts hark back to the division of Kyi-de Nyi-ma-gön's kingdom in the tenth century which, in turn, was undoubtedly based on well-recognized boundary lines long antedating this event.

Another perplexing problem is the question of the exact relationship between Ladakh and Guge after Kyi-de Nyi-ma-gön's death. Francke asserts that the eldest son (i.e., the ruler of Ladakh) was suzerain over his brothers, and that Ladakh thus exercised some form of authority over West Tibet, Zanskar, Spiti, and Lahul.[5] Petech takes issue with Francke, maintaining that the reverse was true. Citing one of the Ladakhi chronicles as his source, Petech argues that the kings of Guge also ruled over Purang and Ladakh until the time of Naga-de (Naga-lde) in the late eleventh or early twelfth century.[6] As further evidence, he cites the "high cultural, political, and religious level attained by Guge's kings," as described by Tucci,[7] and the failure of other Ladakhi chronicles to claim Ladakhi suzerainty over Guge. Petech's thesis is somewhat confusing, for it appears to be based on the assumption that a single dynasty ruled over both Guge and Ladakh from approximately 930–1110. This indirectly contradicts his own analysis of the Ladakhi and other chronicles, nor does it conform with the few historical facts known about the period.

Here again a historical event has assumed unexpected significance in the recent border disputes, for the Chinese and Indian governments adhere to basically divergent interpretations of relevant passages in

---

Jalung) is a well-known gold field. However, if this was a misspelling in the chronicles and the original name was Hgrog or Grog, the pronunciation "might easily have become similar to Thog." Francke also suggests the possibility that Hgog is not a proper name but the ordinary word *hgog,* meaning "pledge," or "deposit." If this were the case, then the chronicles should be translated to read that Pal-gyi-gön "received the gold mines as a pledge," A. H. Francke, *op. cit.*, II, 94–95.

the chronicles. Peking argues, essentially, that no political division of Kyi-de Nyi-ma-gön's dominion occurred, and that the Ladakhi chronicles have in this respect been incorrectly translated by Western and Indian scholars. According to this interpretation, the chronicle refers only to the distribution of manorial estates and not to the establishment of independent kingdoms. Excerpts from the "Blue Annals" (a famous Tibetan work of the fifteenth century) and "The Biography of Atisha" were also cited[8] in support of the Chinese contention that the division of Kyi-de Nyi-ma-gön's kingdom was nothing more than the bestowal of "feudal estates."*

Indian officials disagreed with the Chinese interpretation of the Ladakhi chronicles and questioned the relevance of the two other passages cited. The main disputed point was the Tibetan term *Ngari* (from which the name for West Tibet, Ngari Horsum, is derived), which the Chinese translated as "vassals" and the Indians as "sovereign authority."[9] As for the passage from the "Blue Annals" cited by the Chinese, the Indians noted that this source "states clearly that the elder son who secured Maryul became an independent sovereign. This translation of the text has been declared to be the correct one by the well-known Soviet scholar, the late Professor George Roerich."[10] A similar interpretation was made of the passage from "The Biography of Atisha" which, the Indians argued, "stated clearly that the territories were handed over to them [Kyi-de Nyi-ma-gön's three sons] with full powers."[11]

This disagreement between the present-day governments of India and China over events in Ladakh's dim past is not as ludicrous as it may appear on the surface, for it exhibits clearly China's consistent refusal to concede that Tibet's alleged suzerainty over Ladakh ever lapsed. While China has not yet claimed the whole of Ladakh on this basis, neither has it been willing to admit that Tibet (and hence, China) has no legal or historical claim to Ladakh at all. The available resource materials on the tenth century are both too sparse and too vague to justify drawing more than tentative conclusions on the exact course of events subsequent to Kyi-de Nyi-ma-gön's death. Nevertheless, the history of this area, no matter which sources are used, can only be interpreted as indicating that Ladakh achieved at least *de facto* independence in this and later periods. Whether its independence dates from the death of Kyi-de Nyi-ma-gön in 930, or from the rule of

* The Chinese delegation called Kyi-de Nyi-ma-gön a "local prince of China's Tibet." (*Report of the Officials of the Government of India and the People's Republic of China on the Boundary Question* [New Delhi: Ministry of External Affairs, 1961], p. CR-56.) Even the most exuberant Chinese historians have never claimed that Tibet was part of China in the tenth century.

the great Ladakhi King Utpala in the eleventh century, or from some time between is a matter of historical, but not political interest. On several occasions expansionist rulers of Ladakh laid claim to West Tibet on the basis of past association, but there are no recorded instances in which the reverse occurred. Thus, there is an ancient historic basis for disputes between Ladakh and central Tibet over control of West Tibet, but not for any Tibetan (or Chinese) claims to Ladakh.

During the rule of Kyi-de Nyi-ma-gön and his descendants over West Tibet, Ladakh, and Zanskar, the evidence appears to indicate that none of these areas was culturally oriented toward central Tibet, even though Lhasa had nominal suzerainty over them for a century or two. According to Petech, the "earliest tangible tokens" of Tibetan influence in Ladakh are the Alchi inscriptions, dating no earlier than the eleventh or twelfth century.[12] On the other hand, numerous Indian inscriptions, some dating back to the third or second century, B.C., are found throughout Ladakh, testifying to the widespread contacts that existed with the Indo-Aryan cultures of Kashmir and the plains to the south.[13] However, the "Tibetanization" process apparently proceeded at a rapid pace after a Tibetan dynasty was established in Ladakh. By 982–83, the Persian geographical treatise *Hudud al-'Alam* referred to Ladakh as "Bolorian Tibet."[14] Moreover, Buddhism, which had long flourished in Ladakh, came gradually under the sway of Buddhistic influences from central Tibet.* This process was accelerated, one presumes, by the founding in the first half of the eleventh century of the great Tibetan Buddhist center at Toling in Guge, and monasteries in Ladakh thereafter.

The chronicles and inscriptions indicate that strong cultural cross-currents flowed through the Ladakh-West Tibet area from the eleventh to the thirteenth century. This coincided with violent upheavals in India accompanying the successive waves of Muslim invasions that began in the eleventh century. High-caste Hindus and Buddhist scholars fled in large numbers to the mountainous regions in north India to escape the depredations of iconoclastic Muslim rulers. Most of the sub-Himalayan hill states eventually came under the rule of these refugees—who gained power either by conquest or by their intermarriage with indigenous ruling families. The Himalaya had never constituted an effective barrier to similar movements from the south before and presumably the impact of these new ruling classes—with the prestige attaining to Rajput status—was felt in Tibet and Ladakh

* However, it should be noted that Indian Buddhistic influence continued to dominate in Tibet itself until the destruction of the great Buddhistic centers—such as Nalanda—by Muslim invaders in the late twelfth and thirteenth centuries.

as well. We find, for example, that the Indo-Aryan Malla dynasty (sMal in Tibetan) in the district of Jumla in western Nepal extended its control to West Tibet in the eleventh century and retained its authority there for more than 200 years.[15] That Ladakh was probably affected by these developments is indicated by the fact that in the Ladakhi chronicles, the sixth king in the line established by the eldest son of Kyi-de Nyi-ma-gön is given the Sanskrit name Utpala.

Nevertheless, it appears that Indian cultural and political influences on Ladakh and Tibet declined rapidly after 1300, due to the wholesale destruction of Buddhist religious centers in India. Buddhism, which had flourished as a monastic rather than popular religion under tolerant Hindu kings, lacked the resilience shown by Hinduism under the impact of Islam. Hence, Buddhism virtually disappeared from the subcontinent except in parts of the sub-Himalayan hill area. The close relations that had long existed between Hindu and Buddhist schools, significantly modifying the philosophical systems of both, was reflected in Tibetan Buddhism as well. While Indian influences did not disappear entirely from Tibet after the Muslim conquest, they were greatly reduced in scope and changed in character. Indian Buddhist scholars no longer visited Tibet regularly, nor were there any longer the great Buddhist institutions in India to which Tibetans could come in large numbers.

The same trend could be seen in West Tibet and Ladakh, where cultural, social, and religious patterns from central Tibet became ever more dominant after the thirteenth century. By the fourteenth century, the area had been effectively "Tibetanized," and the traditional relations with India and Kashmir had been drastically circumscribed. Thus, the actual nature and character of Islamic social and political institutions in India far more effectively prevented relations with Buddhist Ladakh and Tibet than the lofty Himalaya.

References to this period in the Ladakhi chronicles are very sparse, consisting of little more than the names of the kings. The one exception concerns King Utpala, who ruled from approximately 1080 to 1110 and was the first of several powerful Ladakhi kings to bring large expanses of surrounding territory under their control. According to the chronicles, during Utpala's reign:

> The united forces of Upper Ladakh and Gsam [Lower Ladakh] invaded Nun-ti [Kulu]. The King of Nun-ti bound himself by an oath, so long as [the glaciers of] Ti-se [Mount Kailasa] do not melt away, nor Lake Ma-phan [Manasarovar] dry up, to pay tribute or dues. . . . He also subjected Blo-bo [a district east of Guge] from Pu-hrans [Purang] downward hither; in the south the country of Bre-sran [?] to [Lake] Chu-la-me-hbar [possibly Badrinath in Kumaun]; in the west, from Ra-

> gan-hgren-sin and Stag-khu-tshur [two villages in Baltistan, west of Skardo] upward hither; in the north, from Ka-sus [?] upwards. [They all] paid an annual tribute and attended the Darbar [literally, see the king's face].[16]

A notable exception from the list of Utpala's possessions is Guge. This seems to constitute final proof that, by this time at least, separate dynasties ruled in both states, neither subordinate to the other.

After King Utpala, the chronicles once again are terse and uncommunicative for nearly 200 years. The tenth king of this dynasty, Tra-shi-gön (Bkra-shis-mgon, *ca.* 1200–1230), ruled while the great Mongol empire under Jenghiz Khan was in the process of formation. Jenghiz Khan made several efforts to bring Tibet (and presumably Ladakh*) under his rule, but with little lasting effect. It was only under his successors that a rather tenuous Mongol suzerainty was established in Tibet through the agency of the Sakya lamas, whose monastic and political center was situated in Tsang province on the main route to Nepal, West Tibet, and Ladakh. The authority of the Sakya lamas was not always recognized by the virtually autonomous Tibetan aristocracy, whose submission to the Mongol (Yuan) dynasty was largely nominal. Civil strife was prevalent in central Tibet after 1375, and the power and influence of the Sakya lamas weakened accordingly.† In these circumstances, it is unlikely that Ladakh and West Tibet ever gave more than nominal submission to the Mongol emperors, and probably not even that. They were reportedly included in the great census carried out by the Yuan Emperor, Kublai Khan, in the latter half of the thirteenth century,[17] but in terms that minimized its significance.

The reign of the thirteenth king in this Ladakhi dynasty, Lha-chen Ngö-trup (Lha-chen Dngos-grub, *ca.* 1290–1320), was notable for one important religious development that must have had political connotations as well. Prior to his reign, the Buddhist monastic system in Ladakh had been closely tied to that in Guge, in whose monastic in-

* A Mongolian chronicle (tr. by G. Huth in *Geschichte des Buddhismus in der Mongolei* [Strasbourg: Trubner, 1892–96], p. 24) states that in 1207 and thereafter, Ladakh recognized the suzerainty of Jenghiz Khan and his successors. The Ladakhi chronicles have absolutely nothing to say about this or, for that matter, on the great Mongol Emperor whose path of conquest brought his armies directly north of Ladakh in Turkestan.

† G. Tucci, *Tibetan Painted Scrolls*, tr., V. Vacca (Rome: Libreria dello Stato, 1949), I, 16–17. This was the first instance of the ruling power in China (on this occasion the Yuan dynasty) attempting to use one of the Tibetan Buddhist sects or religious centers as the instrument through which to influence Tibet. The pattern became a common feature of Chinese policy in later centuries and is still apparent, in somewhat perverted form, in Communist China's policy in Tibet.

stitutions Ladakhi novices were trained. Lha-chen Ngö-trup, however, initiated a system under which novices were sent to monasteries in central Tibet for religious education. This may well have been a period of intense rivalry and hostility between Ladakh and Guge. The political disadvantages of a system that assured Guge a dominant influence over the powerful Buddhistic institutions in Ladakh could well have impelled the ruler of the latter to make some basic changes in this procedure.

Neither the Kashmiri nor the Ladakhi chronicles are very specific about the nature of the relationship between the two states during this time. Several events alluded to in both sources indicate, however, that close contact continued even after religion had ceased to be a unifying factor. The gradual emergence of Islam as the dominant political and cultural force in Kashmir complicated relations between that country and Ladakh, and forced them into a new framework. But basic economic, political, and strategic considerations precluded any great decline in the scope of contact between the two, and the old trading patterns were retained. These factors tied Ladakh's fate more closely to Kashmir and Turkestan than to central Tibet, even though Ladakhi society retained its Tibetan Buddhist character well into later centuries.

# IV

## *CONFLICTING PRESSURES ON LADAKH:* A.D. *1300–1600*

Kashmir, weakened by internal strife and sorely beset on all sides by would-be conquerors, for two centuries did not constitute a serious threat to Ladakh. In 1339, however, an Islamic dynasty was established in Kashmir with the ascension to power of Shah Mir, a Muslim from Swat who had come to Kashmir as a refugee twenty-five years earlier and who had played a vital role in developments in the valley in the intervening time. Buddhist Ladakh did not feel the impact of this change immediately, as the first three rulers of the new dynasty were mainly concerned with consolidating their domestic authority and with their hostilities against the Tughlak dynasty in India and the Tartars to the north. The great Timur, whose capital was Samarkand, invaded India through Afghanistan at the close of the fourteenth century and laid the entire northwest in ruins. Neither Kashmir nor Ladakh was directly affected, but Jammu to the south and Kangra and other hill states to the southeast were ransacked by the invaders. Timur's invasion was a short-lived affair for all its violence, and by 1400, an unfortunate turn in his relations with the Ming dynasty in China forced him to turn his attention in that direction and withdraw his armies from India.

At the beginning of the fifteenth century, then, the political situation in India and Central Asia was marked by chaos and turbulence. The Tughlak empire in India had disintegrated completely under the impact of Timur's invasion. A number of power centers emerged, none strong enough to master the area as a whole. The Tartars in Central Asia were still a threat, but engaged elsewhere for the time being. In Tibet, the temporal supremacy of the Sakya lamas weakened with the decline of their Mongol patrons. Some time earlier, a revival of national fervor in Tibet had brought to power an aristocratic family from U province, the Pha-mo-tru (Phag-mo-gru), and the Mongol Yuan dynasty perforce extended recognition to these lay princes. Then, after a similar "nativist" movement in China had toppled the Yuan rulers, the new Ming dynasty tried and failed to reassert its control of Tibet through the lama hierarchy, and they too extended their support to the Pha-mo-tru princes. The Ming emperors never exerted much influence in Tibet, however, and their nominal support was of no avail to the Pha-mo-tru in a losing struggle against the Rin-pung-pa (Rins-spungs-pa), a rival princely family centered at Shigatse in Tsang province. The struggle between these families was not merely a regional struggle between U and Tsang: Each family had strong support from rival religious sects whose interests extended well beyond provincial boundaries. Furthermore, underlying regional and doctrinal rivalries, there were economic rivalries no less intense, whose significance in shaping the course of Central Asian history has yet to be fully elucidated.

Recent research has laid a foundation for such a study, however, and as our knowledge increases about the flexible manner in which the monastery system played its central role in the economy of Lamaist areas, hitherto baffling developments become easier to interpret. Despite the ancient rules enjoining poverty and forbidding monks even to touch gold or silver, the Mahayana doctrine, with its emphasis on service to others, found no insuperable difficulty in reconciling religion and commerce. An ingenious system was developed, well-suited to the exigencies of the Tibetan environment, by which the abler monks and laymen alike could derive material benefit along with corresponding religious merit.* Economic rewards for the less able might be scanty or nonexistent, but even at worst there was an endless reservoir of religious merits available to all. In practice, this monastic economy fostered trading relations both within and across Tibetan borders. Chains of "daughter" monasteries grew up along the trade routes, serving not only to tap the economic resources of wider areas, but also to

* For further details on the operation of the lamaist economy, and particularly the interesting *jisa* system of decentralized treasuries, see Robert J. Miller, "Buddhist Monastic Economy: The Jisa Mechanism," *Comparative Studies in Society and History*, III, (1961), 427–38. In a useful comment on this article (*Ibid.*, pp. 439–42), George Murphy suggests that the *jisa* system may have had an importance to Inner Asia comparable to double-entry bookkeeping in the West. André Bareau concludes that the *jisa* system is probably of Indian origin, in "Indian and Ancient Chinese Buddhism: Institutions Analogous to the Jisa," *ibid.*, pp. 443–51. See also Miller's earlier study. *Monasteries and Culture Change in Inner Mongolia* (Wiesbaden: Otto Harrassowitz, 1959).

provide caravans with safe haven at night against marauding "bandits" who may well have been connected with a rival trading system. Given these conditions, it can be readily understood that the establishment of foreign enclaves in Tibet and of reciprocal enclaves in neighboring countries were of vital importance to the development of trade, while at the same time devoid of political significance, except insofar as the rivalry between Buddhist sects was injected into the internal politics of a given state.

The first half of the fifteenth century was marked by more than ordinarily intense sectarian rivalry as a result of the zeal and organizing ability of the great religious reformer Tsong-kha-pa (1357–1419), the founder of the Yellow sect of Tibetan Buddhism. This sect later became the instrument of Tibetan unification and the dominant Buddhist sect in most of Central and Himalayan Asia. It began, however, as one in a series of attempts to purify Tibetan Buddhism—which had been forced again and again to come to terms with a shamanistic aboriginal religion—through a return to the precepts of primitive Buddhism. The reasons for the success of the Yellow sect are many and varied, but ranking high among them was surely the unusual degree of cooperation it fostered between the "other-worldly" and "this-worldly" views of life.*

The many-faceted role of the monastery, with its specialized working force of monks and lay brethren, has long been recognized, if often underestimated. But another aspect in which ethical precepts and material well-being reinforced each other has not been given its due. For the monastery to fulfill its important economic role, some sort of capital surplus was needed. In much of the difficult Central Asian environment, grazing was the principal use to which the land was adapted,† and the most important surplus was in herds. Indigenous religious practices, however, had included animal sacrifice—often on a large scale—for various ceremonial purposes, and the evidence suggests that such practices persisted, even in supposedly Buddhist areas, at the time when Tsong-kha-pa instituted his reforms. The prohibition of animal slaughter that Yellow sect doctrine made explicit may have been intended as nothing more than a reaffirmation of the compassionate Buddha's reverence for all life, but it surely resulted in greatly increased wealth in cattle, with consequent material benefit not only to the monasteries but also to the herdsmen who contracted to pasture the surplus animals.

* See the perceptive "Reflections" by David Snellgrove, in his *Buddhist Himalaya* (Oxford: Cassirer, 1957), pp. 275–82.

† F. Kingdon-Ward defined Tibet as a grazing land. ("Tibet as a Grazing Land," *Geographical Journal*, CX [1948], 60–75.)

During the early fifteenth century, the new Yellow sect built many monasteries in important locations along the trade routes. King Trak-bum-de (Grags-'bum-lde) of Ladakh (*ca.* 1410–40) enthusiastically received a Yellow sect mission in the 1420's. A new monastery was built, and the King adopted the doctrines of the reformed sect, issuing the famous Mulbhe edict aimed at abolishing the ritualistic practices of the Dards, in particular animal sacrifice.[1] What the King's motives were we are not told: He may have been interested in counterbalancing the powerful Red sect institutions in Ladakh and Guge (in the upper Sutlej valley), or he may have wished to strengthen his position with respect to threatening developments in Kashmir. But whatever other considerations were involved, we can be certain that Leh's trade links were altered.

The newly established Islamic dynasty in Kashmir was eager to extend its authority over the mountainous areas to the north and east. In 1405, King Sikander of Kashmir invaded and conquered Baltistan, forcing its Buddhist population to embrace Islam. Sikander's death in 1413 temporarily halted Kashmir's expansion, but it was not long until King Trak-bum-de faced a powerful neighbor impelled by aggressive religious drives that reinforced economic and strategic factors which had always made Ladakh of vital importance to Kashmir. Thus, during the reign of the Kashmiri King Zain-ul-abidin (1420–70), at least two expeditions were sent into Ladakh. The most significant of them, which must have taken place between 1440 and 1450, was an invasion of Guge, undertaken with the support (not necessarily voluntary) of the Ladakhi King Lo-trö-chok-den (Blo-gros-mchog-ldan). The Kashmiri army finally withdrew from Guge and Ladakh, both of which rendered their submission to Srinagar.

It is probable that Kashmir maintained nominal sovereignty over Ladakh until the death of Zain-ul-abidin in 1470. King Lo-trö-chok-den may actually have depended on Kashmir for his retention of royal powers, for also in 1470 or thereabouts, he was dethroned by a prince from a collateral branch of the ruling family, Lha-chen Bha-gan* (*ca.* 1470–1500), the founder of the Nam-gyal (Rnam-rgyal) dynasty. Lha-chen Bha-gan apparently took advantage of internal disorder in Kashmir following Zain-ul-abidin's death to depose the puppet ruler and re-establish Ladakh as an independent state.

It was ten years before the Kashmiris could renew their efforts to bring Ladakh under their control again, and then not with much effect. King Hasan Khan (1472–84) sent two armies against Ladakh around 1480, one of which was defeated while the other, after some

* Bha-gan does not appear to be a Tibetan name unless the various Ladakhi chronicles have transcribed it incorrectly.

initial successes, was forced to withdraw.* Ladakh thus preserved its precarious independence. Six decades passed before Kashmir emerged again as a serious threat, for internal disorders became chronic after the death of Hasan Khan and the authorities at Srinagar were too preoccupied with defending themselves against incursions from outside to bother with Ladakh.

The temporary lull in relations with Kashmir did not provide an extended breathing spell for Ladakh. This time it was Mongol-led Turki invaders from Turkestan who descended on the country in successive waves. Around the end of the fifteenth century, the armies of the Khan of Kashgar, Abu Bakr, conquered Kafiristan, Gilgit, and Baltistan, while Mongol parties occasionally raided south of the Karakorams into Ladakh. In 1517, the situation became more critical with the invasion of Ladakh by Mongol forces under the leadership of Mir Mazid. However, the Ladakhi ruler Tra-shi Nam-gyal (Bkra-shis-rnam-rgyal)† defeated the invaders and slew the Mir. This gave the Ladakhis a brief respite, as well as an opportunity to gain control over two of the strategic areas coveted by all strong rulers in Central Asia: West Tibet and Purig (the district west of Leh between Ladakh and Baltistan on the main route to Kashmir valley).

Ladakh had to meet an even greater challenge in September, 1532, when the armies of Abu Sayed Mirza, the new Khan of Kashgar, crossed the Sugat and Karakoram passes into Ladakh and Baltistan, led by Prince Sikander and Mirza Haider Dughlat. The Ladakhis were defeated and Tra-shi Nam-gyal forced to render his submission to the Kashgar Khan. The following year, while Mirza Haider was leading an invasion into Kashmir, a revolt broke out in the Nubra district of Ladakh that was suppressed only with some difficulty. Tra-shi Nam-gyal, evidently implicated in the revolt, was executed by the Mongols,[2] who then placed his brother's eldest son, Tshe-wang Nam-gyal (Tshe-dbang-rnam-rgyal, *ca.* 1533–75), on the throne.

The Kashgar Khan had contemplated the conquest of Tibet for some time; he now decided the time was ripe for such a venture. Mirza Haider was ordered to lead a force into Tibet, apparently with Lhasa as its objective.‡ The Mongol army set out from Leh in early July,

*Curiously, the Ladakhi chronicles do not even mention this victory, while Srivara's *Rajatarangini* describes the Kashmiri defeat in some detail. (Pandit Daya Ram Sahni, "References to the Bhottas or Bhauttas in the Rajatarangini of Kashmir" [Notes from Tibetan sources by A. H. Francke], *Indian Antiquary*, XXXVII [July, 1908], 190–91.)

† Two brothers are said to have ruled jointly, but the real power lay in Tra-shi Nam-gyal's hands.

‡ In Mirza Haider's account, Ursang and its great temple were stated to be the objective. (Mirza Muhammed Haider Dughlat, *Tarikh-i-Rashidi* [A *History of the Moghuls of Central Asia*], tr. by E. R. Ross [London: Low, Marston, 1895].) It has

1533, and quickly pushed its way through Ladakh into West Tibet. No resistance was met with until the army reached Kardung, a strategic spot in Purang between Lake Rakas and Taklakot.* There, a small Tibetan force reinforced by a contingent sent by the Raja of Jumla† engaged the invaders, but was finally defeated. The Mongol army then pushed on across the Mayum Pass into central Tibet, but was finally forced to retreat because of the lack of supplies.‡

Once back in Guge, Mirza Haider found himself facing another disaster. Shortly after the invasion of Tibet had begun the previous summer, the Kashgar Khan had died while crossing the Sugat Pass on his way back to Turkestan from Ladakh. His successor, Rashid Khan, was ill-disposed toward Mirza Haider's family, and he recalled most of the Mongol troops from Ladakh. Deprived of all hope of assistance from Turkestan, Mirza Haider was finally forced to flee from Ladakh. In the winter of 1534–35, the durable Mongol commander made his way up the Yarkand River valley through the Taghdumbash and over the formidable Pamir passes to Badakshan, where he was assured a friendly welcome.

This was not the last that Ladakh heard of Mirza Haider, however. The Moghul emperors in Delhi had been trying for some years to extend their control over Kashmir, and Babur had made one direct effort himself after his capture of Delhi in 1526, but he had been re-

---

been generally assumed that this refers to Lhasa and the Potala Palace of the Dalai Lama. However, it may just as well have been Shigatse and the Panchen Lama's great monastery Tashilhunpo.

* It is interesting to note that both the Mongol invasion of 1533 and the Dogra invasion of 1841 first met resistance at Kardung. This indicates its strategic character and the importance of the area around Taklakot.

† Mirza Haider's account of this battle does not make it clear that it was the Raja of Jumla who lent assistance to the Tibetans. He merely refers to troops sent by a "Rai [Raja] of Hindustan." However, the Ladakhi chronicles refer specifically to Hdzum-lan, or Jumla. (A. H. Francke, "Antiquities of Indian Tibet," *Archaeological Survey of India*, II, 105.) Jumla, the most important of the small principalities in the western area of present-day Nepal, lies directly across the Himalayan passes from Taklakot, to which it is connected by an important trade route. The Raja of Jumla, whose Hindu ancestors had once fled from Islamic persecution in India, could only have viewed with apprehension the approach of Mirza Haider's army so close to his borders.

‡ The actual depth of the Mongol army's penetration into central Tibet is still unclear. Mirza Haider states that his force reached Askabrak (or Astakbark), a place "eight days journey from Ursang" (*op. cit.*, p. 455). This place name is not readily identified on maps of Tibet, but the Ladakhi chronicles shed some light. King Tshe-wang Nam-gyal, whom the Mongols had just placed on the Ladakhi throne, apparently accompanied Mirza Haider on the invasion of Tibet, for the chronicles note that "Tshe-wang, going to war while yet a young man, conquered [all the country] from Nam-rins in the east." (A. H. Francke, "Antiquities," 105.) Nam-rins (Ngam-ring) is on the main Ladakh-Lhasa trade route, only a few days' journey west of Shigatse.

pulsed. The Emperor then played on internal dissensions in Kashmir to achieve his objective, but again to no lasting purpose. His successor, Humayun, intensified the campaign against Kashmir, giving assistance to Mirza Haider, who was poised to invade the valley at the invitation of a powerful Kashmiri faction. Badly divided as it was, Kashmir could do little against the invaders. King Ibraham Shah II was deposed and Mirza Haider placed a puppet of his own on the throne and proceeded to rule Kashmir himself.[3]

Mirza Haider had evidently neither forgotten nor forgiven his experiences in Ladakh, for he twice sent armies across the Zoji Pass. The first expedition in 1545 met with only limited success, but the second in 1548 conquered and annexed Baltistan and Ladakh. Muslim governors were appointed for both states, though it is doubtful if they ever assumed office. Mirza Haider was killed in 1551 by Shia Muslim rebels antagonized by his pro-Sunni policy, and Kashmir once again passed into the hands of weak and ineffectual kings who were hard put to retain control over their turbulent subjects, much less over the uncooperative Baltis and Ladakhis.

There were two more ill-conceived Kashmiri incursions into Ladakh. The first of these in 1553 was led by King Habib Shah and Haider Chak as a reprisal for Balti and Ladakhi raids on Kashmir. In 1562, Ghazi Shah, who had seized the Kashmiri throne from Habib Shah in 1555, sent his eldest son, Ahmad Khan, and several other generals into Ladakh with a small force. The Ladakhis defeated the Kashmiri army and Ahmad Khan was forced to flee in disgrace. His father collected an army to avenge the defeat, but died before this could be accomplished. The next twenty years were marked by extreme factional strife in Kashmir, and when the Moghul Emperor Akbar renewed the campaign against Kashmir in 1585, little resistance was offered. Moghul rule was established in Kashmir in the following year and lasted until 1752.

The two decades from 1555 to 1575 were for Ladakh another remarkable period of expansion under the vigorous leadership of King Tshe-wang Nam-gyal. Having withstood the series of challenges from Kashmir and Kashgar during the century before, Ladakh was geared for war and ready to take advantage of the temporary weakness of its neighbors. Successful expeditions were dispatched against both Guge and Baltistan, and Ladakh once again reasserted its suzerainty eastward over Tibet to the Mayum Pass, and westward over Baltistan and perhaps even as far as Chitral.[4] Tshe-wang Nam-gyal is reported to have contemplated an invasion of Turkestan across the Karakoram Pass but, the chronicles relate, "the people of Nub-ra petitioned him, and he desisted."

This Greater Ladakh Empire was short-lived like its predecessors, and did not long survive the death of Tshe-wang Nam-gyal in about 1575. The King had no sons of his own and the succession to the throne was contested by two younger brothers, with the result that the badly weakened kingdom quickly fell apart. As the chronicles put it, "all the vassal princes in one place after another lifted up their heads." Guge and other principalities in western Tibet regained their independence, as did the Balti states.

The hapless ruler of Ladakh, Tshe-wang Nam-gyal's brother Jam-wang Nam-gyal ('Jam-dbyangs-rnam-rgyal) attempted to retrieve his position by intervening in a dispute between two local rulers in Purig—the key district between Ladakh and Baltistan. However, in this endeavor he met only with disaster. Ali Mir Khan, the ruler of Skardu and probably the ablest of all known Balti chieftains, came to the assistance of one of the local rulers, surrounded and destroyed the Ladakhi army, and captured the king. The chronicles tell us that "the time had now come when the period of darkness should supervene, the period when royal supremacy should well-nigh be destroyed."[5] The Balti armies took advantage of Ladakh's complete helplessness to invade the country and avenge the many times in the past when Baltistan had suffered from Ladakhi ambitions. The Muslim invaders also took the opportunity to gain religious merit: Buddhist texts were burned, monasteries destroyed, and a Muslim wife (the daughter of Ali Mir) forced on Jam-wang Nam-gyal. The King's two sons by a Buddhist wife were barred from the throne and exiled to central Tibet. Subsequently, two sons were born to the Muslim queen, the eldest of whom, Sen-ge Nam-gyal (Seng-ge-rnam-rgyal), became the most illustrious of Ladakh's kings.

The boundaries of the kingdom of Ladakh were greatly circumscribed by Ali Mir. The chronicles describe them as from "Purig upward, and from Bran-rtse downwards."* Jam-wang Nam-gyal did what he could to rebuild and revitalize the monasteries destroyed by the Muslim invaders. This may perhaps be interpreted as a tribute to the vitality of Buddhist mercantile institutions, since Skardu's suzerainty over Ladakh lasted throughout Jam-wang Nam-gyal's reign and the administration seems to have been in the hands of a Muslim minister, Husain Mir. This situation continued even after the King's death (about 1595) and the accession of his son (Ali Mir's grandson) to the throne of Ladakh. In due course, as we shall see, Sen-ge Nam-gyal's joint heritage worked to his advantage, and Ladakh was able to regain its independence early in the next century.

* A. H. Francke, *op. cit.*, II, 107. Bran-rtse is the Tankse of the maps, a well-known village east of Leh on the road to Pangong Lake and Rudok.

# V

## *LADAKH'S RELATIONS WITH TIBET AND INDIA IN THE SEVENTEENTH CENTURY*

The sixteenth and seventeenth centuries were an equally critical and transitional period in the political history of India, Central Asia, and China. In the Indian subcontinent, the anarchy and chaos following the disintegration of the Tughlak dynasty had given place to a new Indian empire under the Moghul rulers. By 1550, their possessions included most of northern India below the Himalaya, and in 1586, the valley of Kashmir was also incorporated into the Moghul empire. But the other mountain kingdoms—from Baltistan and Ladakh in the west to Bhutan in the east—successfully resisted Muslim penetration for nearly another century. Yet for the Moghuls, as for earlier and later Indian governments, the Himalaya was the natural boundary of their empire to the north, and Moghul policy projected the eventual expansion of its political authority to these snow-clad ranges.

In China, the last years of the sixteenth century witnessed the disintegration of the Ming empire. This was the result of both internal dissension and external aggression, for the various Mongol nations on China's northern and western frontiers exerted continuous pressure on the Ming emperors while competing among themselves for the spoils that would fall to the victor. The Ch'ing dynasty's rivalry with the Central Asian states antedates the Manchu conquest of China, and it is evident that imperial policy in Tibet and Central Asia during the Ch'ing period (1645–1911) can be attributed in part to this as well as to the desire for security. Furthermore, it should be remembered that the Moghul dynasty in India originated in Central Asia and retained an interest in developments there for some time after gaining power in India.

In Tibet, meanwhile, the rivalry between the Yellow and older Buddhist sects—reinforced by the rivalry of powerful princely patrons and competing channels of trade—broke into open violence that greatly weakened Tibet. The remarkable early growth of the Yellow sect had been reversed in the late fifteenth and early sixteenth centuries with the rise to power of a new princely family who were patrons of a Red (Karmapa) sect. New Red monasteries were established near Lhasa, and for a period of twenty years (1498–1518), Lhasa itself was closed to Yellow sect monks. War broke out again between the sects in 1537, resulting in further Red sect triumphs, as eighteen Yellow monasteries were forced to change allegiance.* The Yellow sect lamas, however, soon found a new patron in the north—the powerful Mongol chieftain, Altan Khan. After his conversion to Buddhism in 1578, Altan Khan conferred the title of Dalai Lama on Sonam Gyatso, the gifted abbot who had been his preceptor.† From the base provided by this priest-patron relationship, Buddhism spread throughout Mongolia despite opposition from the shamans.

Tibetan influence thus grew apace in Mongolia with the blessing of the declining Ming dynasty, which now looked hopefully to Buddhism to subdue the warlike temper of the Mongols and provide a shield for China. In southern and western Tibet, however, the situation was very different. There, disorders had so weakened Tibetan authority that the price of continued trade across the borders was cession of territory. At some point between 1625 and 1635, Kathmandu acquired authority over sections of the important trading centers of Kuti (Nyalam) and Kerong (Skid-grong), and the hill kingdom of Gorkha forced the cession of another portion of Kerong district.

Ladakh was also able to take advantage of the dissensions weakening Tibet in the early seventeenth century. King Sen-ge Nam-gyal (1595–1645) had inaugurated another period of Ladakhi expansion after the collapse of the Balti kingdom created by his grandfather, Ali Mir Khan. He first declared war against Guge to avenge an insult to the family honor (the King of Guge sent back Sen-ge Nam-gyal's sister, whom he had wedded by proxy, when the bride was only two days from his capital at Tsaparang). Hostilities continued sporadically for

* For further details, see G. Tucci, *Tibetan Painted Scrolls* (tr., V. Vacca; Rome: Librerio dello Stato; 1949), I, 40–44.

† This was the first use of the title, which means ocean (of merit), but as Sonam Gyatso was already the third in a reincarnation series, the title was also conferred on his two predecessors, and he became the third in the succession of Dalai Lamas in which the present Dalai Lama is the fourteenth.

fifteen years, and it was not until 1630 that Sen-ge Nam-gyal, aided by internal dissension at Tsaparang, conquered Guge.

The steady Moghul advance toward his western frontier soon forced Sen-ge Nam-gyal to divert his attention in that direction. When Shah Jahan's Moghul army was used in 1637 to place a puppet on the Balti throne at Skardu, Sen-ge Nam-gyal prepared to move. In 1639, he invaded Purig, annexing it easily, and then advanced on Baltistan. A Moghul army was sent against him, however, and after defeat in battle at Kharbu, he was forced to sue for peace. Ladakh was not required to submit to Moghul supremacy, but Purig had to be relinquished and all claims to Baltistan renounced. The agreement also contained a promise to send tribute, but this provision was neither honored nor enforced during Sen-ge Nam-gyal's lifetime.

The agreement with the Moghuls, unfavorable as it may have been, nevertheless stabilized Ladakh's western frontier and enabled Sen-ge Nam-gyal to turn his attention eastward once again for further conquest. The time was auspicious for such a move, as both Tibet and China were in turmoil. The Manchus, driving south, were engaged in a conquest of China that was soon to culminate in the capture of Peking (in 1644) and the establishment of the Ch'ing dynasty. Meanwhile, the Qosot Mongol chieftain, Gusri Khan, led a successful invasion of Tibet that allowed him in 1642 to assume the title of King of Tibet and to set up the fifth Dalai Lama as the supreme religious head of the country. While the struggle in central Tibet entered its most critical stage, Sen-ge Nam-gyal took advantage of the situation to sweep eastward, first taking Purang in 1641 and then pushing immediately forward across the Mayum Pass into Tsang Province. When his forces were only some ten miles from Sakya monastery, they suffered a setback in an engagement with Tsang forces and withdrew to the Mayum Pass. A peace settlement was negotiated that recognized all of Tibet west of the Mayum Pass as part of Sen-ge Nam-gyal's Ladakhi empire.

Sen-ge Nam-gyal's death in 1645 put a temporary end to Ladakhi imperial ambitions. Indeed, Ladakh was before long once again occupied with preserving its independence against the Moghuls, whose interest in Ladakh arose from its strategic position with respect to the defense of Kashmir. The visit to Kashmir in 1663 of the Moghul Emperor Aurangzeb was viewed in Leh as an ominous development. King De-den Nam-gyal (Bde-ldan-rnam-rgyal) hastily dispatched an embassy to Srinagar with professions of loyalty and promises to pay the tribute specified in the 1639 treaty. Aurangzeb left Kashmir without insisting on more tangible concessions from Ladakh, and De-den Nam-gyal mistakenly assumed that it was once more safe to ignore

Moghul claims. The following year, however, Aurangzeb sent Mohammed Shafi to Leh to enforce the 1639 and 1663 agreements. The envoy carried an imperial decree calling upon the Ladakhi King to accept Moghul suzerainty and to spread the Islamic faith among his subjects. De-den Nam-gyal accepted these terms and agreed to construct a mosque at Leh, which he also promised to protect and sustain.

Ladakh abided by the 1664 agreement only as long as it was necessary. By 1672, Aurangzeb was so deeply involved with the Afridi chieftain Akmal Khan that no diversion of Moghul strength toward Ladakh was possible. De-den Nam-gyal quickly took advantage of the situation to seize Purig in 1673, and the lower Shyok River valley in the following year. Thus, by the time of his death in 1675, the Greater Ladakh Empire included Ladakh and its dependencies of Nubra and Dras, Purig, the lower Shyok River valley, Guge, Purang, Rudok, Spiti, Upper Kunawar, Upper and Lower Lahul, and Zanskar.

Meanwhile in Tibet, the Great Fifth Dalai Lama (1617–82), backed by his Mongol patrons, was engaged in consolidating his authority. The death of Gusri Khan in 1655 greatly reduced Mongol interest in the administration of Tibet, and the Dalai Lama soon took the power of appointing the regent in his own hands. It was not until 1680, however, that he was ready to challenge Ladakh's authority in West Tibet. Ladakhi chronicles assert that the crisis was caused by Ladakh's support of a Red sect lama who held spiritual and temporal sway over Bhutan, in his quarrel with Lhasa.[1] Tibetan sources claim that the Ladakhis were persecuting the Yellow sect in Ladakh and fomenting unrest in the Tsang border districts. Be that as it may, the Dalai Lama and the Mongol chief, Dalas Khan, were probably more concerned with hierarchical disputes and the border disturbances that curtailed Ladakh-Tibet-Mongol trade. War broke out in 1681, and Ga-den-tshe-wang-pal-sang-po (Dga'-ldan-t'she-dbang-dpal-bzang-po) of Tashilhunpo monastery was entrusted with military command by the Dalai Lama.[2] His Ladakhi counterpart was the Shakya-gya-tsho (Shakya-rgya-mtsho), who in 1673–74 had led the successful expeditions against the petty principalities of Purig and the Shyok River valley.

As the Tibeto-Mongol forces advanced toward Leh, the Ladakhi commander prepared to resist. He sent a challenge to his adversary in terms that clarify beyond any doubt the character of the relationship between Ladakh and Tibet:

> A savage like you dares to approach to insult with his envy our Liege Lord! Well, when we fight it out, if you win you may tie your horse to the lion gate of the palace [at Leh]; if we win, we shall tie our horses to the inscription pillar of Lhassa.[3]

The Tibetan commander accepted the challenge and, according to the chronicles, did indeed tie his horse to the lion gate after his army had won two battles and captured Leh. The Tibetan forces penetrated as far as Basgo, the second city of Ladakh (twenty miles northwest of Leh), where the Ladakhis withstood a siege lasting some six months. The King of Ladakh, in desperation, appealed to the Moghuls for aid. Ibrahim Khan, Governor of Kashmir, was apprehensive of the effect that a Tibetan conquest of Ladakh would have on the lucrative Kashmiri shawl-wool trade, and advised the Moghul Emperor to aid the Ladakhis. The Emperor agreed—in spite of his preoccupation with the Marathas in central India—for the Ladakhi plea not only allowed this ardent missionary of Islam to advance the cause of his religion, but also to enforce the tributary status that Ladakhi kings had agreed to in 1639, 1663, and 1664. Thus a Moghul army, reinforced by the Balti forces of Skardu and those of Sam-mi (Lower Ladakh) advanced on Basgo. The Tibetans promptly raised the siege and met the Moghuls in battle on the Kashmir-Ladakh road, just south of the town. The Moghuls were victorious and pursued the Tibetans to the traditional Ladakh-West Tibet border at Tashigong.

The Moghul commander, Fidai Khan, then left the two original adversaries to settle their own problems, stipulating to the Tibetans only that Ladakh proper be left inviolate in the hands of Ladakh's royal family. Before retiring, however, he exacted a number of concessions from the Ladakh authorities as well*—for Ladakh had to pay the price usually demanded of a weak nation which has been obliged to seek the assistance of one powerful neighbor against the threat posed by another. King De-lek Nam-gyal (Bde-legs-rnam-rgyal, *ca.* 1675–1705) was forced into a nominal acceptance of Islam, taking the name Aqabut Mahmud—a title used by his successors until their deposition by the Dogra conquerors in 1842. He further agreed to keep the mosque in Leh in good repair and to carry out the earlier agreements that hitherto had been evaded. He was also required to pay biennial tribute to the Moghul Governor of Kashmir. The most telling provision of all was the requirement that all Ladakhi coins were to be struck in the name of the Moghul Emperor, thus defining Ladakh's political allegiance. Ladakh had also to agree to some territorial concessions to the semiautonomous principalities that had assisted the

* L. Petech, "The Tibetan-Ladakhi-Mogul War of 1681–83," *Indian Historical Quarterly*, XXIII, No. 3, 178. In his article on the 1681–83 war, Petech inadvertently left the impression that Ladakh's agreement with the Moghuls followed the treaty with the Tibetans. A careful reading of the chronology indicates that the Ladakh-Moghul Treaty came first. Fidai Khan's engagement with the Ladakhis preceded his withdrawal to Kashmir in 1683, while the Ladakh-Tibet Treaty was not concluded until 1684.

Moghuls in the war. Raja Bidhi Singh of Kulu was ceded Upper Lahul, while the Balti states conquered by Ladakh a decade earlier were restored to their rulers, who renewed their allegiance to the Moghul emperors.

The continuation of hostilities between Ladakh and Tibet held no promise of advantage to either belligerent. Ladakh was in no position to challenge the much stronger Tibetan force in West Tibet, while the Tibetans were prevented—by fear of renewed Moghul intervention—from renewing their invasion of Ladakh proper. An armistice was arranged and negotiations for a final peace settlement begun. The Tibetans very shrewdly chose a Red sect dignitary, Mi-pam-wang-po (Mi-pham-dbang-po), to negotiate on their behalf, and the Treaty of Tingmosgang in 1684 was the result. The Ladakhis, although ostensibly on the winning side, paid for their victory with some loss of territory. Upper Kunawar went to Bashahr, which had aided the Tibetans, while the border between Ladakh and Tibet was fixed at the Lha-ri stream, which flows into the Indus five miles southeast of Demchok. Lhasa regained its rights in West Tibet, the revenue of which was to be used to meet "the expenses of sacred prayers offered at Lhasa."[4] The use of religious terminology here leaves open the possibility that Ladakh retained some sort of political claim on West Tibet. It is known that small enclaves near Mount Kailash remained under Ladakhi control. In any case, the ambiguity of the treaty provision concerning West Tibet was used 160 years later by the powerful Dogra rulers then in control of Ladakh as the basis for renewed claims to this area.

There can be little doubt that territorial concessions were of lesser importance to Ladakh than trading rights, and such victory as Ladakh achieved was in the provisions governing trade. Under the terms of the Ladakh-Moghul agreement, all Tibetan wool imported by Ladakh had to be sent to Kashmir's skillful craftsmen, but the authorities in Ladakh were guaranteed the right to act as intermediaries in the lucrative wool trade between northwestern Tibet (Chang Tang) and Kashmir through the offices of four Kashmiri merchants at Pitak. Under the treaty with Tibet, Ladakhi merchants received exclusive rights to the wool produced in the Rudok district of West Tibet, while the Dalai Lama's private treasury received a monopoly of the brick-tea trade (*Chaba*) with Ladakh.* What amounted to another com-

* R. Rahul, in his discussion of the structure of the Government of Tibet, notes that a new post of Government Trader in Ari was instituted under the provisions of this treaty. This Government Trader was a non-civil list officer who held his appointment under the Dalai Lama's private treasury. His duties included "the supply of two hundred loads of brick tea to Ladakh." (R. Rahul, "The Structure

mercial arrangement was the provision obligating Ladakh to send missions (*Lapchak*) to Lhasa with presents for the Dalai Lama and other Lamaist authorities.[5] The caravans bearing the gifts were allowed to carry large quantities of other commodities for trading purposes, a profitable enterprise for the Leh officials and monasteries granted a monopoly under this system.

The 1684 treaty is another of the mileposts in Ladakhi-Tibetan history that has aroused controversy in contemporary Sino-Indian relations. The Chinese Communist Government, in line with its policy of refusing to recognize the validity of any of the Ladakh-Tibet border agreements, has attempted to cast doubts on the very existence of the treaty.* The Chinese representatives noted that the "Biography of the Fifth Dalai Lama" does not mention the treaty with Ladakh—scarcely surprising in view of the fact that the fifth Dalai Lama died in 1682, two years before it was concluded. They also cited another Tibetan document, "The Biography of P'olha" (Pho-lha-në), which mentions the "bestowal" of seven forts and their estates on the Ladakhi King by the Regent of the Dalai Lama, but does not, the Chinese claim, refer specifically to the 1684 treaty. Moreover, Peking asserts, even if the treaty were genuine, nowhere does it "concretely define" the border between Ladakh and Tibet.

In the view of the Government of India, there is no doubt about the historical veracity of the 1684 treaty. Scholars of several countries have accepted the authenticity of the various texts of the treaty available, the Indians point out, and this at times when the boundary between Ladakh and Tibet was not in open dispute. Furthermore, they consider the fact that several of the provisions of the treaty continued to be operative until the present day to constitute an indirect verification of the treaty. That it did not "concretely define" the boundary between Ladakh and Tibet is readily conceded. However, the text of the treaty specifies precisely that the boundary to which it refers is the one defined in the terms of the tenth century division of Kyi-de Nyi-ma-gön's kingdom: "As in the beginning King Skyid-lde-ni-ma-mgon gave a separate kingdom to each of his sons, the same delimitations still to hold good."[6]

---

of the Government of Tibet: 1644–1911," *International Studies,* III [January, 1962], 282, 285.)

* *Report of the Officials of the Government of India and the People's Republic of China on the Boundary Question* (New Delhi: [Government of India] Ministry of External Affairs, 1961), p. CR-12. It was only in July, 1960, that the Chinese expressed these rather astounding doubts about the authenticity of the 1684 treaty. In earlier communications, Peking never questioned the existence of the treaty, and the matter apparently has again been allowed to drop.

The governments of China and India are also in fundamental disagreement over the significance of the *Lapchak* missions which Ladakh was to send regularly with gifts to the Dalai Lama and other Lamaist authorities in Tibet. To Peking, these were "tribute" missions that symbolized Ladakh's political subordination to Tibet. The Indians rejected this interpretation, arguing that they were not "one-sided arrangements" as the Chinese implied. If the Ladakhis sent *Lapchak* missions to Lhasa with gifts for the Dalai Lama, it was also true that Tibetans sent *Chaba* missions to Ladakh with gifts for the King. "*Lapchak* . . . [has], therefore, no political significance."[7] On this question, it is important to note that the so-called "tribute" was not paid to the civil authority in Tibet (at that time the representative of the Qosot Mongol Khan) but to the Dalai Lama, and what it symbolized was Ladakh's recognition of the Dalai Lama's spiritual and hierarchical authority as well as the supremacy of the Yellow sect over all other Tibetan Buddhist sects. The "tribute" mission—with the rich trading opportunities such missions always offered—must have seemed more of a privilege than an obligation, the more so since Ladakh's political dependence upon the Moghul Emperor had previously been made explicit. Insofar as its political implications are concerned, the Ladakhi authorities must have looked upon it as a useful counterweight to Moghul suzerain rights in Ladakh—effecting a balance between its two more powerful neighbors and thus permitting Ladakh to maintain *de facto* independence.

# VI

## *THE DOGRA CONQUEST OF LADAKH*

The period immediately after the 1684 treaty with Tibet found Ladakh in the uneasy position of a weak state tolerated by two stronger neighbors. It was not long, however, before each of these neighboring states was fully occupied with other matters. The Moghul empire, under attack from the British East India Company, the Afghans, and the Marathas, soon disappeared as an important factor in Indian affairs. And in 1751, the Afghans, under the leadership of Ahmed Shah Abdali, conquered Kashmir. The tribute Ladakh had formerly rendered to the Moghuls was now paid to the new ruler of Kashmir, who thus retained nominal suzerainty over the dominions of Ladakh's king.

Political developments involving China, Tibet, and Central Asia were no less complex than those in India, and touched Ladakh's vital interests at least as closely. The Great Fifth Dalai Lama had been able not only to achieve Tibetan autonomy under the patronage of the Qosot Mongols, but had extended his influence deep into Mongolia. After his death, the situation began to change. Intrigues between the Tibetan Government and the warlike Dsungar Mongols of the Ili district (in eastern Turkestan) alarmed both the Chinese court and the Qosot Mongols. Matters came to a head early in the eighteenth century, soon after the succession of Lha-sang (Lha-bzang) Khan to the rights and titles of the Qosot ruling family. The new Khan, apprehensive of the compact reached a few years earlier between the Regent of the sixth Dalai Lama and the Dsungar Khan, decided to assert his authority in Tibet. With the tacit support of the Chinese court, he marched on Lhasa in 1705, defeated the Regent, and assumed full ruling powers himself.

A decade passed before Tibet's internal politics gave the Dsungar

Mongols an opportunity to intervene. In late November, 1717, a sizable force was dispatched to Tibet to expel Lha-sang Khan. Both the time of year and the route chosen deserve attention. The route crossed the Kunlun range over the rarely used Yangi Pass, went down the Yarkand River valley and across the Qara Tagh Pass into the Qara Qash basin, traversed the west side of the Lingzi Tang plains, went across the Chang Lang Pass into Chang Chenmo, and finally over the Lanak Pass into the Rudok district of West Tibet—in short, the area of northeastern Ladakh currently in contention between China and India. The invasion of Tibet did not greatly surprise Lha-sang Khan, but the route chosen was unexpected. The Dsungar commander's decision to proceed along the little-known northern route to central Tibet circumvented Lha-sang Khan's defense system and resulted in his defeat, capture, and execution.

The Ch'ing Emperor was not prepared to concede Tibet to the hostile Dsungar Mongols. Chinese expeditionary forces invaded Tibet in 1718 and 1719. The first met with a disastrous repulse, but the second, aided by anti-Dsungar Tibetan factions, succeeded in expelling the Mongols from Tibet in 1720. In Chinese annals, this episode appears as a "conquest" of Tibet. From the Tibetan point of view, the Chinese army assisted Tibet in driving out invaders. It was not in any event a clear-cut conquest against united Tibetan opposition, but the consequence was that Peking appointed two Ambans (Residents) at Lhasa, and Chinese influence in Tibetan affairs gradually became paramount.

The first documented direct relations between Ladakh and China followed the expulsion of the Dsungar Mongols from Tibet in 1720. Ch'ing dynasty records report the arrival of a Ladakhi mission at Peking in 1724.[1] China's interest in Ladakh was due to the latter's strategic position on the southern flank of the Dsungar empire in Turkestan. Peking was not prepared to allow Ladakh to pass under the control of the Dsungar Mongols since this would have given the latter a valuable base for operations against Tibet, as well as control over all the major pass areas between Tibet and Turkestan. Furthermore, the extensive trade between Ladakh and Turkestan made Leh a valuable source of intelligence concerning developments to the north.

Ladakh appeared to welcome relations with China since they provided a powerful source of support against the constant threat of engulfment by the Dsungar Mongols of Turkestan and the Muslims in Kashmir. In 1732, the King of Ladakh wrote to the Chinese Residents at Lhasa: "I am trying to obtain information about Ye-erh-ch'i-mir (Yarkand)."[2] Later missions from Ladakh to Lhasa in 1737, 1738, 1743, and 1751 provided the Chinese with valuable information on developments in Turkestan and insight into the plans of the Dsungar Khan. But with the conquest of Turkestan in 1757–59, China's interest in Ladakh and other frontier states rapidly waned. Ladakhi missions continued to make their way to Lhasa during the next three decades, but after 1785, no mention of Ladakh or of Ladakhi envoys can be found in Tibetan or Chinese documents for nearly half a century.

The question has been raised concerning the precise nature of Ladakh's relationship with Tibet and China during this time. Nothing in the correspondence between the Chinese Residents at Lhasa and the Kings of Ladakh indicates that Ladakh was politically subordinate. The Chinese communications are haughty in tone, but no more so than those addressed to other "barbarian tribes" not under the sway of the Middle Kingdom. So far as is known, both Chinese and Tibetan policy treated Ladakh as an independent political entity. Neither in 1717 nor in 1750, when Dsungar invasions of Tibet appeared imminent, were Tibetan or Chinese forces stationed within Ladakh, even though several practicable invasion routes for an army from Turkestan passed through Ladakhi territory. In asserting that in this period Ladakh was subject to Lhasa and hence ultimately to China, the present Chinese Government relies heavily on an incident in 1753, when a Tibetan incarnate lama of Kha-tak-pa (Ka-thag-po) was sent to Ladakh to mediate in a succession dispute between rival factions of the royal family. Tibetan chronicles, however, make it perfectly clear that this mission was undertaken at the request of the Ladakhi nobles rather than as an exercise by Tibet of suzerain powers.

Throughout the eighteenth century, then, Ladakh was able to sustain its precarious status as an autonomous state owing nominal political allegiance to Kashmir and enjoying commercial and religious relations with Tibet. As a matter of fact, internal dissensions were a much greater threat to Ladakh's existence than ambitious foreign powers during most of this period. A series of weak monarchs and strong ministers seriously diminished royal prerogatives and the authority wielded by Leh officialdom over other areas of the country. A number of rival political centers emerged that paid little heed to the directives of the royal court.

The favorable external conditions that allowed the Ladakhis to indulge in domestic quarrels with impunity did not long continue. The rise of the Khalsa (Sikh confederation) empire in the last years of the eighteenth century and the expansion of British rule in India added new facets to an already complicated problem. When the great Sikh ruler, Ranjit Singh, conquered Kashmir in 1819, Ladakhi authorities promptly sought an alliance with the British to forestall the extension of Sikh ambitions to Ladakh. An East India Company agent, William Moorcroft, was in Leh in 1820–21 and negotiated a trade pact acceptable to Ladakh, but the Company officials in Calcutta rejected it.* This pact was meant to form the basis for a formal treaty which would have brought Ladakh into the British sphere and led to a serious British-Sikh dispute—something Calcutta wished to avoid at that time.

The Sikhs, reassured by the Company's abnegation of any interest in Ladakh, moved to strengthen the defenses of their new Kashmiri possessions by establishing relations with Ladakh on the same basis that had existed when Moghul and Afghans ruled Kashmir. Describing themselves as the heirs of their predecessors, the Sikhs demanded that Ladakh continue to pay "tribute" to the Governor at Srinagar and recognize the suzerainty of the Khalsa Maharaja. Ladakh refused to accede to this demand and terminated all tribute payments. Sikh involvement in hostilities with the Afghans and the cis-Sutlej hill states enabled Ladakh to adhere to this policy successfully for a decade and a half, in spite of its failure to secure support from the surrounding states.

As it turned out, it was the Dogra feudatories of Ranjit Singh led by the redoubtable Gulab Singh, rather than the Sikhs themselves, who were to prove to be the greatest threat to Ladakh. Gulab Singh and his two brothers, Dhyan Singh and Suchet Singh, had first entered the service of Ranjit Singh after the Sikh conquest in 1808 of Jammu, their home state. They quickly came to the conclusion that the way to restore their family fortune was through service to the Khalsa under Ranjit Singh. The Dogra brothers became so useful to their new master that by 1822 Gulab Singh had been made hereditary Raja of Jammu, and his brothers had also been made rulers in their own right.

Both the East India Company and Gulab Singh were well aware that the death of Ranjit Singh would presage the collapse of the Sikh power. While he lived, the British were content to maintain the *status quo* rather than risk defeat at the hands of the powerful foreign-led Sikh army. Ranjit Singh was, after all, a useful if wily ally. More-

* According to Moorcroft (*Travels in the Himalayan Provinces, etc.* [London: John Murray, 1841], I, 255–57), the Ladakhi authorities found it advisable to consult Lhasa and the Tibetan Governor at Gartok on this issue. However, the significance of this gesture has been greatly overestimated by Petech ("The Tibetan-Ladakhi-Mogul War of 1681–83," *Indian Historical Quarterly*, XXIII, No. 3 [September, 1947], 191), who assumed it implied some form of political subordination to Tibet. That this was not the case Moorcroft makes amply clear; he notes, first, that the Ladakhi officials stressed to him that this was a mere courtesy and, second, that the Ladakhis did not abide by the advice given them by the Governor.

over, his strong state acted as a buffer against possible Afghan or Russian incursions. Ranjit Singh's departure from the scene would change all this, but the Company could afford to wait.

Gulab Singh's ambitions necessitated a more active policy. While conquering territories to the north of the Punjab ostensibly in the name of Ranjit Singh, he was, in fact, creating a dominion for himself that could survive the expected collapse of the Sikh empire on the plains. Claude Wade, a British agent deputed to Ranjit Singh's court at Lahore, kept a wary eye on the activities of the Dogra brothers. He feared that Gulab Singh might attempt to seize all Punjab upon his master's death[3] or at least "would attempt to seize Kashmir which they have now almost surrounded."[4]

Gulab Singh's only path for expansion in the circumstances lay north and northeast—in Kashmir and Ladakh. Kashmir was, no doubt, his primary objective, but while Ranjit Singh lived and the Khalsa empire thrived, he could do little more than maneuver a frequent change of Governor to prevent any one of them from strengthening his authority in the valley. Ladakh was a riper plum, however, and ready for the plucking. The strategic value of Ladakh was apparent to Gulab Singh: It would give him new avenues of access to the Kashmir valley, while at the same time isolating it even further from the Sikh authorities in Lahore and the British possessions in the sub-Himalayan hill area.*

Ladakh's internal dissensions, combined with its inability to assert authority effectively in many sections of the country, presented the Dogras with numerous opportunities to intervene in support of one or another disputant. Some of the Sikh officials viewed with alarm the possible consequences of a Dogra conquest of Ladakh and possibly even Ranjit Singh had mixed feelings on this score.[5] However, Sikh involvement in an increasingly serious disagreement with the British over Sind and in dynastic disputes in Afghanistan made it inexpedient for the Lahore Durbar to interfere with the projects of its powerful Dogra feudatory.

British policy after 1830 also served to channel Gulab Singh's ambitions toward Ladakh. British officials in Calcutta apparently viewed the projected Dogra invasion of Ladakh with some enthusiasm. Not only might it lead to a rift in Dogra-Sikh relations—thus weakening the only powerful rival the British then faced in India—but the po-

* With regard to Gulab Singh's conquest of Ladakh, Wade wrote: "It was a wanton act of usurpation in order to strengthen his means of seizing Kashmir itself when the expected opportunity may offer." (National Archives of India [New Delhi], *Political Consultations,* January 17, 1838, No. 26; Wade to Macnaghten, November 17, 1837.)

litical instability that was bound to follow might divert a larger portion of the Tibetan wool trade to British possessions. The Company had been trying to achieve this end since 1815 at least, when a "factory" was established at Kotgarh on the Sutlej River to coax the lucrative shawl-wool traffic (normally a monopoly of Kashmir and Ladakh) directly into British territory. The Sikh conquest of Kashmir in 1819 and the ensuing famine drove many of the Kashmiri weavers into British India, and the Company redoubled its efforts to gain direct access to Tibetan products and to establish contacts with the Tibetan Government, but all its attempts to upset the traditional trading relations were rebuffed.

Such were the circumstances when, in 1834, Gulab Singh sent 4,000 men under his ablest general, Zorawar Singh, to conquer Ladakh. The Dogra commander advanced through Kishtwar into the key district of Purig, and then along the traditional route to Leh, via Kargil. The Ladakhis were unable to put up a successful resistance, and their desperate appeals to the British went unheeded. After a disastrous defeat at Lang Karchu where the Dogra force had encamped for the winter, King Tshe-pal Nam-gyal (Tshe-dpal-rnam-rgyal) was forced to sue for peace. An arrangement was finally agreed on, under the terms of which the King promised to pay an indemnity of 50,000 rupees, and an annual tribute of 20,000 rupees.

This treaty did not, however, end Dogra difficulties with Ladakh. Zorawar Singh spent much of the next five years suppressing revolts in various parts of Ladakh, periodically changing kings in an effort to find a satisfactory puppet ruler. A further complication arose from the fact that a number of Sikh officials were less favorably disposed toward the Dogras than Ranjit Singh. It was soon discovered that many of the difficulties encountered by Zorawar Singh in Ladakh had been instigated by Mian Singh, the Sikh Governor of Kashmir, who found the supply of shawl wool to Kashmir diminished by the Dogra incursions. Ranjit Singh himself had long coveted Ladakh, but he was evidently content to see its conquest accomplished by the Dogras, especially as Raja Dhyan Singh presented him with its tribute of 30,000 rupees. He received a deputation in Lahore sent in the name of Ngö-trup-ten-zin (Dngos-grub-bstan-'dzin), the current puppet ruler of Ladakh, and thus recognized Gulab Singh's conquest.*

In 1839, Zorawar Singh was once again back in Ladakh to frustrate

* *Political Consultations*, August 8, 1838, Nos. 28–29; Wade to Macnaghten, March 1, 1838. Gulab Singh arranged the payment of the Ladakhi tribute directly to Ranjit Singh rather than to the Governor of Kashmir, presumably because he did not wish to provide the Srinagar authorities with any basis for a claim to Ladakh after the expected dismemberment of the Sikh empire.

a plot between dissident Ladakhi elements and the ruler of Baltistan, Ahmed Shah.* After pacifying Leh, he invaded Baltistan with a mixed force of Ladakhis and Dogras. Taking advantage of the ambitions of the Sultan's son, Mohammed Shah, Zorawar annexed Baltistan, deposing Ahmed Shah in favor of his son and levying an annual tribute of 7,000 rupees.

Thus, by 1840, the Dogras had firmly established their authority throughout Ladakh and Baltistan, and were ready for fresh conquests. The Khalsa empire was still too strong to challenge directly by a movement against the Kashmir valley, but there were other important objectives in Tibet and the sub-Himalayan hill states, after which it would be feasible to turn north toward Turkestan. Gulab Singh's ambitious Governor of Ladakh was soon ready to turn his attention eastward.

* Ngö-trup-ten-zin was suspected of complicity in the plot and was deposed. The child King, Tshe-pal Nam-gyal (Tshe-dpal-rnam-rgyal), who had himself been deposed in 1835, was reinstated on the throne.

# VII

## *THE DOGRA-TIBETAN WAR OF 1841–42*

Gulab Singh's chief objective in the conquest of Ladakh and Baltistan had been two-fold: to encircle the Kashmir valley—in anticipation of the day when the dissolution of the Sikh empire would permit him to claim Kashmir as well as Jammu—and to gain access to the lucrative wool trade that normally flowed from the plains of northwestern Tibet (Chang Tang) through Ladakh to the looms of Kashmir. Control of the wool trade was desirable not only for sound economic reasons, but also because possession of this vital key to Kashmir's prosperity would provide him with a superior position in future negotiations with Kashmir. The hostilities and subsequent disorders attending his conquest of Ladakh had permitted the British to divert the shawl-wool trade to Bashahr—a state of affairs that Gulab Singh could not long afford to tolerate. With Ladakh in his hands, all he needed to achieve a monopoly of the coveted wool trade was to annex those areas of Tibet from which the wool came. If Ladakh's ancient claim to West Tibet could be enforced, it would give him the complete control he sought.

In 1841, the time seemed ripe for the attainment of Gulab Singh's ambitions. Ranjit Singh's death in 1839 had left the Sikhs absorbed in their own internal dissensions. The British were preoccupied elsewhere, as trouble was brewing in Afghanistan and Burma. Peking's attention was diverted by war with the British. Nepal, once a power to be reckoned with, was weakened by severe factionalism. In Tibet itself, there was considerable turmoil arising from a power struggle between the Regent of the Dalai Lama and the Tibetan ministers.

Relatively favorable circumstances prevailed, then, when Zorawar Singh, military governor of Ladakh and Gulab Singh's foremost commander, advanced on Tibet in the summer of 1841 with a force of some

4,000 men—a mixed group of Ladakhis, Baltis, and Kistwaris around a Dogra nucleus. He attempted initially to disguise the invasion as a pilgrimage to Mount Kailash, but Tibetan border officials, alarmed by the size of his forces, sent a warning to Lhasa. The Dogra forces were in three divisions: One moved up the Indus valley toward Tashigong, another through Rupshu, and the third into Rudok district via the route south of Pangong Lake. The first two contingents plundered Buddhist monasteries at Hanle in Ladakh and Tashigong in Tibet. The third unit captured Rudok and then moved south where it joined forces with the first division and captured Gartok, district headquarters for West Tibet. Zorawar Singh then announced his intention to conquer in the name of the Jammu Raja all of Tibet west of the Mayum Pass, on the ground that this territory had rightfully belonged, since ancient times, to the ruler of Ladakh. He then proceeded to make good his threat by advancing along the old caravan route between Ladakh and central Tibet. His forces cut the trail between West Tibet and Bashahr, and one contingent reached Taklakot, on the western extreme of the Nepal-Tibet border, by September 6, after garrisoning several stations along the way. The Tibetan general who had hurried to Taklakot when the first alarms reached Lhasa was unable to hold it with the local forces at his disposal, and had to pull back behind the Mayum Pass after only token resistance.

Hitherto, the British had not been greatly concerned by Gulab Singh's conquests in the mountain areas around Kashmir. Disorders in Ladakh had in fact been advantageous for British-protected Bashahr. The invasion of Tibet, however, threatened both the commercial and political interests of the East India Company. The initial effect was a sharp drop in the flow of wool to the factories of Bashahr. The Governor General's displeasure was conveyed to the Sikh court along with a request that Gulab Singh be ordered to recall Zorawar Singh from Tibet.[1]

Overshadowing the loss of the wool trade, however, was the Dogra capture of Taklakot, close to the Nepal border. When Gulab Singh had first annexed Ladakh, it had been rumored that his real aim was to establish direct relations with Nepal in the hope of promoting a mutually advantageous alliance.[2] Current intelligence reports stated that Zorawar Singh intended to build a chain of forts from Ladakh to the Nepal border and was attempting to gain Nepali cooperation in this endeavor. It was conjectured that Nepal hoped to obtain from this alliance a means of recapturing Kumaun.*[3]

* Kumaun, directly west of Nepal, had been conquered early in the Nepali westward sweep (*ca.* 1790) that was finally checked by the Sikhs at Kangra on the Sutlej River in 1809 and pushed back to the present boundary by the British in the Anglo-

These developments were understandably alarming to the British, who were well aware of the extensive network of anti-British intrigue that reached out from Nepal to every important ruler in India and to such foreign courts as Burma and Afghanistan.[4] For many years, also, the British had watched with apprehension the continued expansion of Nepal's disproportionately large army. It was a cardinal objective of British policy to see that Nepal did not obtain a common frontier with any other "powerful and aspiring hill state,"[5] and above all to prevent any coalition between Nepal and the Sikh empire.

Despite Nepal's obvious desire to turn the power struggle in the trans-Himalayan area to profit, however, it is open to question whether Zorawar Singh, in taking Taklakot, was as concerned with a possible alliance with Nepal as he was with forestalling any hostility from that quarter. He must have known that a Ladakhi mission whose objective was to overthrow Dogra rule had been well received in Nepal's capital. He may even have known that the Nepali King had requested Chinese sanction for such a scheme.[6] Once the Dogras took Taklakot, however, the King of Nepal authorized his personal appointee, the Governor of Jumla (a district in northwestern Nepal) to negotiate an alliance with them,[7] but nothing came of it. Again, when a large Tibetan army surrounded the Dogra forces in late November, 1841, Nepali troops stationed at Jumla reportedly had orders to prevent the Dogras from wintering in Nepali territory.[8] After the recapture of Taklakot by the Tibetans, the King of Nepal quickly offered to aid the Tibetans in expelling the Dogra forces from Tibet.[9]

These opportunistic tactics had in the end little result beyond contributing further to the mistrust with which neighboring countries regarded Nepal. Yet during the fall of 1841, while Zorawar Singh was still advancing triumphantly, the threat posed by a possible Dogra-Nepali coalition took on nightmarish proportions in British minds. This threat was two-pronged. When Zorawar Singh threatened to march on Lhasa if Ladakh failed to receive its time-honored monopoly of the shawl-wool trade,[10] more than financial loss to the Company was at stake. The inevitability of war with Nepal was coming to be accepted by British policymakers.* When the time came to subdue

Nepali war of 1814–16. One important aspect of British interest in Kumaun was the desire to put a wedge of Company-controlled territory between these two powerful states.

* Twice during October, 1841, the new Governor General designate Ellenborough, who had expected to take up his duties in November, 1841, had consulted Wellington concerning how best to conduct a campaign against Nepal. Reference was made to the coming campaign in various secret letters of the period. Brian Hodgson, the harassed British Resident at Kathmandu, wrote to his father earlier in 1841 that his aim was to hold things together "until the return of the season of

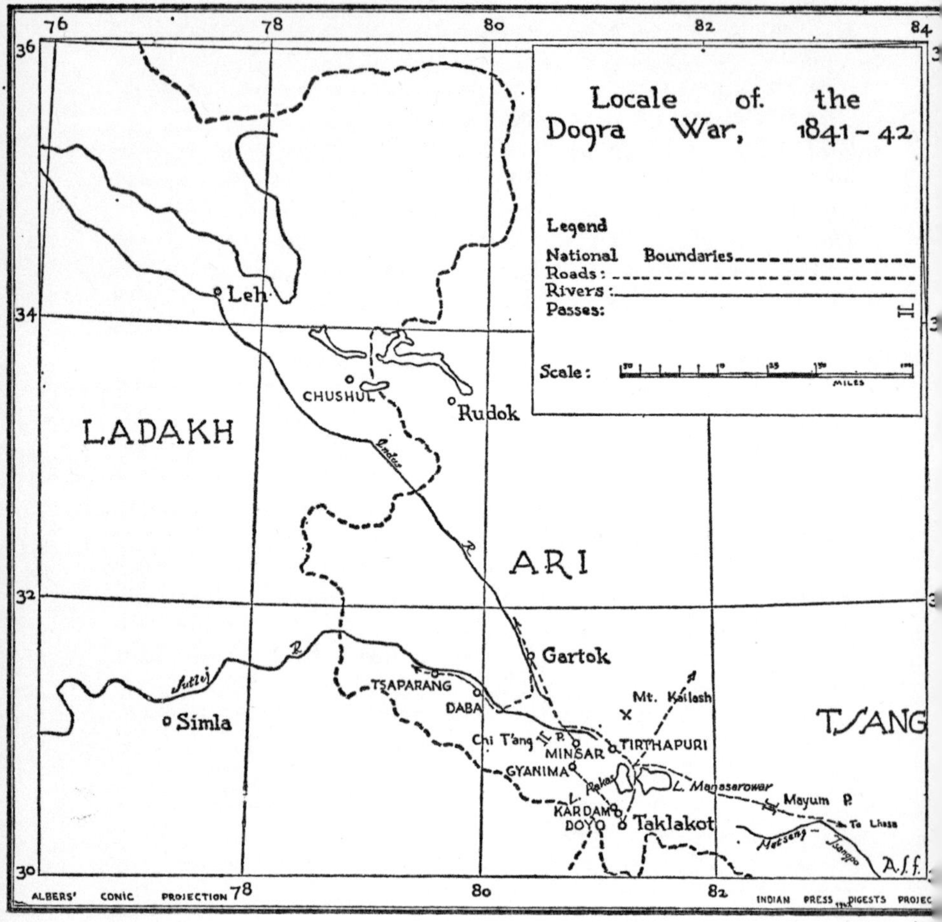
Locale of the Dogra War, 1841-42
Legend
National Boundaries
Roads :
Rivers :
Passes:
Scale :
MILES
LADAKH
ARI
TSANG
Leh
CHUSHUL
Rudok
Indus
R.
Gartok
Sutlej
R.
Simla
TSAPARANG
DABA
Chi T'ang
P.
MINSAR
TIRTHAPURI
Mt. Kailash
GYANIMA
L. Rakas
L. Manasarowar
Mayum P.
KARDAM
DOYO
Taklakot
To Lhasa
Matsang - Tsangpo
A.S.f.
76
78
80
82
84
36
34
32
30
ALBERS' CONIC PROJECTION
INDIAN PRESS DIGESTS PROJEC

that troublesome kingdom, they did not wish to be confronted with a Nepali-Dogra-Sikh coalition, nor did they wish Chinese attention to be fixed on this region as a result of Zorawar Singh's rashness. The Governor General brought heavy pressure to bear on the Sikhs to recall their Dogra feudatory, and set a deadline of December 10, 1841, for the withdrawal of the Dogra forces to Ladakh.[11]

With winter approaching, the Dogras were not unwilling to withdraw—but for a price.[12] What indemnity they demanded from the Tibetans we are not told, but it was presumably too high. Since the Mayum Pass was blocked by snow, it first appeared that the campaign would languish until spring. But the Tibetans found a bypass that permitted them to advance on Taklakot and continue the war. After severe fighting, Taklakot was retaken on November 9, 1841, and detachments were sent forward to cut Dogra communications and invest their fortifications. Reconnaissance parties sent out by Zorawar Singh were annihilated. Deciding to risk everything on a campaign to recapture Taklakot, Zorawar Singh broke camp and led his army from the Tirthapuri camp. Fighting raged indecisively in the Taklakot area for about three weeks, until the Tibetans, aided by a heavy snowfall, were able to ambush the Dogra forces on December 14. Zorawar Singh himself was killed, and his army suffered a crushing defeat. The remnants of his army fled, and except for pockets of resistance here and there along the line of fortified posts, the invasion was at an end. The Governor General's deadline was very nearly met, if not in the manner he had expected. There had been no Nepali-Dogra coalition, but a large Tibetan army had been sent into action with orders to seek out all fugitives and exterminate them. By the end of March, the Tibetans reported that all forts had been recaptured and the last of the invaders driven from Tibet. The Emperor of China expressed his satisfaction, and promotions and decorations were eventually distributed with a lavish hand.

These arrangements had hardly been completed, however, when the situation considerably altered. Among the prisoners taken by the Tibetans during their unexpected advance had been Gön-po (Mgon-po), the steward of the powerful Hemis monastery near Leh. The death of Zorawar Singh aroused in him the hope of freeing Ladakh from Dogra rule. He sent a secret letter to Ladakh with the information that Zorawar Singh was dead, that the remnants of the Dogra

action in November, when I sadly fear it will be indispensable to inflict the long-merited and long-provoked punishment." (W. W. Hunter, *Life of Brian Houghton Hodgson* [London: John Murray, 1896], p. 89.) The disaster in Afghanistan made an attack on Nepal unthinkable in 1841–2, however, and Nepal's potentially explosive instability was brought to an end by internal developments a few years later.

army were being pursued by the Tibetan army, and the time had come for Ladakh to prepare for war. He sent another letter to the British asking for aid in establishing an independent Ladakh.[13] The British replied that in their opinion Ladakh should belong to the Sikhs,[14] but before this reply had even been written, the Tibetan Kalons (cabinet ministers) had been busy. A delicately worded petition from the Ladakhi "aborigines" and the Balti Khan and his people, asking to be allowed to "pledge allegiance to the Tibetan 'shang-shang,' "* was duly forwarded to the Emperor by the Chinese Resident, who added his endorsement to that of the Kalons. The advantage to trade and to increased security of the borders was stressed, and it was also suggested that if this request were rejected, "at some later date they might have to submit to others. Then more trouble might result and another of our enemies would be strengthened." Nothing was said about any military operation. The Chinese Emperor gave his assent on May 31, 1842.† According to Nepal's representative at Lhasa, 5,000 additional Tibetan troops left Lhasa for Ladakh in June,[15] which suggests that the Emperor's consent, which would normally require five weeks to reach Lhasa, was something of a formality.

Be that as it may, the Emperor received no further reports on affairs in the Ladakh area until the war was over and the peace had been signed. The Ladakhi King's ministers wrote to the British in late May that they had given the country to the Chinese Emperor: "We had no other remedy—what could we do?"[16] In the middle of June, a letter went to Sher Singh in the name of the King of Ladakh, saying that the Ladakhis had always had relations with China through Lhasa until the Dogra had interfered. Now the Dogras must leave Ladakh, as the Tibetans demanded it, along with the usual tribute to Lhasa and the recognition of Chinese supremacy. If Gulab Singh would cooperate, the letter went on, shawls, wool, and tea would once again pass through Ladakh and Kashmir to Lahore.[17] But presumably "cooperation" was not forthcoming.

The Ladakhi chronicles have nothing to say about this correspondence, but they do give details of the fighting. The Tibetans, the Ladakhis, and Ahmed Shah, the deposed ruler of Baltistan, joined forces, invaded Ladakh, and laid siege to the Dogra garrison at Leh. The siege had been in effect for some six weeks when word reached Leh that Dewan Hari Chand and Wazir Ratanu, two prominent Dogra officials, were marching to the relief of the Dogra garrison with a huge army and several guns. The Tibetans retreated along the Indus River trade route, making a brief stand where they could. They set up their

* See Appendix, p. 156.
† See Appendix, p. 169.

camp in the Pangong Lake area,* and the pursuing Dogras set up camp a few miles away. The Tibetans received reinforcements numbering about 5,000† and a battle was fought at Chushul, possibly on the site of the present Indian airfield. The Tibetans were defeated and retired to their camp. Fighting raged indecisively for about ten days. The war was brought to an end only when the Dogra forces managed to dam up a stream and flood the Tibetan camp, after which the Tibetans surrendered. Dewan Hari Chand and Wazir Ratanu carried General Pi-hsi, the two Kalons, and some fifty other officers and men to Leh, where a peace was concluded.‡

As the Ladakhi chronicles report it, "conquered Ladakh," with the frontiers it had during the time of the Ladakhi kings, was annexed by the "high government"—Sher Singh's Sikh empire. Everything on the Tibetan side of the border remained under Tibet, that is, the ancient Ladakhi claim to West Tibet was relinquished. The biennial trade was to go on as before.§ Ladakhi merchants were to be allowed to travel to Gartok, Rudok, and wherever they pleased, and Tibetan merchants from Chang Tang were to be allowed to go to Ladakh. Everything was arranged exactly as it had been during the time of the former Ladakhi kings.

The Ladakhi chronicle agrees well with the Persian and Tibetan versions of the treaty that have come down to us. The treaty took the form of an exchange of documents, on September 17, 1842. The Tibetan note, incorporating the concessions made by the Dogras, was handed to Gulab Singh's representative while the Persian note, detailing the obligations assumed by the Tibetans, was presented to the Tibetan officials.||

* This area, in which most of the heavy fighting of 1842 went on, was also the scene of considerable fighting in 1962.

† Here the Ladakhi chronicles corroborate the report sent to Kathmandu by Nepal's official at Lhasa.

‡ There are conflicting stories about the death of Kalon Ragasa who, according to the Ladakhi chronicles, "swallowed the diamond of his golden finger-ring and died," while crossing the pass at Hanle on the way to Leh. Kalon Surkhang, after the signing of the contract, was taken to Jammu where he was presented to Gulab Singh, who gave him "a brocade suit [*kinkhāb*], a golden ring, a girdle, and several other suits," after which the Kalon returned to Tibet. (See A. H. Francke, "Antiquities of Indian Tibet," *Archaelogical Survey of India*, II, 136–37.)

§ Francke (*op. cit.*, p. 137) puts in parentheses the Tibetan words used: *lo-phyag* and *gżuṅ-tshon*. These refer to the *Lapchak* mission from Leh to Lhasa, and the Government Trader in Ari who was responsible for the *Chaba* mission that took tea to Leh. These arrangements had been in force since the 1684 treaty. (See pp. 39–40.)

|| The Tibetan Government sent a copy of the Persian note to the Government of India in 1921 during a minor dispute over the Tibet-Ladakh border. (*Report of the Officials of the Government of India and the People's Republic of China on the*

In both notes, the existing situation was recognized—i.e., the Tibetans accepted the Dogras as the legitimate authority in Ladakh, while Gulab Singh surrendered all claims to West Tibet. The "old, established frontiers" were reaffirmed and the two states agreed to respect them. The Tibetan document proclaimed that perpetual friendship should prevail henceforth between the Dogras and Tibet. The Ladakhi King and his family were guaranteed the right to reside peacefully in Ladakh as long as they refrained from intrigues against the Dogra rulers. The King was also granted permission to continue to send the annual gifts (*Lapchak*) to the Dalai Lama and his ministers if he so desired, though the treaty made it absolutely clear that this was in no sense to be interpreted as constituting political subordination to Lhasa. Two important provisions concerning trade relations were included in the Tibetan document. The first stipulated that "no restriction shall be laid on the mutual export and import of commodities—e.g., tea, piece goods, etc., and trading shall be allowed according to the old, established custom." The second obligated the Ladakhis to provide transportation (i.e., *ula* or *begar:* free porterage) and accommodations for Tibetan traders in Ladakh, a privilege Ladakhi traders in Tibet also enjoyed under a reciprocal arrangement.

In the Persian document, the Tibetans guaranteed that Ladakh "will absolutely and essentially not be the subject of our designs and intention." They bound themselves not to aid or abet the opponents of Gulab Singh and pledged to "carry on the trade in wool, shawl and tea, in accordance with the old customs, via Ladakh year by year." The treaty between Gulab Singh and Tibet did not bind the former's suzerain, and a supplementary treaty with similar provisions was concluded between the Governor of Kashmir (representing the Lahore court) and the Lhasa officials, in the name of the Emperor of China.

It was the duty of Meng Pao, the Imperial Resident at Lhasa, to report these developments to the Chinese Emperor. It is instructive to note the manner in which this task was accomplished.* Writing on December 8, 1842, he began by quoting a report from Kalon Surkhang, covering events from early September to the signing of the treaty on the 17th. Nothing whatever is mentioned concerning the Tibetan army's foray into Ladakh, and the language used strongly implies that the Dogras were attempting to invade Tibet again only to avenge the death of Zorawar Singh. The flooding of the Tibetan

---

*Boundary Question,* [New Delhi: (Government of India) Ministry of External Affairs, 1961] p. 53.) The Persian text has been published in A. N. Sapru, *The Building of the Kashmir State,* Appendix II.

* See Appendix for texts of Meng Pao's three memorials dated December 8, 1842.

camp is recounted, but in terms of a "retreat to a higher, more strategic spot, where it was possible to resist them." It continues that the Dogras then requested peace, "and when it was found that the Shen-pas [Dogras] were actually afraid of us, a truce was agreed upon." On September 17, "the officers from the aboriginal tribes of Gulab Singh and Ranjit Singh and Kashmir repented, and came with statements of submission and also signed an agreement calling for permanent peace, and pledging never to start trouble again. Subsequently, all the enemy forces were disbanded by their chiefs."

Meng Pao then recapitulated events and delicately interpreted them. The period during which the Tibetan army marched into Ladakh and laid siege to the garrison at Leh is obfuscated as follows:

> The possibility that the Shen-pas would seek revenge aroused apprehension, and it was necessary to take precautions against this contingency. The termination of the military campaign was therefore delayed, even though all our posts had been recaptured by the first month of this year [February-March, 1842]. The Kalons were ordered to remain in the area both to supervise the reconstruction work and to keep a careful watch at all times over the frontier defenses. They were strictly warned not to bring the campaign to a close or to shirk their duties until they had a firm control over the situation and were confident of the security of the frontier. Now it is evident that the Shen-pas returned in the seventh month [August-September, 1842] to avenge themselves on us, in unlawful association with the turbaned Muslims of Kashmir. After more than 350 of the enemy were killed in successive battles, the Shen-pas withdrew out of fear of our strong force, and signed an agreement promising never again to cause disturbances. According to the customs of the barbarians and aborigines, once they are willing to take an oath in signing an agreement, they can be relied upon to abide by their word. As the aboriginal Shen-pa and Kashmir officers have signed an agreement vowing permanent peace, things will now be safe for us.
>
> With regard to the Ladakhi Khan, who is still very young, General Pi-hsi was previously sent to pacify the country, and make suitable arrangements with his advisers. The Khan and all of his chiefs have already signed an agreement in which they vowed to guard the frontier and maintain permanent peace. The reports from our military posts there have not been solely relied upon. Our own deputies have also been secretly sent to the area to study and investigate the actual situation. The report of these deputies was submitted on the third day of the 11th month [December 4, 1842], and it verified what the Kalons had reported.

Promotions and honors were duly awarded to the higher officials concerned and to the son of the deceased Kalon, and everything was officially described as "very well managed." But Peking could read between the lines, as the Imperial reply conveyed by Court Letter from the Grand Council, made amply clear:

> The memorial of December 8th was received and understood. The most important thing for the safeguarding of the frontier is to bring peace and order through demonstrating good intentions. But if the aborigines and barbarians should cause frequent disturbances because of their insubordinate attitude, of course they should be punished and brought under control. It is my fear that the Kalons posted there took advantage of their fortunate victory to win Imperial awards and to make use of their position as a pretext for further action, with the result that the aborigines and barbarians were frequently offended. Consequently, they were given ground for complaint and therefore contemplated revenge, allying themselves with other barbarians and thus giving rise to fresh complications. All these considerations should be taken as a warning. Now that the peace agreement has already been signed by the tribes, they should be pacified with great care in the hope that this would ensure permanent security. The Kalons should be very strongly advised to keep a strict guard hereafter and never again allow the aborigines to encroach on our territory, but they should also handle this situation with great caution and never cause any further unfortunate incidents. After these strict instructions have been made known to them, if they should dare to presume on anything in order to earn merit without caring for the possibly disastrous consequences, we will grant them no more favors. The rest of the memorial is approved as proposed.

As they did with earlier agreements between Ladakh and Tibet, the present Chinese and Indian governments have put different constructions on the 1842 agreements. Chou En-lai at one time implied that his government did not recognize the validity of the 1842 peace treaty because of lack of Chinese participation,* but at the 1960 border talks, the Chinese officials found it more convenient to argue that Tibet had not acted independently of China than to run the risk of conceding that Tibet then had independent treaty making powers.[18] For the same reason, presumably, they also abandoned, at least for the purposes of the 1960 report,† the objection that Sinkiang had not been a party to the 1842 treaty. The only objections they raised in 1960

* Chou En-lai wrote on September 8, 1959, that "local authorities of China's Tibet" had concluded a treaty with Kashmir but "the then Chinese Central Government did not send anybody to participate in the conclusion of this treaty, nor did it ratify the treaty afterwards." (*Notes . . . Exchanged Between the Governments of India and China* [White Paper No. II (New Delhi: [Government of India] Ministry of External Affairs, 1959)], p. 28.)

† The untenable objection concerning Sinkiang received fresh currency in November, 1962, in [China, People's Republic] *The Sino-Indian Boundary Question* (Peking: Foreign Languages Press, 1962), p. 55.

concerned not the treaty's validity, but its relevance, arguing that it was no more than a mutual nonaggression pact.[19]

The Indian officials pointed out that the Tibetans had promised " 'neither at present nor in the future [to] have anything to do or interfere at all with the boundaries of Ladakh and its surroundings as fixed from ancient times,' "[20] and said this could only refer to the tenth century division of Kyi-de Nyi-ma-gön's kingdom that had been reaffirmed in the 1684 treaty.[21]

It is clear from the evidence as preserved in the Ladakhi chronicles and Indian and Chinese archives that the Ladakhis disliked Dogra rule, and would gladly have accepted help from any quarter—Chinese, Tibetan, British, or any other—to overthrow it. In particular, they were anxious to continue their old relations with the Dalai Lama's Government Trader in West Tibet. The Dalai Lama and the King of Ladakh were at the time both young children, but their officials arranged for Tibetan aid in ousting the Dogras, and the formal assent of the Chinese Emperor was obtained.* The Dogras, however, drove the Tibetan army out of Ladakh, although unable to enforce Ladakh's ancient claims to West Tibet. A peace treaty was signed that appears to have been mutually satisfactory to both the Dogra Raja of Jammu and Kalon Surkhang of Tibet. Ladakh's political subjugation to Jammu, and through Jammu to Lahore, was made explicit, but the trade relations between Leh and Lhasa, which the Dogras had for a time upset, were restored and the ancient boundaries reaffirmed. The Chinese Emperor's consent to the dispersal of the Tibetan expeditionary force was obtained, together with an Imperial warning that the Tibetan Ministers should henceforth take care to avoid further unfortunate incidents, and not try to earn merit for themselves with no care for the possibly disastrous consequences.[22] The Imperial relief was obvious. The *status quo ante* was re-established by the 1842 treaty. Under prevailing circumstances, this was as much as could well have been hoped for by any of the participants.

* Dated May 31, 1842. (See Appendix.)

# VIII

## *LADAKH AND GREAT POWER RIVALRY: 1845–1950*

The conflict with Tibet settled, Gulab Singh shifted his attention once more to developments in the Punjab. As he and the British had anticipated, the Sikhs were not able to maintain the efficiency of their government after Ranjit Singh's death in 1839, and the inevitable conflict with the Company came to pass in 1845. Gulab Singh ingratiated himself with the British by refusing to fulfil his obligations as a feudatory of the Lahore ruler and by acting instead as an intermediary in the dispute. Therefore, in Article XII of the Treaty of Lahore, signed on March 9, 1846, he was recognized as an independent ruler by both the Lahore and British Governments. The attainment of this long-sought goal was facilitated by the inability of the Sikh Government to pay the full 15 million rupee indemnity assessed by the Company. The Sikhs were forced to cede to the British the territories between the Beas and Indus rivers, including Kashmir and Hazara, and the Company, in turn, transferred these areas to Gulab Singh for the sum of 10 million rupees. This amount was later reduced to 750,000 rupees, as the British kept Kulu and Mandi, two districts originally part of the ceded territory, because of their potential importance in the trade with Tibet. This arrangement was mutually advantageous for the Company and the Dogras. Gulab Singh at last saw the fulfillment of his ambition for an independent Dogra state, while the British were able to conclude quietly what could have been a most difficult war. Not only did they gain a sizable financial profit, but they also avoided something for which they were by no means prepared at this time: the conquest of Kashmir and the burden of defending its frontier.

A week later the Treaty of Amritsar signed by Gulab Singh and the

British Government formalized the agreement in greater detail. The Dogra position with respect to the British Raj was more favorable than that of most princely states, for the Company did not guarantee the internal security of the state and thus could not as readily interfere in its affairs.* Gulab Singh and his heirs were guaranteed "all the hilly or mountainous country with its dependencies situated to the eastward of the River Indus and the westward of the River Ravi including Chamba and excluding Lahul."[1]

The eastern boundary of the Dogra domain was left for later determination, inasmuch as the traditional location of the frontier seemed well-known. Travelers such as Vigne, Moorcroft, Henderson, and Cunningham, who had traversed much of this area in the preceding three decades, had found no difficulty in describing the traditional boundaries, which appeared to be so well established through custom and tradition that formal demarcation was not considered necessary. Districts might change hands with the fortunes of war, but it was noted that "the natural boundaries of a mountainous district generally remain unaltered, in spite of changes wrought by war and religion."[2] The British thought it well to have a formal demarcation of the eastern border of the Dogra dominions, nevertheless. They still feared the possible renewal of Gulab Singh's ambitions in West Tibet, the realization of which would not only have brought the wool trade to a complete stop, but might also have embroiled the Company in disputes with China.

In 1846, the British were ready to attempt again to gain further access to the Tibetan wool market. Lord Hardinge informed the Chinese Resident at Lhasa that Article XI of the Dogra-Tibetan treaty, under the provisions of which all the wool trade was to pass through Ladakh, had been cancelled, and assured him that Tibetan traders would have free access to British territory and that no duty would be charged on shawl wool or other Tibetan products entering British territory.[3] Hardinge had more than limited commercial objectives in mind, of course, in pursuing this policy. For several decades, the British had demonstrated an interest in establishing contacts with Lhasa, but had been frustrated by the refusal of either Tibetan or Chinese officials to allow such a development. Any situation that was likely to lead to contacts between British and Tibetan representatives was accordingly avidly seized by the British in the hope that it would lead eventually to the establishment of full diplomatic and commercial relations.

To further the Company's objectives, the Governor General ap-

* This did not prevent the British from deposing Maharaja Pratap Singh and establishing a Residency in 1889, however.

pointed two commissioners to proceed to Ladakh in August, 1846, to "ascertain the ancient boundaries" between Ladakh and Tibet, and to lay down the boundary between the newly acquired British territory that had previously constituted the southern districts of Ladakh, and the districts belonging to Gulab Singh.[4] The Company was ready to be generous to Gulab Singh in terms of mere territory in order to obtain "a clear and well defined boundary in a quarter likely to come little under observation."[5] The commissioners were also reminded that it was one object of their mission to prevent the turning of the British flank to the northeast by troops or traders from Jammu.[6]

To facilitate matters, the Maharaja of Kashmir was asked to aid the British party. It was even more important to the success of this operation to gain the cooperation of the Tibetan and Chinese officials. The Bashahr Raja was prevailed upon to send a letter to the Tibetan Governor at Gartok who, after some display of reluctance, finally forwarded it to Lhasa. At the same time, the British Plenipotentiary in Hong Kong, Sir John Davis, approached the Chinese Viceroy at Canton, K'e-ying. Initially, Davis was confident that the Chinese would agree not only to the joint demarcation of the Ladakh-Tibet border but also to a reassessment of Chinese trade policies toward India.[7] But the Chinese officials, well aware of their country's intrinsic weakness, were unwilling to demarcate the border. Protecting China's position with a policy of evasion and procrastination—to which succeeding governments in China, down to the present, have adhered with considerable success—the Chinese and Tibetans thwarted British objectives.

In early 1847, long after the survey was to have commenced, a much less confident Davis wrote to Lord Hardinge that K'e-ying was away in the western provinces and that no progress had been made.[8] K'e-ying further frustrated Davis by claiming that a liberalized Chinese trade policy in Tibet would violate the Treaties of Nanking, which gave to the British special rights in only five Chinese ports. With respect to the frontier question, K'e-ying remarked that "the borders of these territories have been sufficiently and distinctly fixed so that it will be best to adhere to this ancient arrangement and it will prove far more convenient to abstain from any additional measures for fixing them."[9] Under considerable pressure, K'e-ying finally promised to convey the British view on commerce to the Emperor, but stated that the actual investigation of the situation was a matter for the commissioner in Tibet, who was unfortunately a great distance away.[10]

In August, K'e-ying intimated that the Chinese were willing to send a delegation to cooperate with the British in the demarcation of Tibet's western frontier.[11] When the British commissioners arrived at the border at the end of August, however, not only were there no Chinese officials awaiting them, but they met with active hostility from the Tibetans.[12] The commissioners were instructed to proceed with the inquiry on existing boundaries on their own initiative. The results, as depicted on the map prepared by one of the commissioners,[13] conform essentially with what is presently claimed by the Government of India as the boundary between Ladakh and Tibet from the Lanak Pass to the southernmost tip of the border.

The remainder of the nineteenth century was a period of comparative stability and amicability in Ladakh's relations with Tibet, virtually devoid of complications over boundaries or trade. There was some trouble in 1851, centered largely on the *Chaba* mission from Lhasa to Leh. The matter was settled readily by a reaffirmation that long-established rules and custom were to be observed in all particulars, and that "the boundary between Ladak and Tibet will remain as before."[14] The episode is of interest only as one more illustration of the stability of the boundary and of the trouble caused whenever there was any deviation from established custom in the border trade.

By 1860, interest in Ladakh centered around new and critical developments in Turkestan which threatened the precarious balance of power between the British, Russian, and Chinese empires. As the British Government in Calcutta steadily extended its control to northwestern India, it came in contact with Russians advancing against the small principalities in Western Turkestan. A clash between these two great powers seemed likely, and the situation was aggravated by misconceptions entertained on each side about the intentions of the other.

The situation became acute in the mid-1860's with the collapse of Chinese rule in Eastern Turkestan. The Ch'ing dynasty, torn asunder by the T'aiping rebellion, was still in the process of surmounting this catastrophe when new insurrections among the Muslim tribesmen in the western frontier areas undermined its authority. Both the British and the Russians wanted order restored there, but each great power was suspicious of any moves made by the other.

In these circumstances, Yakub Beg, a Kokandi official who had been forced to flee to Eastern Turkestan when Russia conquered his homeland, managed by 1867 to unify most of this former Chinese territory under his authority. He then attempted to insure the integrity of his domain by establishing good relations with the Russians and British, and with other neighboring states. (In 1866, he had written to the Maharaja of Kashmir proposing the establishment of friendly relations,[15] and shortly thereafter he expressed a desire to encourage trade with India.[16])

Unrealistic notions of the wealth of Central Asia persisted in

England throughout the Victorian era, and Yakub Beg's overtures seemed to supply the key to a storehouse of treasure, as well as a means of counteracting possible Russian advances. The Viceroy, Lord Mayo, encouraged by optimistic reports received from a tea planter who had recently visited Turkestan, urged the establishment of an India-Yarkand trade route.[17] As it was expected that most of the trade would go through Leh and then via either the Chang Chenmo or Karakoram routes to Turkestan, a treaty with the Maharaja of Kashmir, providing for the survey and construction of a new "free highway" through his territories to the domain of Yakub Beg,[18] was signed on May 2, 1870. The Maharaja was, however, less than enthusiastic about a "free highway"—an unheard-of innovation in Central Asian trade. When the first British mission to Yarkand suffered great losses in livestock through the failure of the Kashmir Government to provide the promised supplies, it was taken to be part of a deliberate plan to impede the progress of the mission, and in particular to prevent the opening of the Chang Chenmo route.[19] But in spite of the numerous difficulties, the British persevered. Eventually a Central Asian Trading Company was established, but its success was not spectacular. The Yarkandis were interested in British goods, but had little to give in exchange.

Yakub Beg also welcomed Russian missions, and a commercial treaty was signed in May, 1872, well before arrangements had stabilized with the British. Both Britain and Russia were content to have an independent Eastern Turkestan as a buffer, especially since trading relations promised to be less exacting than they had been when China controlled the area. But Eastern Turkestan's independence was short-lived. Yakub Beg died in September, 1877, when Chinese forces were already within his borders.

The Chinese reconquest of Eastern Turkestan did not put an end to Yarkand's trade with Russia and India. The British succeeded in placing a special officer on duty in Kashgar, and eventually a consulate, although they were never able to equal the level of Russian influence in Eastern Turkestan.

While all this was taking place, Ranbir Singh saw fit to take advantage of the disturbances in Turkestan to expand the boundaries of Kashmir. In 1863, a Kashmiri garrison was set up at Shahidulla, slightly to the north of the Sugat Pass in the Kunlun mountain range. In effect, this brought the Yarkand River valley between the Karakoram and Kunlun ranges under Ranbir Singh's control. Whether or not it constituted an expansion into Turkestani territory is hard to say. The valley was uninhabited, and largely uninhabitable. Both Ladakhi and Turkestani merchants plied the trade route between the

Karakoram and Sugat passes, having to depend upon their own resources for protection against Balti and Hunza robber bands. If Kashmir's claim to the area was insubstantial, Turkestan's was hardly better.

The whole question was destined to become little more than an academic exercise, however, for Ranbir Singh's "forward" policy had only a brief life. In 1866, when Yakub Beg conquered Khotan and unified Eastern Turkestan, the garrison at Shahidulla was hastily withdrawn south of the Karakoram Pass (partly as a result of British pressure), and Turkestani troops seized control of it. With the Chinese reconquest of Turkestan in 1877, this post passed into the hands of a Mongol detachment subordinate to the Chinese Amban at Khotan. However, no attempts were made to establish posts south of the Sugat Pass, and the Yarkand River valley remained a virtual no man's land over which none of the surrounding states exercised effective authority. While no permanent civil or military administration was set up by the Chinese in this area, neither the Kashmir, British, nor the Indian Governments have disputed their claim since 1866, and it is not an issue in the present Sino-Indian border dispute.

That Ladakh was contiguous not to Russian but to Chinese-held territory was an important factor in the formulation of British policy in this area. For the most part, the British were quite prepared to entrust to the rulers of Kashmir the conduct of Ladakh's relations with neighboring powers, although a joint commission was maintained at Leh during the summer months to supervise the trade between India and Turkestan. China, hard-pressed to retain possessions it already held, was not considered a threat. As a matter of fact, China's very weakness redounded to its advantage, as the British preferred to shore up Chinese rule against Russian encroachment rather than become themselves the warders of Eastern Turkestan. The Russians were for many years content with this situation, since it allowed reasonably full exploitation of Russian economic advantages.

Until late in the nineteenth century, the British were also willing to leave the Dard states north of Kashmir and west of Ladakh in the charge of the Dogras. British policy on the frontier area was generally determined by their attitude toward Russia. Most of the Dard area rested in the weak hands of the Kashmiri *Wazir-i-Wazarat* stationed at Gilgit. Since the early 1840's, he had held nominal but sporadic sway not only over Gilgit, but also over Astor, Hunza, Nagar, Punyal, and the states of the upper Indus valley. His motley Kashmiri forces, however, were no match for hardy mountaineers, and disaster inevitably resulted from any Dogra attempt to enforce physically the state's claims to suzerainty.

All this was of little consequence to the British, who felt that the lofty Hindu Kush and Pamir ranges made the area safe from Russian invasion, which, after all, was their chief concern. Their feeling of security was reinforced by complacent reports of British agents such as Johnson, Biddulph, Hayward, and Shaw, who periodically wandered through the Hindu Kush and Pamirs. During the course of Forsyth's second visit to Yarkand in 1873, Thomas Gordon, his second in command, led a mission into the Pamirs to check on routes that might be used by an invading Russian army. He later wrote:

> It was tolerably well known that the wide extent of lofty mountains between Eastern (or Chinese) Turkistan and Ladakh barred the passage of a modern army in that direction, but it was open to question regarding the Pamirs and the passes leading to India through Gilgit and Chitral.[20]

Gordon's explorations, which helped "to gauge accurately the difficulties that would confront an invader,"[21] apparently assuaged British fears about the strength of the mountain barrier, for no efforts were made to create additional defenses. Evidently, the opinion expressed by Sir Henry Rawlinson in 1867 still held good as far as British official attitudes were concerned. Rawlinson had stated that he

> did not believe there could be the slightest danger of collision with Russia in this direction. . . . With so many other lines open, no army would ever think of attempting to force a way . . . across the enormous mountain belt extending from Karakorum Pass to the Punjab, where you have a succession of passes varying from 15,000 to 19,000 feet in height. It is the most impassable of any part of the north-west frontier of India; consequently the most unlikely to be the scene of any collision between the two empires.[22]

In 1885, however, continued Russian advances in Central Asia alerted the British to the possibility of a Russian invasion of their dominions via Kashmir. Later in that year, a British officer, Colonel Lockhart, visited Hunza on a reconnaissance tour, and in 1888, Algernon Durand was sent to the same area by Lord Dufferin, ostensibly to check on the cause of hostility between Hunza-Nagar and Kashmir. The main purpose of Durand's journey, however, was to work out a plan for the defense of the Hindu Kush that would utilize the projected Kashmir Imperial Service Troops.[23] On his return to Lahore, Durand reported to his brother, the Foreign Secretary, that as he passed Gilgit he heard that a Russian officer had just been in Hunza. He was quite right; the officer was Captain Grombchevsky, who had found his way through a gap between the Pamirs and Eastern Turkestan. Thus, as Durand observed, "The game had begun."[24]

Now the problem was to strengthen the position of the Kashmir Government with respect to the northern marches. Durand contended that "as the suzerain power the responsibilities became ours and it was recognized that the Hindu-Kush for these hundreds of miles must be our natural frontier."[25] The formation of the Imperial Service Troops, already agreed to in 1888, would increase the military capacity of Kashmir, but security requirements suggested the reopening of the British Political Agency in Gilgit, which had functioned briefly during Lord Lytton's term of office. The time was ripe for it, so in 1889 the Gilgit Agency was reopened, with Durand as agent. The objects of the Agency were declared to be, "the watching and control of the country south of the Hindu-Kush and the organization of a force which would be able in time of trouble to prevent any *coup de main* by a small body of troops acting across the passes."[26] Durand quickly drew up an agreement with the rulers of Hunza and Nagar under which they agreed to keep open the Kashgar road and allow free passage of mail. In recompense, both chiefs were granted a subsidy.

In 1890, another Russian delegation visited Hunza and allegedly not only promised aid to Hunza against the British, but confidently foresaw the eventual absorption of Hunza by the Czar.[27] Safdar Ali, the Mir of Hunza, was well pleased with the visit and sent a mission with presents to Russia, as he wished to counteract the growing British influence in the Pamirs. To make matters worse, Colonel Francis Younghusband, who was undertaking a journey through the Pamirs, was stopped by the Russians at Bozai-Gumbaz and expelled by Colonel Yonoff, who claimed that Younghusband was on Russian territory. A similar experience befell Lieutenant Davison at Alichur Pamir.

But the danger that Safdar Ali would come to terms with the Russians did not persist for long. In May, 1891, together with Uzr Khan, the heir apparent of Nagar, he stopped the mails on the Kashgar road and prepared to expel the Kashmiri troops stationed in Hunza and Nagar.* A short but sanguinary war ensued, in which Durand himself was severely wounded. The intensity of the fighting was attested by the awarding of three Victoria Crosses to British officers involved in the campaign. Safdar Ali waited vainly for Russian or Chinese aid, and was finally forced to flee to a small estate in Yarkand granted earlier to his father by the Chinese. He was deposed by his half brother, Nazim Khan, who had British support. Nazim Khan, however, on British advice, continued to make the annual payment for the trans-

* The British had already decided to remove Safdar Ali. See India Office Library (London), *Foreign Department, Secret Frontier,* No. 1C, October 25, 1891; "Memo of Information Regarding the Course of Affairs Beyond the Northwestern Frontier."

Shimshal areas to Chinese authorities at Kashgar. Uzr Khan was exiled to Kashmir, but his father continued as ruler of Nagar, although the subsidies to both Hunza and Nagar were withdrawn until 1895. As part of the new arrangement, an assistant political agent was stationed in Hunza and functioned there until 1897.

Generally speaking, the northern frontier of Kashmir did not cause the British any real problems after the 1890's, and was consequently left under the nominal control of the Kashmir Government until the transfer of power. The Ch'ing empire was faced with internal and external problems of too pressing a nature to allow the diversion of much energy to either Ladakh or the Dard area. The British were satisfied with the Karakoram frontier, and the danger of a collision between Russia and Britain was lessened by a number of factors: the establishment of a friendly ruler on the throne of Hunza; the northeastern extension of Afghan territory in 1893 to form a buffer zone; and the defeat of Russia in the war with Japan.

The question of the border between Hunza and Sinkiang remained unsettled. The main area in contention was the long, narrow Raskam valley running from the Topa Pass to Bazar Dara, south of the Muztagh and Aghil Mountains. This area was uninhabited for most of the year, but in the summer months Hunza tribesmen moved in and cultivated the arable lands. Chinese officials in Sinkiang raised no questions until the British began to establish themselves in the area. British authorities were not yet directly involved in the dispute, being content to allow the Mir of Hunza to settle the issue on his own initiative. Representatives of the Mir and the Chinese Amban at Kashgar met in 1898 to negotiate their differences, but without success.[28]

The British now stepped in, anxious not only to settle the border controversy, but to delimit the whole northern frontier of Kashmir. Included in any comprehensive boundary settlement would be the Aksai Chin plateau, which had never previously been discussed by the British and Chinese. A bleak, uninhabited area whose salt deposits were regularly exploited by both Ladakhi and Turki traders, it was otherwise crossed only occasionally by European hunters. Indeed, there was considerable confusion among British cartographers in defining the limits of the Aksai Chin plateau. Several maps prepared by British explorers had depicted the plateau as stretching beyond Ladakh's northeastern boundary to include a similar area in northwestern Tibet, thus incorporating in "Aksai Chin" a larger area than appears in present-day maps. It had been as late as 1896 that Chinese officials in Sinkiang—reportedly with Russian instigation—challenged the British maps. Interestingly enough, they contended that the Aksai Chin was part of "*Chinese Thibet*."[29] This claim is in obvious conflict with the often-repeated Chinese Communist assertion that the Aksai Chin *has always been a part of Sinkiang*, but it does not bear out the Indian contention that Chinese authority had not been extended south of the Kunlun range by the end of the nineteenth century.

The British agent in Kashgar transmitted the views of the Chinese officials in Sinkiang to his superiors, commenting further that "Aksai Chin was a general name for an ill-defined and very elevated table land at the northeast of Ladakh and it was probably the case that part was in Chinese and part in British territory."[30] The Viceroy did not think it advisable to raise the issue with China at that time, however. He noted that it might well involve "real risk of strained relations with China, and might tend to precipitate the actual intervention of Russia in Kashgaria, which it would be our aim to postpone as long as possible."[31]

In 1898, British interest in the Aksai Chin was outweighed by concern over the Raskam valley and the Taghdumbash Pamir, where the claims of Hunza and China clashed, and the threat of Russian intervention at the doorway to India seemed imminent.[32] Accordingly, in October, 1898, the Indian Government wrote London suggesting that the Aksai Chin and Qara Qash basin be conceded in exchange for Chinese recognition of Hunza's claims to the western end of the Taghdumbash.[33] The British Government agreed to this proposal, and in March, 1899, made an offer to Peking to demarcate the boundary on these terms.[34]

This proposed border agreement would have entailed major territorial concessions by the British, since the Government of India had demonstrated both on maps and through the exercise of authority in the Aksai Chin that they considered the Kunlun range to be the *de facto* boundary between Sinkiang and Kashmir. Indeed, most of the territory currently in dispute between New Delhi and Peking would have been conceded to China under this settlement. The Chinese Communists must indeed find it galling that the Ch'ing Court did not even formally reply to the British offer, thus rejecting it by default.*[35] In retrospect, it is clear that China missed an excellent opportunity; for the British never repeated their offer, and subsequent British maps continued to depict the boundary along the Kunlun range. One can only guess at the motives behind Peking's lack of receptivity to this

* Chinese propaganda still tries to create the erroneous impression that the 1899 proposals *annexed* the Aksai Chin to Ladakh. ([China: People's Republic] *The Sino-Indian Boundary Question* [Peking: Foreign Languages Press, 1962], p. 55.)

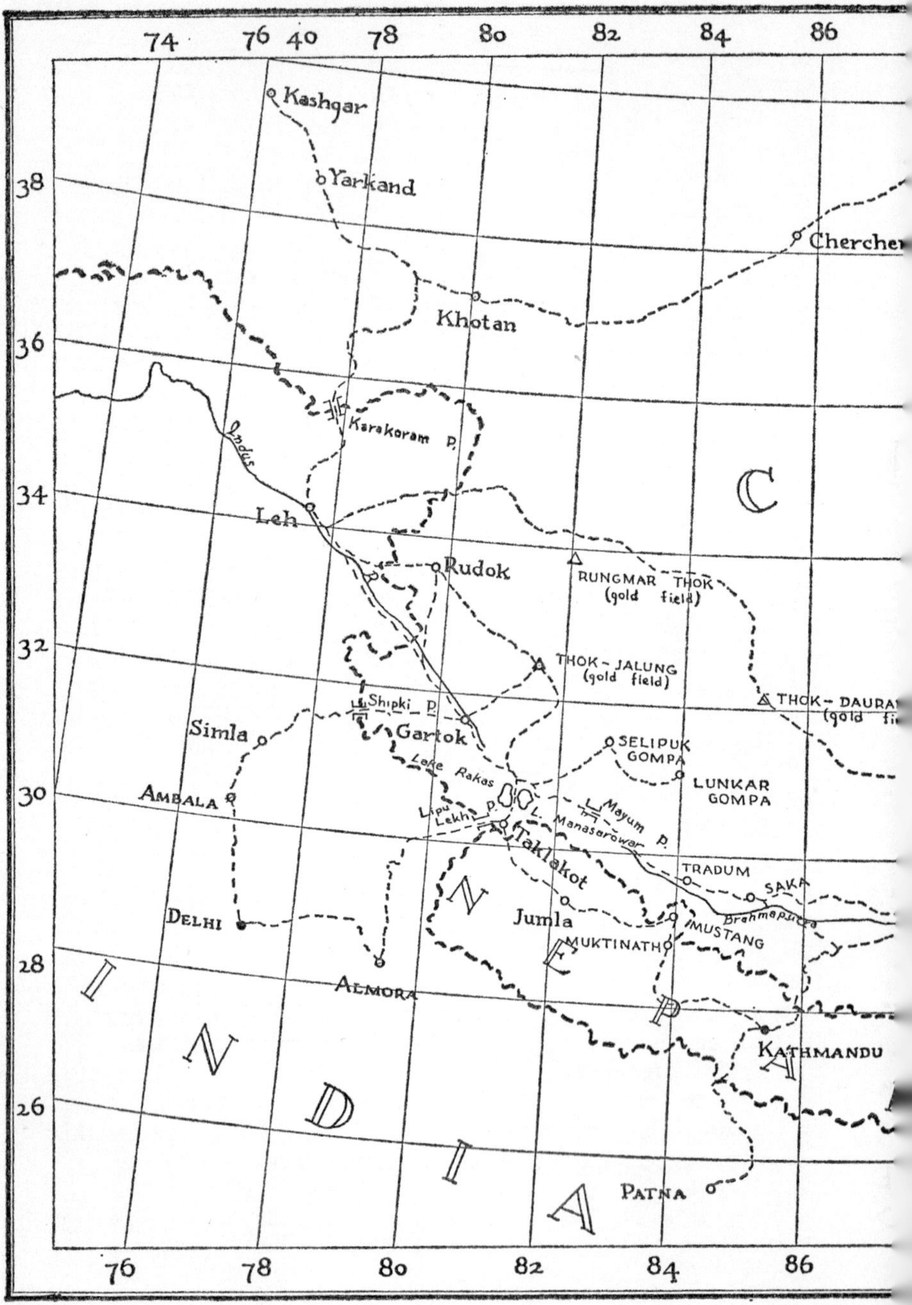
74
76
40
78
80
82
84
86
38
36
34
32
30
28
26
Kashgar
Yarkand
Khotan
Cherchen
Karakoram P.
Indus
Leh
C
Rudok
RUNGMAR THOK (gold field)
THOK - JALUNG (gold field)
THOK - DAURA
Shipki P.
Simla
Gartok
SELIPUK GOMPA
LUNKAR GOMPA
Lake Rakas
AMBALA
Lipu Lekh P.
L. Manasarowar
Mayum P.
Taklakot
TRADUM
SAKA
Brahmaputra
DELHI
Jumla
MUSTANG
MUKTINATH
ALMORA
N
E
P
A
KATHMANDU
I
N
D
I
A
PATNA
76
78
80
82
84
86

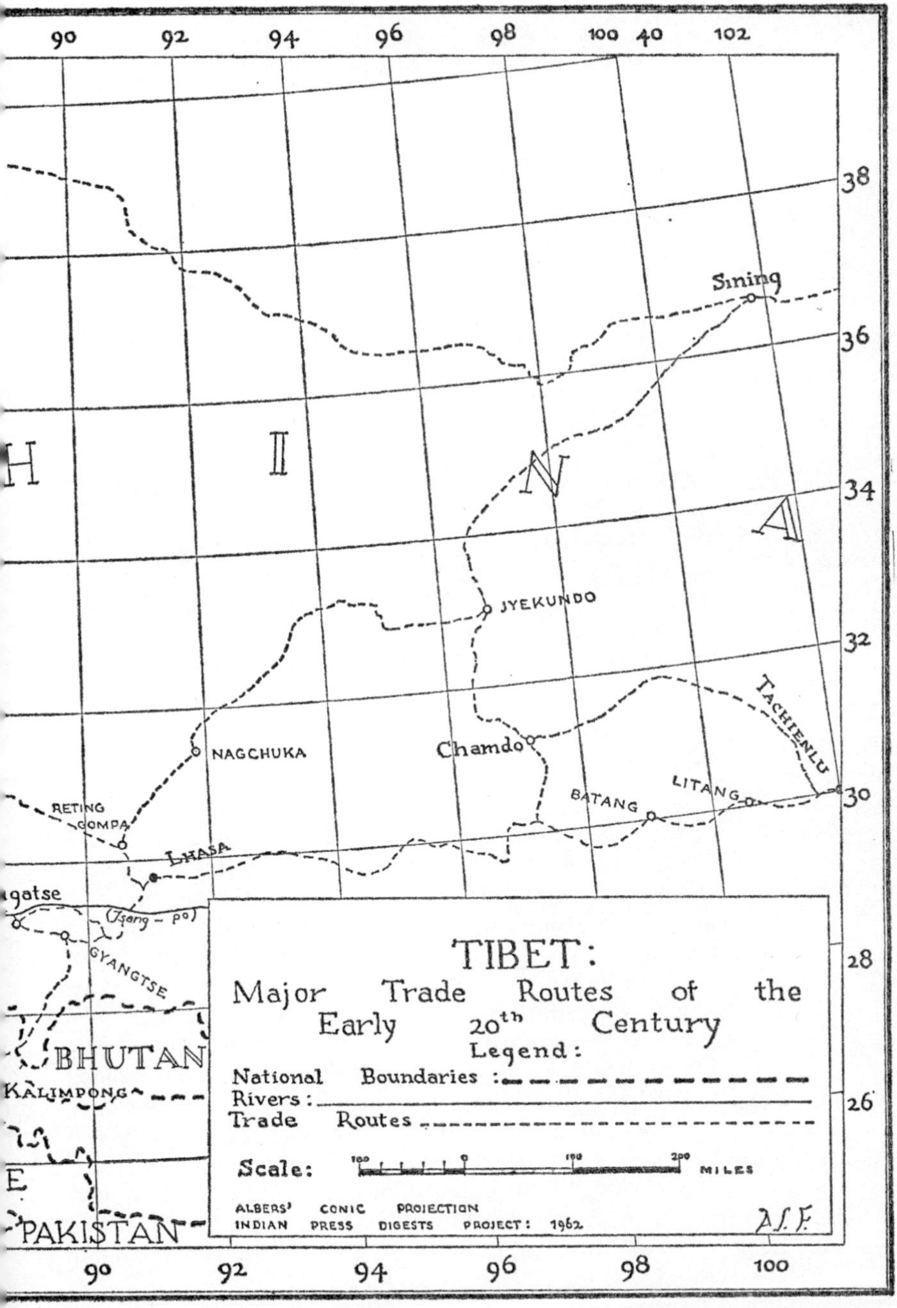
TIBET:
Major Trade Routes of the Early 20th Century
Legend:
National Boundaries
Rivers
Trade Routes
Scale:
100 0 100 200 MILES
ALBERS' CONIC PROJECTION
INDIAN PRESS DIGESTS PROJECT: 1962
A.L.F.
Sining
JYEKUNDO
NAGCHUKA
Chamdo
TACHIENLU
LITANG
BATANG
RETING GOMPA
LHASA
gatse
(Tsang – po)
GYANGTSE
BHUTAN
KALIMPONG
PAKISTAN
H
I
N
A
E
90
92
94
96
98
100
40
102
38
36
34
32
30
28
26

favorable offer. Perhaps it is to be explained by suspicion, or perhaps it is attributable to a general policy of refusing all proposals for boundary agreements during periods of Chinese weakness, on the assumption that a revival of Chinese strength would allow better terms to be extracted later.

Yet the Chinese were neither uninterested nor inactive. In 1890, the fort at Shahidulla was pulled down and another military post established eight miles further south, near the summit of the Sugat Pass. Two years later, the Chinese official at Sugat set up a pillar 64 miles to the south of the new fort, proclaiming Chinese authority over the area.[36] Later, a Chinese detachment set up a notice at the Karakoram Pass, asserting it to be the boundary between Chinese and British territory.[37] While these developments were noted by the Kashmir and British governments, no protests were made to Peking, as no conflict with the British conception of the boundary was involved.

The first four decades of the twentieth century were marked by comparatively amicable relations between Kashmir and neighboring states. There were minor eruptions occasionally, but none that was genuinely threatening. Although Central Asia became an arena for intense rivalry among the major powers, Ladakh, seemingly an observation post, remained outside the actual field of conflict. Yet in retrospect, it is obvious that the present ominous conflict over Ladakh stems in part from events that took place at some distance from its borders during this time. The most important of them occurred in Tibet.

The weakening of authority on the periphery of the Chinese Empire—in evidence even before the T'ai-ping rebellion of 1850–65—had given Tibet the conveniences of nominal Chinese suzerainty with very little restraint on freedom of action. Beginning in 1895, when the thirteenth Dalai Lama reached majority and assumed full ruling powers, the trend toward even greater independence was strengthened. The influence of the Dalai Lama extended throughout Mongolia as well as Tibet, making him a figure of considerable political importance, especially in regard to the expansion of Russian influence east into Mongolia. Various ties between the Russian court and the Dalai Lama gave rise to rumors of a possible threat to the security of India that caused great apprehension among the British. The threat loomed the larger because the British were not themselves able to communicate with the Dalai Lama, even by letter. They attempted to establish relations of some sort with the Tibetans by means of treaties signed with the Chinese, but it soon became obvious that the Chinese suzerain was unable, or in any event unwilling, to bind the Tibetans to any treaty to which they themselves were not a party. When circumstantial reports reached India concerning Chinese consent to a Russian protectorate over Tibet,[38] it was soon decided to open direct relations with Tibet, by force if need be.

The first attempt to open negotiations in 1903 failed. Tibet could be opened only by force, it was clear, and force was applied, opening the way to Lhasa for Colonel Younghusband in the summer of 1904. As British troops approached the Tibetan capital, the Dalai Lama fled to Mongolia, but the Lhasa Convention was quickly signed with the principal officials of his government. The treaty reaffirmed earlier ones signed with China dealing principally with trade relations and the boundary between Sikkim and Tibet, provided for the payment of indemnities, and contained several clauses intended to exclude all Russian influence from Tibet.*

The expeditionary force quickly withdrew from Lhasa, but repercussions echoed for some years throughout Europe and Asia. Britain—engaged in negotiations that it hoped would lead to a general settlement with Russia—had reluctantly sanctioned a limited expedition, and was embarrassed by the penetration to Lhasa. Furthermore, although the Chinese Resident had been present when the Lhasa Convention was signed, his signature had not been obtained. Negotiations were set afoot at once to obtain Chinese adherence. However, the supposedly moribund Ch'ing dynasty, no doubt shocked into decisive action by the ease with which the British had marched into Lhasa, lost no time in strengthening and extending its formerly lax hold on Tibet. By the time an Anglo-Chinese Convention was finally signed on April 27, 1906, Chinese troops had succeeded in breaking the back of Tibetan resistance in the borderlands, and a Liberal Government had come to power in England. Although Peking's demand that the British recognize Chinese sovereign rights over Tibet was denied, and although Chinese officials later conceded that the treaty stipulations prevented Tibet from being turned into a Chinese province,[39] the Lhasa Convention was considerably modified in favor of the Chinese.

This reversal of Curzon's policy was continued in the Anglo-Russian Convention of August 31, 1907. Recognizing both Chinese suzerainty and Great Britain's "special interest in the maintenance of the *status quo* in the external relations" of Tibet, the treaty placed restrictions on both British and Russian freedom of action in Tibet. The Russian specter—already diminished by defeat in the Russo-Japanese War—was thereby laid to rest, although at some cost to the British position in Central Asia.

* For an informed account of this affair, sympathetic to Tibetan as well as British problems, see H. E. Richardson, *A Short History of Tibet* (New York: Dutton, 1962), pp. 82–97.

The Chinese, meanwhile, exerted themselves to the utmost in an effort to strengthen their frontier and further weaken the British position. The British likewise busied themselves with the consolidation of their Himalayan frontier. The tribes of the Assam territories were brought under control, and a treaty was signed with Bhutan on January 8, 1910, giving the Indian Government control over its foreign affairs, but guaranteeing internal autonomy—a guarantee still honored today.

By this time, the Tibetan borderlands had been sufficiently reduced to enable the Chinese to move toward Lhasa. The Dalai Lama, seeking aid in vain from the King of England, the Czar of Russia, and other foreign rulers, sought to arrange terms with the Chinese. In return for assurance on his own status, the treatment of the Tibetan people, the number of troops to be brought in, and the purposes for which they were coming, the Dalai Lama gave orders not to resist the entry of Chinese troops into Tibet. Once the Chinese were in Tibet, however, it became clear that their promises had meant nothing. The Dalai Lama and members of his government fled once again—this time to Sikkim and British protection. The Chinese, as they had done in 1904, issued a decree deposing the Dalai Lama and calling for the selection of a successor. This decree was as fruitless as the earlier one. Manchu rule over China had nearly reached its end, in fact, at the very time when it was asserting its most extensive territorial claims along the Tibetan frontier area, including rights over Nepal, Bhutan, and Sikkim. These claims were firmly rejected. It should be noted that even at this period of expansion, the Chinese denied any intention to change the form of the Tibetan Government, and expressly conceded that they were precluded from reducing Tibet to provincial status by the Anglo-Chinese Convention of 1906.[40] It is also worth noting that no pretense to sovereignty over Ladakh was mentioned at this time, nor was any disagreement stated concerning the border between Ladakh and Tibet as depicted on British Indian maps.*

In 1911, the Tibetan cause was aided by the outbreak of revolution in China. By November, the Chinese troops at Lhasa had mutinied and were engaged in looting and killing. The Tibetans rose throughout the country, and the Chinese—civilians and military alike—were forced to surrender, deliver up their arms, and leave the country under a guard provided by Nepal's representative at Lhasa.[41] The Chinese official with whom the agreement permitting peaceful departure was negotiated was executed in March, 1915, for having "disobeyed orders and left Tibet, thus rendering the situation past remedy."[42] This ex-

* It is known that a Chinese High Commissioner saw British maps of the Ladakh border area in 1906. (See [Great Britain] House of Commons, *Further Papers Relating to Tibet* [Command Paper No. 5240] pp. 54–56.)

pulsion of the Chinese marked, in fact, the end of Chinese authority in Tibet until some forty years later, when it was again imposed by the Communist masters of China with the aid of an overwhelming expeditionary force.

The Chinese Republic—which in April, 1912, had proclaimed the provincial status of Tibet, Mongolia, and Sinkiang—did not at once give the situation up as hopeless, and made attempts to cajole the Dalai Lama back into the Chinese fold. He had learned by bitter experience, however, to distrust Chinese promises, so instead he declared Tibet independent. None of the great powers with influence in Central Asia, however, was prepared to recognize Tibetan independence. In January, 1913, Tibet and Mongolia signed a treaty recognizing each other's independence and promising mutual aid, although it is not certain that this treaty was ratified.[43]

At this juncture, British policy was obviously crucial. The British were convinced by developments since their march on Lhasa in 1904 that the Tibetans were in no position to maintain their independence against an invading army, but were equally incapable of submitting quietly to any attempt to rob them of it. The British had no confidence in the ability of the Chinese Republicans to re-establish the atmosphere that had characterized Manchu relations with Tibet at the zenith of the Ch'ing dynasty, but they were most anxious to avoid the protracted instability along their northern frontier that had marked that dynasty's decline. They also wished to put an end to the warfare then raging in the Sino-Tibetan borderland. The British had never at any time been prepared to take responsibility themselves for the defense of Tibet. Their one consistent solution throughout was to combine ultimate Chinese suzerainty with internal Tibetan autonomy. The problem was to get both sides to agree to such a compromise simultaneously.*

In the hope of ending the border war and bringing both Tibet and China to an agreement that would settle all outstanding questions concerning their political relations and boundary lines, the British proposed a tripartite conference. The response from Lhasa was favorable, once Tibet had been assured an equal status with China and Britain at the conference table. China's initial reaction was cautiously negative, but a combination of internal and external factors finally obliged the Yuan Shih-kai Government to agree to participate in the meetings, essentially on the terms proposed by Britain. Representatives of the three governments met at Simla in October, 1913, and began discussions that did not end until July, 1914.

* See the comment by H. E. Richardson ("The Myth of 'Suzerainty,'" *United Asia*, XII, No. 4 [1960], 384).

The initial claims of the two sides were far apart. The Tibetans demanded complete independence of China and restoration of the ancient border between Tibet and China. The Chinese claimed Tibet as an integral part of the Republic of China, but pledged not to convert Tibet into a Chinese province; rather, Tibet was to be guided by China in foreign and military affairs and not enter into independent negotiation with any foreign power, except for direct relations with British commercial agents as provided in the Lhasa Convention of 1904 and confirmed by the Anglo-Chinese Convention of 1906. The question of the Sino-Tibetan border proved to be the thorniest issue of all. The divergence between China's and Tibet's territorial claims was extensive—in its most extreme form involving an area approximately 500 miles wide, from Gyamda on the border of Lhasa province to Tachienlu in Szechuan.

It is important to note the position assumed by the Chinese on one aspect of the border question—namely, the *political* significance of the Dalai Lama's *religious* authority in certain border districts. On June 13, 1914, Sun Pao-chi, China's Minister for Foreign Affairs, informed the British Minister in Peking that "the Tibetans affected to think that they had rights over all places inhabited by Lamaists, but this was not so. The Lamas might have ecclesiastical authority, but this did not necessarily mean that these places belonged to Tibet."[44] The contrast between this viewpoint—essentially the correct one—and that of Communist China concerning areas inhabited by Lamaists in the sub-Himalayan regions of India is striking. It has a bearing on the whole question of Tibet's relationship with Ladakh, Sikkim, Bhutan, and the tribal areas of Assam, an issue that the Chinese have persistently kept in the background during negotiations with India in the current border conflict.

The Simla Conference was unable to conciliate the divergent Chinese and Tibetan positions on the boundary question, although the British offered a compromise setting off an Inner Tibet where Chinese authority would be stronger than in an autonomous Outer Tibet. The Tibetans reluctantly agreed to the reimposition of Chinese suzerainty under these conditions, but Peking repudiated the draft, although the Chinese plenipotentiary had initialed it. The sole reason they gave for not accepting the Convention was their unwillingness to accept the Sino-Tibetan boundary.* By refusing to sign it, however, the Chinese lost an opportunity to become the acknowledged suzerain of

* H. E. Richardson is undoubtedly correct in suggesting that although the boundary question was the only *stated* reason, it was in actuality symptomatic of deeper emotional reactions against the entire basis of these proposals (*A Short History of Tibet*, p. 113).

Tibet. The Tibetans were therefore free to make their own agreement with the British. Both plenipotentiaries signed the Convention, including a boundary agreement between Tibet and India (the McMahon Line), and a further declaration barring the Chinese Government from enjoying any rights under the Convention so long as its signature to the document was withheld. The opportunity was left open, but China never signed it.*

None of the available sources on the Simla Conference (including the Chinese) gives the slightest hint that the Ladakh-Tibet border was ever a subject of the extensive discussions between the British and Tibetan representatives.† Evidently neither government felt that there was any issue concerning it that warranted consideration. A minor dispute over the ownership of pasture land in the border area north of Pangong Lake occurred in 1917, and joint investigations were held. No final settlement was concluded, but the Tibetans apparently allowed their claim to lapse after 1927. At least the subject was not raised again until 1947, when Tibet, attempting to take advantage of the change in the international situation resulting from civil war in China and the withdrawal of Great Britain from the Indian subcontinent, proffered a statement of their most extreme territorial claims to both governments. But the pasture lakes north of Pangong Lake continued to fall within the confines of the Kashmir administration system, and it was only with the Chinese Communist encroachment in 1959 that this situation changed. China has asserted claims to this area based on the position assumed by Lhasa in the 1917–27 period, although it should be noted that the former are more extensive than any previously pressed by Tibet.[45]

This comparatively minor dispute was the only incident of any significance marring the good relations between Kashmir and Tibet from 1900 to 1950. Similarly, Kashmir's relations with Sinkiang never proved particularly troublesome in this period. Following the revolution in 1911, Chinese authority in Sinkiang had suffered a significant diminution, but did not completely disappear as it had in Outer Mongolia and Tibet. The period after 1911 might have witnessed a renewal of Anglo-Russian rivalry over Sinkiang had it not been for the series of

* A full treatment of the Simla Conference is not warranted here. The archives of the period are not yet open, but a selection of important documents was published anonymously in Peking in 1940. (*The Boundary Question Between China and Tibet: . . . 1913–1914.*) Consult Richardson, *op. cit.*, Chapter VII, for an evaluation of the results of the Simla Conference, including the advantages of which the Chinese were deprived by withholding signature.

† The Simla Conference map signed by the Chinese representative depicted the Sinkiang-Ladakh boundary as lying along the Kunlun range, *i.e.*, in conformity with the present Indian claim.

events that led to the outbreak of World War I. But in 1917, as a consequence of the revolution in Russia, Anglo-Russian competition erupted again. Yang Tseng-hsin, the "Governor" of Sinkiang, who had established control over the province in 1912 and made himself a virtually autonomous ruler, followed a cautiously pro-Soviet policy after 1918. Extensive Soviet economic penetration followed, under which Russian consulates were established in various centers. Yang's successors retained a pro-Soviet orientation until midway through World War II, when circumstances permitted the Kuomintang to establish tenuous authority in Sinkiang.

The contest for influence in Sinkiang continued to play a major role in Sino-Soviet relations, however. During the first half of 1949, Stalin's negotiators attempted to extract from hard-pressed Kuomintang representatives long-term economic concessions that would safeguard Russian interests in Sinkiang, whatever the outcome of the Chinese civil war. It is reported that before negotiations finally collapsed, the Soviet Consul General in Urumchi made one final effort to save his government's position in Sinkiang, proposing that the Nationalists declare Sinkiang independent, in return for which the Russians would order the Chinese Communists to desist from advancing into Sinkiang.[46] Highly circumstantial reports continue on Soviet backing of anti-Chinese guerrilla forces in Sinkiang, including a "pitched battle" in the strategic Altai region as recently as March, 1960.[47]

Source materials detailing British policy toward Sinkiang from 1920 to 1949 are still limited. The sketchy data presently available indicate that the British did what they could under basically unfavorable conditions to minimize Russian influence and, when feasible, to extend their own influence in districts immediately adjacent to India and to bolster Chinese authority elsewhere. In addition, the Government of India attempted, although with limited success, to secure for Indian merchants (mostly Ladakhis and Kashmiris) commercial privileges equivalent to those enjoyed by Russians.

Boundary questions never assumed any importance in the relations between Kashmir and Sinkiang in this period, presumably because the real center of conflict lay in the northern and western sections of Sinkiang in the districts bordering on the Soviet Union and Outer Mongolia. A joint Russian-Sinkiang survey of the northern and western borders of Sinkiang was carried out in 1940–42. This survey was extended on a very restricted basis to the border area between Gilgit and Sinkiang, but though a small survey team did visit the area between Shahidulla and the Karakoram Pass,[48] no detailed survey was made of the border areas now in dispute between India and China.

The years after the surrender of Japan in August, 1945, were marked by flux and change throughout Central Asia. As far as Ladakh was concerned, the most significant development was British withdrawal from South Asia and the partition of the Indian empire between the two new states of India and Pakistan.

The problem that most seriously complicated relations between India and Pakistan was the disposition of Indian princely states that had never been directly absorbed into the British administrative system, and particularly Kashmir, where the descendants of the Hindu Dogra dynasty established by Gulab Singh still ruled. Kashmir as a whole had a large Muslim majority, though in Jammu province the Hindus and Sikhs were the dominant element in the population, and in Ladakh Buddhists were in the majority.

The reluctance of the Maharaja's government to decide one way or the other intensified the crisis. The breaking point was reached on October 22, 1947, when Muslim tribal forces from the northwest frontier area of Pakistan invaded Kashmir. Both the Hindu Maharaja and the Muslim leaders of the National Conference* appealed to the Government of India for assistance in repelling the invaders. On October 26, India finally decided to intervene and three companies of Indian troops were flown to Srinagar. Although heavily outnumbered, they were successful in blunting the advance of the invaders until reinforcements had arrived and the safety of Srinagar had been secured. In early November, the Indian army under General Thimayya seized the offensive and quickly succeeded in expelling the invaders—now openly assisted by the Pakistan Army—from the greater part of the Kashmir valley and Jammu.

Thus, at the end of 1947, pro-Pakistan forces held only the Gilgit Agency in northwestern Kashmir and small pockets in the valley and in Jammu province. Frustrated in their designs on Kashmir itself, they turned to Baltistan and Ladakh in an effort to circumvent the Indian defense system in the valley. Skardu, the leading town in Baltistan, was besieged in January, 1948, and fell shortly thereafter. A few weeks later, Kargil, the strategic center on the 200-mile mule track (via the Zoji Pass) between the Kashmir valley and Leh, was captured, cutting off central Ladakh from the most easily accessible area under Indian control.

The Ladakhi authorities sent out urgent appeals for assistance to General Thimayya's headquarters in Srinagar as the Pakistani forces converged on Leh itself. An improvised air strip was hastily constructed at Leh and the Indian Air Force, pioneering a new route at

* The National Conference, the strongest Muslim political organization in Kashmir, had first opposed the partition of India and then the accession of Kashmir to Pakistan.

more than 23,000 feet above sea level, flew in Gurkha reinforcements. These arrived just in time to save Leh from the 1,000-strong Pakistani force, which was repulsed in an engagement a few miles west on July 11.

By this time, an alternative land route to Leh, some 200 miles long, from Manali in East Punjab through the 16,200-ft. Bara Lacha Pass, had been opened and thousands of porters and mule convoys brought up urgently needed supplies. However, it took two months to go over the road, and Ladakh's safety depended on the recapture of Kargil and the reopening of the much shorter land route through the Zoji Pass. In October, General Thimayya launched a relief drive. Tank-led Indian forces broke through the strongly-held Pakistani defenses at the Zoji Pass and on November 23, Kargil was recaptured and the invaders expelled from Ladakh.

Full-scale war between India and Pakistan was only averted when the Government of India requested of the United Nations Security Council that Pakistan be declared an aggressor. Under the auspices of the United Nations, a cease-fire was arranged, effective January 1, 1949. In subsequent months, a cease-fire line was established by a United Nations Commission, bringing about an uneasy division of Kashmir between Pakistan and India. The northern and northwestern areas, including Gilgit, Hunza, Nagar, and Skardu, came under Pakistan's control, while the Kashmir valley, Jammu, and Ladakh remained with India. The territorial alignment devised in 1949 assumed a semi-permanent *de facto* status as it became clear that neither Pakistan nor India was prepared, for urgent security reasons, to permit all of Kashmir to come under the sole jurisdiction of the other. Chinese encroachments on Ladakh near the Karakoram Pass have reopened the dispute in an acute form, involving all three powers in complexities that will be discussed at greater length in the closing chapter.

# IX

## *THE CHINESE COMMUNIST CONQUEST OF TIBET AND ITS IMPACT ON LADAKH*

By 1950, the center of interest in the Himalaya had once more shifted to Tibet. China had never relinquished claim to ultimate suzerainty over Tibet, even though it had bowed to the expulsion of the Chinese mission in 1912, and to Tibetan insistence on neutrality in World War II. With the defeat of Japan and the British withdrawal from India, the balance of power that had enabled Tibet to resist Chinese encroachment for nearly four decades collapsed. The People's Republic of China, like its Kuomintang predecessor, asserted a claim to Tibet.* Unlike its predecessor, the new government was in a position to press this claim in direct action.

Threats to "liberate" Tibet were first issued by high officials of the Peking Government on January 1, 1950.† The actual invasion was launched on October 7, 1950, at several points along Tibet's eastern border. Within a few weeks, the Chinese had routed key elements of the Tibetan Army, opened the main highway to Lhasa by capturing the border garrison town of Chamdo, and seized control of the major

* Chiang Kai-shek, in his address on August 23, 1945, to a joint meeting of the Supreme National Defense Council and the Central Executive Committee of the Kuomintang, said that the Sixth National Kuomintang Congress had decided to grant Tibet autonomy, and that if the people of Tibet expressed an aspiration for independence, the Government would not hesitate to accord them full autonomous status. (Aitchen K. Wu, *China and the Soviet Union* . . . [New York: John Day, 1950], p. 290.) The Communists began with an assertion of sovereignty, combined with what appeared to be a guarantee of internal autonomy.

† These threats followed almost immediately on the official announcement of December 28, 1949, that Sinkiang Military Headquarters had been established under the direction of Generals Peng Teh-huai and Chang Chih-chung, Chairman and Vice-Chairman, respectively, of the Northwest Military and Administrative Committee (*Ibid.*, p. 262).

eastern passes into Tibet. Despite the many rumors spread from Kalimpong on the progress of the Chinese armies, no further advances were undertaken during the winter from the east—the direction from which the Chinese attack would normally be expected. Instead, the Chinese made their deepest immediate penetration into Tibetan territory in the far northwest. Armed Chinese units that had been operating in Sinkiang—making use of the almost forgotten route through the Aksai Chin in Ladakh—were able to take the Tibetan defenses completely by surprise, and quickly overpowered the small garrisons at Rudok and Gartok. From these vantage points, they were able not only to control the western passes to India, but also to threaten to cut the main route from Lhasa southward by a quick drive on Shigatse from the west.*

It is doubtful that the Chinese were then present in a great enough force to make such a threat good against determined resistance, but the Tibetans were in no position to meet simultaneous threats from north, east, and west without immediate and substantial military assistance, and such aid was not forthcoming from any source. When Tibet's final recourse to the United Nations proved unavailing, December was well along. Nevertheless, the young Dalai Lama, who had meanwhile been invested with full powers as temporal and spiritual head of Tibet, fled south with his entourage to Yatung, on the Sikkim border, before his escape route could be cut.

At Yatung, the question of whether the Dalai Lama should go into exile or come to terms with the Chinese became the subject of protracted debate. In the end it was decided that he should return to Lhasa. An agreement establishing Chinese suzerainty over Tibet—but also containing provisions that purported to guarantee Tibetan regional autonomy and religious freedom—was signed at Peking on May 23, 1951. However, the Dalai Lama remained at Yatung until well into July, and did not enter Lhasa again until August 17. This meant that he reached Lhasa more than a week after the Chinese General Chang Ching-wu. The Tibetan Assembly, emphasizing the fact that Tibet had capitulated under duress, delayed its final ratification of the agreement until November 19, after Chinese troops had entered Lhasa itself in force.

The Chinese military occupation of Tibet—in such force as to belie the Communist claim of "peaceful liberation"—created anxiety in India on a number of counts. One was the manifest difference be-

* The route used by the Chinese is presumably the one taken by the Dsungars in their successful surprise attack on Lhasa, which they captured on the first day of December, 1717. Both invasions took place in early winter, when conditions were favorable for crossing the dreaded Aksai Chin desert.

tween Chinese and Indian maps, particularly with respect to the border between Tibet and India's northeast frontier province. Premier Chou En-lai informally assured the Indian Ambassador on September 27, 1951, that China intended in every way to safeguard Indian interests in Tibet, adding that "there was no territorial dispute or controversy between India and China."[1] Another was that the Indian Mission at Lhasa, unlike Gyantse and other lesser posts, was without treaty foundation. Chinese and British Missions had for years existed at Lhasa on Tibetan toleration, legitimatized by reference to the will of the late Dalai Lama, in which it was laid down that China and Britain were to be treated exactly alike. In the past, this informal arrangement had worked satisfactorily enough, but the situation had changed radically with the ratification of the 1951 Sino-Tibetan agreement. The British had long since discovered that without a permanent Mission at Lhasa, their treaty-based privileges at other Tibetan centers were of little value. It was therefore important to the Indian position in Tibet that an agreement was reached between the Chinese and Indian Governments that converted the Indian Mission at Lhasa into a Consulate General. Such an agreement was announced on September 15, 1952. In return, the Indian Government agreed to the opening of a Chinese Consulate General in Bombay. It carried with it implicit recognition of China's suzerain rights, and gave no written guarantee of Tibetan autonomy. At this point, however, the Chinese were still talking in terms of an autonomous Tibet. In any event, the military situation, both in Tibet and India, was the reverse of what it had been in 1914. In recognizing the hard facts of the situation, India at least managed to retain an important window in Central Asia that might otherwise have been lost.

The agreement did not bring to an end, however, the many frustrations suffered by Indian traders, pilgrims, and scholars who attempted, in accordance with time-honored custom, to enter Tibet. On Indian initiative, formal discussions began in late 1953 between Indian and Chinese representatives that culminated in the Sino-Indian Agreement on Tibet of April 29, 1954. The Panch Shila, or "Five Principles" of peaceful coexistence, were declared to form the basis of Sino-Indian relations. The treaty concerned mainly economic relations between India and Tibet, and particularly the improvement of facilities for merchants and pilgrims in both countries. Long before negotiations began, the Indian Government had given wide publicity to its intention to give up extraterritorial rights in Tibet that it had acquired as a legacy from the British. But if the Indians hoped to evoke a friendly response by making such generous overtures, they had much to learn of the nature of the regime with which they were dealing.

The behavior of the Chinese negotiators was such that their Indian counterparts, who were ready to make a gift to the Chinese of their postal, telegraph, telephone, and rest-house facilities in Tibet, held out for a stipulation that China should pay a "reasonable price" for them. On the day following the signing of the Agreement, having made its point, the Government of India waived payment as a "gesture of good will"—a gesture that Indians undoubtedly found more persuasive than the Chinese did. On their part, the Chinese conceded to India the right to retain the lease to lands within the trade agency compounds at Yatung and Gyantse, and agreed to provide "every possible assistance for housing the Indian trade agency at Gartok."* Further provisions intended to protect the position of traders and pilgrims in both countries were also incorporated.

Since then, the Government of India has come under heavy criticism for failing to obtain more favorable terms, and in particular, for not insisting on the inclusion of a boundary provision in the 1954 Agreement. Much of this criticism appears to be based more on an understandable dissatisfaction with the subsequent course of Sino-Indian relations than on a realistic appraisal of the possibilities then open to the Indian Government. Unsatisfactory in several respects as the Agreement undoubtedly was, it was nevertheless remarkable that any agreement could be obtained. In any event, Prime Minister Nehru, who had made his own position on the boundary very clear and furthermore had received assurances from Chou En-lai that no territorial dispute existed, could see no useful purpose in raising a problem that supposedly did not exist. To be sure, Chinese maps did not accord with Chinese statements, but the discrepancies were always explained away as being based on old maps which there had not been time to revise. The continued publication of these maps, each of which was immediately challenged by India, engendered considerable uneasiness at New Delhi, but the Indian position remained that if the Chinese disagreed with the clearly-stated Indian boundary, it was their obligation to bring the matter up.

In the course of negotiating the 1954 Agreement, the issue of the Indo-Tibetan boundary did arise indirectly—in connection with the pass areas in the middle sector of the boundary, east of Ladakh and west of Nepal. In the original Chinese draft of the Agreement, the wording was: "The Chinese Government agrees to open the following passes." To this wording, with its apparent implications that the passes were Tibetan, the Indian representative objected, claiming that the passes were Indian. After some discussion, both sides agreed to

* Difficulties were always put in the way, and no permanent agency was ever established at Gartok.

adopt the following wording: "Traders and pilgrims of both countries may travel by the following passes . . . (1) Shipki La Pass, (2) Mana Pass, (3) Niti Pass, (4) Kungribingri Pass, (5) Darma Pass and (6) Lipu Lekh Pass." This indirect recognition that the passes were in fact border passes drew from the Chinese representative the comment that "this was the fifth concession on our part."[2]

If India believed that China would henceforth give up claims to territory south of the passes, however, such an idea was upset almost immediately after the Agreement was ratified. On July 17, the Chinese Government protested to New Delhi against the stationing of Indian troops at Wu-Je (known to the Indians as Barahoti), an area southeast of the Niti Pass. This protest did not at first appear to challenge the Indian concept of the border, since the Chinese erroneously described Wu-Je as lying *north* of the Niti Pass. If Indian officials assumed that a correction of this error would lead the Chinese to abandon the claim, however, they had yet more lessons to learn about the Chinese Communists. The latter, although forced to admit to an embarrassing lack of geographical information, nevertheless persisted in claiming the area. It was the first instance in which the People's Republic of China specifically laid claim to Indian territory lying south of the great Himalayan barrier. Talks on this question began in 1955, but no settlement was ever reached.

It is obvious that the emergence after 1950 of a new pattern of interregional relations in Central Asia was bound to have a direct impact upon Ladakh. One immediate effect was a decrease in Ladakh's commerce with its neighbors, although this consequence was at first attributed to Chinese policy in Sinkiang rather than in Tibet. The Indian consulate at Kashgar was obliged to stop functioning, as the Chinese Communists moved to exclude all foreign interests—including Russian—from the area that had been for so long an arena of power rivalries. Trade between Ladakh and Sinkiang virtually ceased. Another setback to Ladakh's economy came with the termination in 1951 of the *Lapchak* missions from Leh to Lhasa that for nearly three centuries had played such an important role in the trade between Ladakh and Tibet.* On the other hand, trade between Ladakh and West Tibet increased somewhat as a consequence of the presence of Chinese forces in the area adjacent to the border, needing goods that could most easily be supplied through Ladakh.

* The termination of these missions seems to have occurred on the initiative of the Government of India, presumably to obviate any possibility that Peking might misinterpret the significance of these missions and use them as a pretext for political claims on Ladakh.

Another disagreement between India and China centered on the border of Ladakh with Tibet and Sinkiang. For several decades prior to the Communist triumph in China, Chinese maps had diverged on several basic points from the boundary depicted on Indian maps. The Communist Chinese appear to have been reluctant initially to provoke a crisis with India, evidently preferring to conceal their true intentions until they could present the Indian Government with a *fait accompli.* Indeed, the very existence of a border dispute in the Ladakh area was allowed to emerge indirectly, without a public statement specifying Chinese claims.

The first public indications of potential trouble in Ladakh appear to have come from the reports of Kushak Bakula, the Head Lama of Ladakh, who visited Tibet in the early summer of 1957 and found evidence of intensive road-building activity between Tibet and Sinkiang. A few months later, Peking announced the completion of a Tibet-Sinkiang road, without specifying the route taken. Shortly thereafter, a Chinese newspaper published a small-scale map giving a rough approximation of the road. It was impossible to determine whether or not the new road ran through territory claimed by India, but since the presumption was strong that it did, the Government of India sent small reconnaissance parties to the Aksai Chin in 1958, as soon as the snows had melted. One detachment was captured by Chinese frontier guards but another was able to carry out its mission, and New Delhi learned that Chinese troops were firmly entrenched in the Aksai Chin. India thereupon sent a strong protest to Peking on October 18, 1958, reaffirming India's sovereignty in this area. In a reply dated November 3, 1958, the Chinese for the first time positively and publicly asserted their claim to the Aksai Chin.

It was the spread of the Tibetan revolt to Lhasa in March, 1959, and subsequent developments, including the escape of the Dalai Lama to India, that intensified the Sino-Indian border disputes and gave them a new character. With guerrilla fighting widespread in eastern Tibet, the road through the Aksai Chin became the only land route to Tibet available to the Chinese Communists, and possession of the Aksai Chin a matter of desperate urgency. With the Dalai Lama safe in India, the hopes of the Tibetan people for eventual freedom were being kept alive and a major propaganda defeat had been inflicted on the Chinese.

From this point on, relations between Peking and New Delhi deteriorated rapidly. All trade across the Indo-Tibetan border was soon affected. Ladakh, already hard hit by the curtailment of trade with Sinkiang, now faced an equally drastic reduction of commerce with West Tibet. When the border crisis worsened, the Indian Government imposed a strict ban on the export of strategic goods to Tibet, defining "strategic" to include any commodity that might conceivably be of value to the Chinese in developing their military strength along the frontier regions. (For example, certain cosmetics used for dressing the hair were on the proscribed list because they could be used as lubricants for motor vehicles.) The Indian Government was faced with the difficult task of creating new employment opportunities for hundreds of Ladakhis who had depended, directly or indirectly, on this commerce. The situation soon deteriorated further, with the presence of Tibetan refugees who could not easily be assimilated into Ladakh's already overstrained economy.

Another problem that assumed some urgency after the 1959 revolt concerned the position and nationality of Ladakhis temporarily resident in Tibet. It had long been customary for many Ladakhi monks, including some of the most important incarnates, to study in Tibetan monasteries. The Indian Government considered that the 1954 Sino-Indian Agreement included Chinese recognition that these Ladakhis were Indian nationals entitled to certain rights and privileges during their residence in Tibet, and the Chinese had appeared to assent to this interpretation. At least no nationality question arose in specific form prior to 1959. During the revolt in Tibet, however, a number of Ladakhis were imprisoned and mistreated by the Communists. New Delhi strongly protested this Chinese action as a violation of the 1954 Agreement. The Chinese initially argued that Ladakhi residents were Chinese nationals. In September, 1959, they conceded on the question of nationality, but then charged the Ladakhis with being in Tibet illegally, and placed various restrictions on them. Ladakhi residents were pressed to accept Chinese nationality, and those who refused were subjected to forced labor. Several monks, including the Head Lama of Hemis monastery, Ladakh's most influential Buddhist center, were detained in Tibet and refused permission to leave. It was only in 1961 that this policy was relaxed and Ladakhis allowed to return to India of their own volition.

While trade and nationality questions were most distressing to numerous individual Ladakhis and other Indian traders, public interest in India and elsewhere has centered primarily on the border dispute. Before 1959 was over, the Chinese Communists had dropped their evasive manner, and pressed an open and bitter challenge of the validity of the entire Sino-Indian boundary as it was conceived by India. This change in attitude was not immediately evident. Nehru's letter of March 22, 1959, protesting Chinese incursions into Indian territory and drawing Chou En-lai's attention to the international agreements upon which the Indian maps were based, went unanswered until September 8—nearly six months. When a reply finally came, it was couched in friendly terms, but served notice that China, which had hitherto given the impression that the McMahon Line (the eastern portion of the border) would not be violated, was now prepared to challenge the entire boundary as a product of former British aggression against China. However, the Chinese Government retained its evasive attitude concerning its own territorial claims, and the extent of these claims remains uncertain even now. As we shall point out in greater detail in Chapter XI, Chinese maps—even those submitted officially to the Indian Government—have varied significantly with respect to the position of the boundary.

During 1959, however, whatever the accuracy or the consistency of Chinese maps, it became clear that Chinese military control was being extended more and more deeply into Ladakh. While awaiting a reply to Nehru's letter of March 22, the Indian Government placed before Parliament on September 7, 1959, a White Paper containing the texts of notes, memoranda, and letters exchanged between the governments of India and China from the time of the 1954 Sino-Indian agreement through August, 1959. The Indian public, acquainted now for the first time with the seriousness of the situation, reacted strongly. Their indignation rose even higher in October, when Chinese border guards ambushed an Indian reconnaissance unit within Ladakh, killing or capturing most of its members.* Some Members of Parliament demanded immediate military retaliation, including the expulsion of Chinese forces from Ladakhi territory. The Government, more aware than its critics of the military exigencies of the situation, firmly rejected these suggestions, and continued efforts to improve the Indian military posture in the area. The pace of development, although gaining momentum, was still distressingly slow, mainly because adequate supply roads were virtually nonexistent.

Although relations between China and India were severely strained by these episodes, the flow of official communications between the two governments continued. India was concerned to make clear the factual data supporting its position, and made several unsuccessful attempts to obtain an equally clear statement from the Chinese. China,

* See *Notes . . . Exchanged Between the Governments of India and China* (White Paper No. III, March 10, 1960, pp. 10–22), for the statement of Karam Singh, the officer in charge of the captured detachment. He relates in detail the method used by the Chinese to fabricate a false version of the entire affair, which the prisoners were forced to act out before movie cameras (a type of Chinese Communist practice frequently utilized during the Korean War). Karam Singh's report was sent to Peking along with a strong Indian note of protest. The Chinese Government, after nearly two months' delay, made an unconvincing denial (*Ibid.*, pp. 29–44).

on the other hand, tried several times to gain Indian agreement to proposals put forward ostensibly to prevent the possibility of border clashes, but which would have created important military advantages for the Chinese. On November 7, 1959, for example, Chou En-lai suggested the demilitarization of the entire Sino-Indian border to a depth of twenty kilometers, using the McMahon Line in the east and a line based on areas under "actual control" in Ladakh. Acceptance of this proposal would have seriously jeopardized Indian defense positions in the east and would have at the same time made a gift to the Chinese of the vital Aksai Chin area.

Nehru quickly responded, pointing out that in the east there were no Chinese south of the Indian border, except at Longju, and therefore no withdrawals were necessary to prevent clashes except at Longju, which India could not allow the Chinese to continue to occupy. He made a counterproposal applying only to Ladakh, requiring Chinese troops to withdraw behind the border claimed by India, and Indian troops to withdraw behind the border claimed by China,* leaving an unadministered no man's land between. He later made it clear that Chinese *civilian* traffic would be permitted to pass through the area. In a reply of December 17, Chou En-lai rejected Nehru's proposal as unfair to China, but in so doing, he committed himself to an explicit statement that the 1956 Chinese map correctly showed the "traditional boundary" in Ladakh—a commitment that was to endure only some six months.

During this exchange of letters, the Chinese continued to press for an early meeting of the two Prime Ministers. Nehru's immediate response was unfavorable. His experience with Chinese double-dealing could only have made such a proposal distasteful. However, despite a presentiment that a meeting was unlikely to accomplish anything, Nehru finally agreed to meet with Chou En-lai, and discussions were held in New Delhi from April 19–25, 1960. After the talks had ended, the Chinese Prime Minister held a press conference in New Delhi at which he stated that he had sought unsuccessfully to obtain Indian agreement to the following six points as a basis for further negotiations:

1. There exist disputes with regard to the boundary between the two sides.
2. There exists between the two countries a line of actual control up to which each side exercises administrative jurisdiction.
3. In determining the boundary between the two countries, certain

* Nehru's letter also pointed out that the Government of India was unable to find out where the Chinese thought the boundary was.

geographical principles, such as watersheds, river valleys and mountain passes, should be equally applicable to all sectors of the boundary.

4. A settlement of the boundary question between the two countries should take into account the national feelings of the two peoples toward the Himalayas and the Karakoram mountains.

5. Pending a settlement of the boundary question between the two countries through discussions, both sides should keep to the line of actual control and should not put forward territorial claims as preconditions, but individual adjustments may be made.

6. In order to ensure tranquility on the border so as to facilitate the discussions, both sides should continue to refrain from patrolling along all sectors of the boundary.[3]

Chou En-lai also stated that the "so-called McMahon Line was absolutely unacceptable to China," but that the Chinese were nevertheless willing to maintain the present state of the boundary in that sector, would not cross the line, and had never put forward territorial claims. He then suggested that since China was prepared to accommodate the Indian point of view in the eastern sector, India should accommodate China in the western sector.[4]

As Nehru pointed out to newsmen on the following day, what Chou En-lai had attempted to do was to link acceptance of the actual position (i.e., the McMahon Line) in the northeast frontier area to Indian recognition of the fact of Chinese occupation of Ladakh, but Nehru firmly stated that there could be no question of barter in such matters.[5]

It was agreed by the two Prime Ministers that officials of the two governments should meet and discuss the evidence available to each underlying their respective claims, beginning in Peking in June, 1960. Once this had been agreed on, Nehru suggested that "it might be done here and now," but Chou En-lai objected that most of their material was in Peking.[6] Indeed, when Nehru brought up the matter of the new Aksai Chin road west of the original caravan route, of which he had positive evidence, Chou En-lai professed ignorance, saying, "I do not know; I can say nothing about it."[7]

The atmosphere of the discussions gave little reason to believe that the forthcoming talks between Chinese and Indian officials could have any positive results, "unless," as Nehru put it when discussing the matter in the Indian Parliament, "some slight clarification takes place about certain basic facts."[8] In the event, as we shall see, the primary result was further obfuscation of the basic facts.

# X

## *THE SINO-INDIAN BORDER TALKS*

The joint communique of April 25, 1960, issued at the conclusion of the Nehru–Chou En-lai talks, specified that:

> Officials of the two Governments should meet and examine, check and study all historical documents, records, accounts, maps and other material relevant to the boundary question, on which each side relied in support of its stand, and draw up a report for submission to the two Governments. This report would list the points on which there was agreement and the points on which there was disagreement or which should be examined more fully and clarified. This report should prove helpful towards further consideration of these problems by the two Governments.[1]

In conformity with this agreement, teams of officials from both governments met in Peking from June 15 to July 25, 1960. The venue was then shifted to New Delhi, where they held nineteen sessions between August 19 and October 5. It had been expected that their work would be completed by then, but this was not the case and the two Prime Ministers agreed to an extension of the talks, this time in Rangoon. The third and final series of talks began there on November 7 and lasted until December 12, 1960.

At the end of the Rangoon meetings, a joint report was issued embodying the position taken by each side on the issues in dispute and summarizing the proofs advanced in support of their respective claims. The Chinese and Indian teams were each responsible for the preparation of sections of the report and, as the jointly signed preface stated, the results "faithfully explain each side's understanding of the factual material furnished and the discussions held during the meetings."*

* *Report of the Officials of the Government of India and the People's Republic of China on the Boundary Question* (New Delhi: [Government of India], Ministry

This joint report was published in its entirety by the Government of India in February, 1961. An invaluable document—containing a great deal of new information never previously available to the public and clarifying many of the issues in dispute—it warrants a detailed summarization of the sections relevant to Ladakh.

Reaching an agreement on the agenda was the first task facing the conference and proved an unexpectedly complex problem. The first session in Peking on June 15 showed that India and China disagreed both on objectives and procedure. The Chinese representatives proposed three points as the basis for the agenda: (1) whether the Sino-Indian boundary had been formally delimited; (2) the location and terrain features of the traditional boundary and its basis; and (3) the line of present actual control between the two countries. The Indians considered the first and third points beyond the competence of the conference, and they argued that:

> The core of the problem for the officials was to ascertain the location of the alignments claimed by the two Governments and then for both sides to bring forward evidence to sustain the claim where it overlapped with the alignment of the other, and thus to vindicate that it was Indian or Chinese territory—as the case may be. The question of actual control was unconnected with the task of deciding as to which country had legitimate title to the area claimed by the other.[2]

The Indians then offered a counterproposal, suggesting that the agenda comprise the following topics for each of the three sectors of the boundary: (1) location and natural features of the Sino-Indian boundary; (2) basis in Treaties and Agreements; (3) basis in tradition and custom; (4) basis in administration and jurisdiction; and (5) miscellaneous. In the fifth session at Peking, an agenda formulated along the lines proposed by the Indian Government was finally adopted.

Another question concerned the exact extent of the borders to be discussed. The Indian officials argued that they should not limit the talks strictly to territories under India's direct authority, but should also include China's borders with Bhutan and Sikkim and the border west of the Karakoram Pass (presently under Pakistani jurisdiction). The Chinese refused to assent, maintaining that Sikkim and Bhutan did not fall within the scope of the Sino-Indian boundary question, and that "in view of the present actual situation in Kashmir, it was also inappropriate for the two sides . . . to discuss the boundary west of the Karakoram pass between China's Sinkiang and Kashmir."[3] This

of External Affairs, 1961), p. 3. Both sides presented their reports in English but the Chinese later stated that their English version could not be considered "official."

interpretation was not acceptable to India, but no consideration was given to these sectors of the border during the talks, although India was careful to reaffirm the right to negotiate for these areas at appropriate points in the discussion.

Meanwhile, the Chinese persisted in their efforts to introduce one of their basic tenets—namely, that the Sino-Indian border in its entirety had never been formally delimited and that there was only a "traditional customary line" between the two countries that still required delimitation. The Indian representatives refused to discuss this question, considering it beyond the purview of the conference. Nevertheless, they had to take it into account, for it had a direct bearing on the validity of several treaties concerned with the Indo-Tibetan boundaries. The Indian position was that though there was obviously no single treaty between India and China that had delimited the entire boundary, there were treaties between India and Tibet delimiting certain sections, while the rest of the boundary was well-known and established through custom and tradition.

One tactic used by the Chinese that the Indians found particularly irksome was their tendency to confuse delimitation of boundaries with demarcation and to use the two terms interchangeably. In the normal parlance of international relations, delimitation refers to the general description of a boundary which can be defined in various ways—by watersheds, rivers, mountain ranges, or other natural or artificial features. Demarcation is the on-the-spot marking of a boundary in conformity with principles established in delimitation. The use of the term "delimitation" in situations where "demarcation" is obviously meant is one of the ways that Peking has attempted to bolster its case, since otherwise the Chinese position that the entire border has never been delimited would have to be abandoned.

The significance of natural features in the formation of boundaries was another point on which the Indian and Chinese representatives could not agree. The Indians relied heavily on the watershed principle:

> It was natural that people tended to settle up to and on the sides of mountain ranges; and the limits of societies—and nations—were formed by mountain barriers. . . . But if mountains form natural barriers, it was even more logical that the dividing line should be identified with the crest of the range which forms the watershed in that area. Normally where mountains exist, the highest range is also the watershed; but in the few cases where they diverge, the boundary tends to be the watershed range.*

* *Ibid.*, p. 236. The Chinese could not fail to catch the implications of this statement, as the major portion of the boundary running east from Ladakh follows the Himalayan crest, rather than the true watershed which is considerably farther north.

The Indian representatives also argued that the interpretations of the boundary diverged only in areas where the Chinese concept of the border "arbitrarily swung westwards or southwards, away from the watershed line, and always towards India and never towards Tibet."[4]

The Chinese refused to accept the watershed principle, arguing that

> geographical features have a certain bearing upon the formation of a traditional customary line, but they are by no means the only or decisive factor. . . . Therefore, as a rule the natural features of a traditional customary line follows different natural features in different sectors in accordance with the actual situation throughout the years of administrative jurisdiction and activities of the inhabitants of a country, and there is no reason why it should precisely run along the single feature of watersheds.[5]

The *Report of the Officials* does much to clarify the nature and extent of China's and India's conflicting claims in the western sector (i.e., Ladakh-Tibet-Sinkiang), as the agenda required both sides to define as precisely as possible their concept of the border. The Chinese divided it into two portions with the Karakoram Pass as the dividing line. In conformity with their decision not to allow discussion of the sections of the Kashmir-Sinkiang boundary presently under the jurisdiction of Pakistan, the Chinese refused to define the border west of the Karakoram Pass. The Indian representatives, on the other hand, were careful to include a description of this part of the border in view of their claim to the entire state of Kashmir. In the westernmost section, they described the border as running through the pass areas on the watershed of the Hunza River flowing into the Indus system in India, and the Qara Chukar River flowing into the Yarkand system in Sinkiang. From there it continued, they said, to the northwestern bend of the Muztagh River, which it crossed, ascending to the crest line of the Aghil Mountains and following this watershed to the Karakoram Pass.

It was the boundary immediately east of the Karakoram Pass where the Chinese and Indian alignments diverged so widely. The Chinese defined the boundary as running east from the Karakoram Pass along a mountain ridge to a point east 78° east longitude, turning southeastward along the high ridge of the Karakoram Mountains on the east bank of the Shyok River and northern bank of the Kugrang Tsangpo River down to the Kongka Pass. They contended that this constituted the border between Sinkiang and Ladakh and that it was only at the Kongka Pass that the border between Tibet and Ladakh commenced. Aksai Chin, Lingzi Tang, and the eastern portion of the Chang Chenmo valley were thus incorporated into Sinkiang province.

The Indian representatives took strong exception to this description, whose impreciseness they were quick to point out. In reply to their questions, the Chinese admitted that at a certain, unspecified, point, their alignment left the highest range of the Karakoram Mountains and followed several of the lower ranges to the Kongka Pass. Thus, Peking's insistence that its version of the boundary followed the Karakoram watershed was shown to be specious. The Indians also pointed out that the Chinese alignment zigzagged from range to range, for the various peaks given in the Chinese description were in different ranges. The Chinese maintained that these ranges were linked by spurs, but were unable to substantiate this assertion when questioned closely. In short, they failed to demonstrate much knowledge of an area they claimed had been roughly surveyed by Chinese parties in 1941–42.

The Indians described the boundary east of the Karakoram Pass as lying along the watershed between the Shyok and Yarkand rivers. After running through the Qara Tagh Pass and crossing the eastern bend of the Qara Qash River (northwest of Haji Langar), the boundary ascended to the crest of the Kunlun range—which is the watershed separating the Yarungkash basin in Sinkiang from those of the lakes in Aksai Chin. At a point approximately longitude 80° 21′ E, the line left the Kunlun Mountains and descended in a southwesterly direction, separating the basins of the Amtogar and Sarigh Jilganang lakes in India from those of the Leightan and Tsoggor lakes in Tibet, down to the Lanak Pass. In the Indian view, Ladakh's boundary with Tibet commenced at the point where the boundary left the Kunlun range—rather than at the Kongka Pass as China contended.

The Chinese representatives disputed the Indian assertion that their alignment followed the principal watershed in this sector, pointing out that the boundary as defined by India "jumps from the Karakoram Mountains to the Kuen Lun Mountains, cuts across the main river in the area, the Qara Qash River."[6] The proper definition of a watershed was one of the issues upon which the two sides disagreed. For the Indians, the fact that the Qara Qash River pierced the major watershed did not make the latter any less a watershed:

> It was not necessary for a watershed that no river should cut across it. The main watershed in any region was that range which divided the greater part of the volume of the water of two big river systems; and it was the Kuen Lun Range which divided the greater part of the volume of waters of the two big river systems in this area.[7]

The Chinese said this was "totally inconsistent with the well-known understanding of the term," and argued that a watershed is necessarily the line that divides two river systems completely.[8] There would appear to be an inner contradiction, however, between the Chinese definition of a watershed and their assertion that their boundary alignment from the Karakoram to the Kongka passes lay along the major watershed. For the map produced to substantiate the Chinese claim showed that every river in the area cut across the alignment. In any event, the Indians denied that their alignment "jumped" from the Karakoram to the Kunlun Mountains, and argued that it followed the watershed formed by the Qara Tagh range of the Karakoram Mountains up to the point where they met the Kunlun range.

It is understandable that the Chinese and Indians could not agree on the major watershed in this area, for the topography is most complex: Several major mountain systems intersect and major river systems cut across these ranges and subranges at a number of points. In these circumstances, the "major" watershed is not easily determined. The most that can be said is that the Indian alignment follows one of several plausible watershed divisions, while that of the Chinese makes no serious attempt to apply any consistent geographical principle.

Several parts of the western sector of the boundary south of the Chang Chenmo valley up to the southernmost limits of the Ladakh-Tibet border were also disputed. The Chinese said the boundary between Ladakh and Tibet started at the Kongka Pass where it turned southwest along a mountain ridge, crossed the junction of the Chang Chenmo and Silung Barma rivers, ascended the mountain ridge again, which it then followed through the Ane Pass and finally to the northern bank of Pangong Lake. Crossing the lake, it ran southeast along the watershed dividing the Tongada River and the streams flowing into Spanggur Lake, up to Mount Sajum. It then followed the mountain ridge south across the Indus River and ran along the watershed east of the Keyul Langpa River and south of the Hanle River up to Mount Shinowu. Turning west, it crossed the Pare River and continued to the point where it reached the junction of Ladakh, Tibet, and the Punjab.

The Indian alignment commenced at the Lanak Pass (rather than the Kongka Pass), ran south through the Kone and Depsang passes which lie along the watershed between the Chang Chenmo and Chumesang rivers in Ladakh and the streams flowing into the Dyap Tso in Tibet. Thereafter, it followed the southern bank of the Chumesang and the eastern bank of the Chang-lung Lungpar, bisected Pangong Lake, ran along the watershed between the Ang stream flowing west and other streams flowing east (Numkum, Aghlung Trong Trong, and Azhrong), cut across the eastern part of Spanggur Lake, and followed the northern and eastern watershed of the Indus—

through the Chang Pass up to the Jara Pass. Then it turned southwestward, crossing the Indus about five miles southeast of Demchok, and following the watershed between the Hanle River and the tributaries of the Sutlej River through the Charding, Imis, and Kyungzing passes. Thereafter, it turned westward and crossed the Pare River about five miles south of Chumar to the point where it reached the Tibet-Punjab boundary.

The boundary dispute between Ladakh and Sinkiang thus involves the whole of the Aksai Chin plateau, Lingzi Tang, and the easternmost part of the Chang Chenmo valley. Between Ladakh and Tibet, the disputed land includes a number of pasture lands to the north of Pangong Lake, the territory immediately west of Spanggur Lake, and the eastern section of Hanle district, including Demchok village, along the traditional trade route between Ladakh and Tibet up the Indus River.

# XI

# *ANALYSIS OF CONFLICTING BORDER CLAIMS*

The report finally submitted to the governments of India and China by the officials deputed to examine the evidence upon which each nation relied in support of its border claims consists of two reports, one prepared by the Indian officials and the other by the Chinese. The only joint portion is a brief statement setting forth details such as the names of the officials, number of sessions, and where and for how long the sessions were held. The lack of agreement was such that each group provided its own summary even of the discussion that led to the adoption of the agenda. The Chinese and Indian reports each follow the same general pattern and are anything but easy reading. Their pages (some 600) are filled with a plethora of geographic and historical detail culled from largely unfamiliar sources, interspersed with acrimonious controversy. There is a great deal of information—and misinformation—in this remarkable document, but anyone might well quail before the task of sifting through the evidence in an attempt to come to an independent judgment on the merits of the conflicting border claims.

The original intention of this study was to assist the reader by bringing together in a single narrative a summary of the important evidence and major lines of argument pursued by the two sides, in such a way that the essentials of the Sino-Indian debate over Ladakh would be brought into sharp focus—a task the report by its very nature could not fulfill satisfactorily. The expectation was that the statements of the two sides would speak for themselves and require a minimum of editorial comment. But first, it was necessary to check the sources cited—a task all the more essential because of the controversy over facts. Some of the sources were unpublished and unavailable archival material, but most of the published material has been checked. This routine check revealed that statements made by the Chinese could not be left to speak for themselves because they often misrepresented the cited sources. We have therefore found it necessary to supply not only the general lines of argument but also an explanation of the distortions —to put it kindly—the Chinese practised. In the conclusion of this chapter, China's probable intention will be discussed; suffice it to say here that an essential part of our narrative will document our conclusion that the case the Chinese presented was a shoddy piece of work, betraying—if only to those in a position to consult the sources cited—a fundamental contempt for evidence.

When the Chinese and Indian delegations met to present evidence in support of their respective concepts of the boundary, both sides agreed that Ladakh had a traditional and customary boundary with Tibet and Sinkiang.* The disagreement was over the exact alignment of the boundary, and the purpose of the conference was to present and examine evidence substantiating the conflicting claims advanced by the two powers. The discussions of the materials submitted centered around five distinct types, based on treaties, maps, tradition, custom, and administrative jurisdiction. For the purpose of convenience, the various categories will be analyzed separately in this study. However, it should be remembered that the interrelation between the several categories is of great importance in comprehending the positions taken. As the Indians were quick to discover, the Chinese occasionally utilized this separation of categories to argue opposite conclusions from the same evidence.

### *Basis in Treaties and Maps*

The various treaties relevant to the Ladakh border question have been discussed in their proper chronological order (i.e., those of 930, 1684, 1842, and 1852) and the positions taken by the disputants have been summarized and analyzed. But it should be noted that those treaties affected only Ladakh's eastern boundary with Tibet from the Lanak Pass south. The border with Sinkiang to the north has never been delimited in an international agreement. Curiously enough, the

* The apparent contradiction between the Chinese statements that the Sino-Indian boundary has never been delimited and that there is a "traditional customary line up to which each side has exercised jurisdiction throughout the years" (*Report of the Officials of the Government of India and the People's Republic of China on the Boundary Question* [New Delhi: (Government of India) Ministry of External Affairs, 1961], p. CR-155) disappears when it is understood that by "delimitation" the Chinese mean "demarcation."

Chinese on several occasions have placed great emphasis on the fact that Sinkiang was not a party to the 1684 and 1842 treaties. Their motives in asserting this are somewhat obscure, but the argument can be dismissed as irrelevant, at least for the latter treaty, for in 1842, China claimed and exercised effective jurisdiction over Sinkiang. Under any interpretation of international law, China's assent to the 1842 treaty (proved by the Meng Pao documents*) made the agreement binding throughout all Chinese territory, including Sinkiang.

In the 1960 border talks, both China and India submitted several maps to support their respective claims to the territory in dispute. The India representatives referred to a number of eighteenth-century maps of Sinkiang prepared by Chinese cartographers after the Ch'ing conquest of Eastern Turkestan in 1757–59, as well as to an earlier map of that area prepared by a Buddhist priest and published in 1607. All these maps showed what is called the Tsungling range as the southwestern boundary of Sinkiang. China and India have disagreed over the proper identification of the Tsungling Mountains, the Chinese insisting that they are the Karakoram and the Indians the Kunlun range.† China's case is largely based on statements made by early nineteenth century British explorers who utilized these Chinese maps and, with their inaccurate knowledge of the topography of the area, assumed that the Tsungling Mountains must be the Karakorams—since they were still unaware of the existence of the Kunlun range to the north. However, by the mid-nineteenth century, British surveyors had recognized their error and correctly identified the Tsungling Mountains as the Kunlun range—a conclusion that was accepted at that time by Chinese map-makers. Indeed, agreement with the present Chinese view on this issue would require the patently absurd assumption that Chinese cartographers in Sinkiang in the eighteenth century knew of the Karakoram Mountains but did not know of the more northerly Kunlun Mountains, as only one range is shown on Sinkiang's southern border area in these maps.

The motives underlying the stubborn insistence of the Chinese on this point is readily apparent. Unless they argue that the Tsungling and Karakoram Mountains are one and the same system, they will have to admit that no Chinese maps prior to the twentieth century

* See Appendix.

† The Chinese quoted a passage from the 1820 edition of the *Chia-Ch'ing Chung-Hsiu Ta-Ch'ing i T'ung-Chih* (*Official Annals of the Empire of the Great Ch'ing Dynasty*), which they claimed proved that the Nimangyi mountains were, in fact, the Karakorams. The Indians pointed out that this passage proved quite the opposite, for it showed the Nimangyi mountains lying immediately south of Khotan; this could only be the Kunlun and not the Karakoram range.

ever depicted Sinkiang's border to be south of the Kunlun range. Even more recent Chinese maps—such as the "Postal Atlas of China," published in 1917 and 1933, and the *Peking University Atlas* published in 1925—put the Aksai Chin in India. The latter map, incidentally, supposedly showed China's maximum expansion prior to 1911 under the Ch'ing dynasty. It is only after the 1930's when nationalist enthusiasm reached a high pitch in China, that there is any consistency in Chinese cartographic practice with reference to the Aksai Chin.

Confusion as to the extent of the Chang Chenmo valley between the Lanak and Kongka passes continued to be a feature of Chinese cartography even after the Communists came to power. In 1950, a map published in *People's China* showed the whole Chang Chenmo valley as part of India. In 1951, the "New Map of China" published by the Ta Chung Society showed an alignment cutting across the Shyok valley, while the maps published by the Ya Kuang Map Publishing Society in 1953 and the Map Publishing Society in 1956 reverted to an alignment between the Qara Qash and Shyok rivers, thus incorporating part of the disputed portion of the Chang Chenmo valley in India. This led the Indian officials to declare:

> With such a bewildering variety of alignments shown by official Chinese maps published in the course of a decade, it was not surprising that one could not be certain as to what was the alignment claimed by China, let alone be convinced that it had a traditional and customary basis over a period of centuries.[1]

The Chinese replied that the "Indian side tried its utmost to exaggerate the divergences of delineation on Chinese maps," which were described as "only those found between some peaks of the Karakoram range, between some sections along a short stretch of the Chang Chenmo River."[2] But these "divergences" amounted to several hundred square miles. Moreover, the flexibility shown by official Chinese cartographers here and on other sections of the border makes mockery of China's oft-repeated claim that its concept of the border has a solid basis in history.

For their part, the Chinese brought to the border talks a number of Survey of India maps dating back to the nineteenth century in which the northern boundary of Kashmir was alleged to be at variance with the alignment presently claimed by India. The earliest of these maps, presented by John Walker in 1825 and by John Strachey in 1851, showed the Kashmir border extending only to the Karakoram range, thus excluding the northeastern portion of Ladakh. The Chinese also referred to other Survey of India maps published between

1865 and 1945 that did not show the Ladakh boundary at all, or only showed it in an ambiguous way. In some—such as "India and Adjacent Countries," published in 1945—the eastern borders of Kashmir were marked "frontier undefined."* The Chinese charged that it was not until 1954 that official Indian maps showed a delimited boundary along the entire Sino-Indian frontier.

This last was a gross distortion, as reference to other Survey of India maps (not cited by the Chinese)—including John Walker's later maps of 1866 and 1868, the Imperial Gazetteer of India maps of 1886 and 1907, and the Gazetteer of Kashmir and Ladakh published in 1890, all of which showed the alignment just as it is presently claimed by the Government of India—will demonstrate. The Chinese had selected those maps that were intended to show only internal divisions or physical divisions. The Indian representatives argued that it was "accepted cartographic practice" not to show external boundaries in such cases, and that the maps that carried the notation "frontier undefined" in the Ladakh-Tibet-Sinkiang border area only indicated that the boundary had not been demarcated on the ground, or defined in detail. This did not detract, they continued, from their position that the boundary had been delimited through treaty, tradition, and custom. As for the pre-1865 maps by Walker and Strachey, neither of them had surveyed the northeastern border of Ladakh, so the border they drew could not be considered accurate. Once the Great Trigonometrical Survey had been extended to Ladakh's northern boundary and a proper survey completed, every Survey of India map has shown the Aksai Chin, Lingzi Tang, and the Chang Chenmo valley as part of Ladakh.

Both sides to the dispute have had to justify the cartographic practices of their predecessor governments, and the explanations advanced have not been completely satisfactory. Nevertheless, it is quite evident that as far as consistency is concerned—and the length of time

* Once again, the distinction between the "delimitation" and the "demarcation" of a boundary was in dispute. The Chinese noted that some Survey of India maps showed the northeastern frontier area as "boundary undemarcated," but the Ladakh border area as "frontier undefined." This, Peking argued, proved that the western sector of the Sino-Indian border had never been delimited. The Indians rejected this interpretation of the terminology used in the maps. They explained that the phrase "boundary undemarcated" had been used in the eastern sector because although the boundary had been delimited in an international agreement (Simla Conference), it had never been demarcated on the ground. The western sector of the border had been marked "frontier undefined" because it had never been demarcated, nor was there any treaty that had delimited the entire boundary from point to point. This did not mean, however, that the boundary had not been delimited through tradition, custom, and, in some sections, treaties.

the claims have been advanced—the advantage lies with the Government of India. China can explain away some of their earlier maps as "imperialist relics" not binding upon the present government of the People's Republic, but this does not explain why *no* official Chinese maps, according to their own report, ever depicted the Aksai Chin as part of China until late in the 1920's.

The same general remarks referring to cartographic practices on Ladakh's northeastern boundary can also be applied to those on the eastern boundary with Tibet. The Chinese, again referring to Survey of India maps, asserted that even the Government of India must not have considered the Ladakh-Tibet border as delimited, since in several instances they marked it as "frontier undefined." Once again, the Indians had to point out that there was a difference between delimitation and demarcation of a boundary and that the significance of the terminology used in these maps was limited to the demarcation process.

The Chinese claim to disputed areas on Ladakh's eastern frontier was asserted cartographically even later than their claim to the Aksai Chin. As late as 1947, the "Map of the Administrative Areas of the Chinese Republic," issued by the Ministry of the Interior of the Kuomintang Government, showed the eastern border cutting across the middle of Pangong Lake and the entire Spanggur area within India, thus conforming with India's concept of the boundary. The first map published by the Communists after their conquest of China followed this same practice. It was only in 1951 that the "New Map of Tibet" included a part of the western portion of Pangong Lake and the Spanggur area within Tibet. However, the "Big Map of the People's Republic of China" published in 1956, reverted to the alignment shown on the 1947 Kuomintang map. It is important to note that Chou En-lai, in a letter of December 17, 1959, stated that the 1956 map "correctly shows the traditional boundary between the two countries in this sector."[3] But by the time the border talks were under way, in June, 1960, the Chinese Government had replaced the 1956 map with a new one that once again showed the alignment running west of Pangong and Spanggur lakes. As the Indian representative concluded, "there was a divergence . . . not merely among Chinese official maps but between the alignment confirmed by Premier Chou En-lai last year and that claimed by the Chinese side this year at these meetings."[4]

The Chinese were not able to point to any Survey of India map published after the first surveys were made of Ladakh in the mid-nineteenth century that showed Ladakh's eastern boundary as different from the one now claimed by India, although they did cite an unofficial map appearing in Sir Charles Bell's *Tibet: Past and Present,** which showed Demchok in Tibet.

*Basis in Tradition, Custom, and Administration*

The documents submitted by China and India as evidence of the traditional validity of their respective boundary alignments were primarily travelers' accounts containing descriptions of the borders as actually encountered. Evidence of the boundaries as accepted in custom comprised such items as proofs that the disputed areas had been used by nationals for purposes of grazing, hunting, or mining, or that trade routes across these territories had been maintained and controlled by the government concerned. Assertions of administrative jurisdiction were based on official documentary material such as revenue and census records, reports of survey teams, or records of military and police control.

With regard to the accounts of travelers, most of whom were British, the question arose as to the reliability of their information. The Chinese strongly denounced the imperialist character of British policy in the nineteenth and early twentieth centuries, and devoted several pages of their report to allegations that the British Government of India had held expansionist ambitions toward Tibet and Sinkiang, and that the borders between the British and Chinese possessions had been altered substantially as the result of this imperialist activity. Interestingly enough, the Chinese advanced contradictory arguments in other sections of their report, when they claimed that China had maintained continuous administrative jurisdiction over all territories within the alignment presently claimed by Peking. Obviously, two such contradictory lines of argument cannot both be valid, but the Chinese appear to have had little regard for consistency in compiling their report.

The Indian representatives were not prepared to accept the thesis that British imperialism was relevant to the subject under discussion. British policy in Sinkiang and Tibet had no bearing on the Ladakh border question unless it could be proved that the traditional boundary had been affected by it, and the Indians contended that this was not the case and that the Chinese had presented no substantial evidence to support their allegations to the contrary. They pointed out that nineteenth-century British Indian official records were open to the public "but the Chinese side had not cited a single British official record of that period to prove deliberate *malafides* and an interested effort to change the then existing alignment."[5] Moreover, as Prime

* London: The Clarendon Press, 1924.

Minister Nehru had pointed out on more than one occasion, the charge of imperialism was a double-edged weapon, for the Chinese were no less "imperialist" than the British in their relations with the people of Central Asia.

The Chinese employed a blatant double standard in choosing which sources to attack for "imperialist" unreliability. They tended to discount all Indian evidence based on accounts of Western (including non-British) travelers, arguing that these accounts were not only biased but had been deliberately falsified to conform with British expansionist ambitions. On the other hand, a large proportion of the evidence they themselves offered as reliable was of the same type; whenever the Indians were able to show that the Chinese were misquoting these Western sources, however, the only Chinese answer was to repudiate their erstwhile evidence as unreliable documents inspired by imperialist motives.

An objective survey of the accounts written by Westerners who traveled through this area shows that this is an unwarranted allegation. Certainly many of these men ardently advocated the extension of British rule to areas beyond the Indian empire. Nevertheless, their accounts are of value in determining the location of the traditional border precisely *for* this reason. No traveler was more careful to note the areas under the effective jurisdiction of Kashmir, Ladakh, Tibet, or Sinkiang than those with imperialist inclinations. Moreover, after 1870, all British travelers were well aware of the concept of the borders held by the British Indian Government and nothing would have aroused them more than to see Tibetan or Chinese officials exercising jurisdiction in territories they considered British. Yet, none of the numerous travel accounts describing the areas presently in dispute includes complaints or warnings of this nature, even in unpublished reports to the Government of India. The Indian contention that these accounts are reliable for the purpose of determining the *de facto*, if not necessarily the *de jure*, situation of any given time appears to be eminently reasonable.

For an analysis of the traditional, customary, and administrative evidence submitted by the Chinese and Indian Governments, the western sector of the boundary will be divided in two sections: (1) Demchok, the territory around the Spanggur and Pangong lakes, and the Chang Chenmo valley (i.e., the border between Ladakh and Tibet); and (2) the Aksai Chin and Lingzi Tang (i.e., the border between Ladakh and Sinkiang).

THE LADAKH-TIBET BORDER. The Indian representatives cited a number of documents that stated that the Ladakh-Tibet boundary on the southern border lay between the Ladakhi village of Demchok and the Tibetan village of Tashigong. The earliest of these was the account by an Italian Jesuit, Ippolito Desideri, who traveled this route in 1716 and who described "Trescy-Khang" (Tashigong) as a "town on the frontier between Second and Third Tibet [i.e., between Ladakh and Tibet]."[6] In 1820, J. B. Fraser published an itinerary of this same route which indicated that "Donzog [Demchok], thus far in Ludhak" was reached on the eleventh stage and on the following day "Tuzhzhee-gong (a Chinese fort)."[7]

The Chinese did not comment on these or on other statements by travelers in the nineteenth and twentieth centuries who had followed the traditional trade route from Ladakh to Tibet. But, in support of their contention that Demchok is in Tibet, they cited several British sources, in particular, the reports of Captain Henry Strachey and Major Alexander Cunningham, who had explored the Ladakh-Tibet border from 1846 to 1851, and both of whom, the Chinese claimed, said that Demchok lay in Tibet. This Chinese claim is simply not true. Strachey, in describing his journey up the Indus River, noted that the farthest point he reached was "Demchok, on the frontier of Ladak and Nari-Khorsum [West Tibet]."[8] By itself, the statement is ambiguous as to the location of Demchok, but this ambiguity disappears when the remark is put in context; elsewhere in his account Strachey stressed the fact that he did not cross the border into Tibet on this trip. The Chinese use of Cunningham's report is equally fallacious. The Chinese tried to use as evidence the fact that the *village* of Demchok was not included by Cunningham in his list of the major administrative sub-divisions in Ladakh—a curious form of verification of a border claim, to say the least. Furthermore, Cunningham made clear that Demchok (Dechhog) was within Ladakh.[9]

The Chinese citation of two twentieth-century British publications is more substantial—a handbook on Tibet prepared by the British Foreign Office and Sir Charles Bell's *Tibet: Past and Present*.[10] The Foreign Office handbook states that "the frontier crosses the Indus about 25 miles below Demchok (33° north)." Bell, citing the handbook as his source, gives the same description. This coincides approximately with the border presently claimed by China. Indian representatives were unable to explain why the Foreign Office and a British government official had described the boundary in terms at variance with the official position of the British Government of India, but noted that these were only two exceptions in a mass of official publications.

In addition, the Chinese submitted two Tibetan documents pertinent to the dispute over Demchok. One was the report of the Tibetan incarnate Lama of Kha-thag-pa who was sent to mediate a dispute in the Ladakhi royal family in 1753. A passage from his report says: "I arrived on the tenth day of the second half of this month (seventh month of the Water–Male Monkey year) at the sacred place of the Guru—Lari Karpo of Demchok—which is the boundary of the King of Tibet with the King of Ladakh."[11] According to the Chinese interpretation, "sacred place of the Guru" meant a possession of the Dalai Lama.

The second Tibetan document was a covenant signed between the "headmen of Ladakh" and the "headmen" of Demchok Lari Karpo in 1850, which reads: "Demchok Lari Karpo and the waters, grass and sheep enclosures, etc. in this valley belonged to the Tibet Government in the past and naturally will still belong to the [Tibet] Government in the future."[12] The Chinese claim that these documents prove that "Demchok Lari Karpo" was the boundary between Ladakh and Tibet.

The Indian delegation found these two documents (neither of which had been known to them previously) extremely interesting, for they supported the Indian rather than the Chinese description of the border. "Lari Karpo" was identified as the "Lha-ri" stream described as the boundary between Ladakh and Tibet in the 1684 treaty that the Indians claim is the traditional border in this area. When confronted with this interpretation, the Chinese asked the Indians to provide the coordinates for the Lhari stream. These were given as the point approximately five miles southeast of Demchok, where the Lhari stream joins the Indus River.

The Indian representatives then asked the Chinese to give their version of the coordinates of "Lari Karpo." At that time the Chinese refused to do so and merely reiterated their view that "Lari Karpo" lay west of Demchok. The Indians pointed out that the Chinese said the boundary crossed the Indus River north of Demchok rather than west, and requested further clarification on its exact location. The Chinese deferred their reply but later somewhat modified their description to identify "Lari Karpo" as a natural feature near 33° latitude. They were unable either to identify the natural feature or provide its coordinates, however, when pressed to do so by the Indians.

The evidence of "tradition" presented by both sides with respect to the disputed areas in the vicinity of Spanggur Lake and north of Pangong Lake was somewhat less substantial than for Demchok. The Indians cited the works of several travelers in the nineteenth and twentieth centuries, including the account by Major Roger Kennion who hunted in the vicinity of Fort Khurnak near Pangong in the early twentieth century. Kennion noted that the boundary lay between the two halves of Pangong Lake. "Of its 80 or 100 miles in length, half is in Tibet proper and the remaining westerly half in Ladak."[13] For the disputed Niagzu pasture lands, the Indians referred to the accounts by Nain Singh in 1874 and M. S. Wellby in 1898,[14] both of which described the Niagzu stream as the boundary, thus placing the Niagzu pasture lands in Ladakh.

For their part, the Chinese cited only two documents to support their claims, both of which turn out to be of questionable value. The first was a passage from the journal of Kishen Singh, an Indian explorer employed by the Survey of India who traveled through the Tibet-Ladakh border area in 1873–74. The Chinese first maintained that Kishen Singh stated that Fort Khurnak belonged to Tibet. The Indian representatives then read out the relevant passage, which said merely that he had camped "on south side of the Pangong. Road crosses the lake by a shallow ford near encampment. About two or three miles northwest is ruined fort of Khurnak. Water, fuel and grass plentiful."[15] They asked how this passage could possibly be considered to verify the Chinese claim. The Chinese later modified their interpretation, and said the passage meant that Kishen Singh had camped in Tibetan territory and that Fort Khurnak was nearby. Even if the claim that Kishen Singh camped in Tibetan territory—which he never stated—were accepted, it was not made clear how this could conceivably support the Chinese claim to Fort Khurnak.

The second piece of evidence submitted by the Chinese was a passage from a Tibetan document dated 1865 that stated that "Chulsul is very close to the Naga of Mordo of Rudok Dzong."[16] The Indian representatives argued that such a statement was no proof of the boundary in this area, since it could apply as much to the Indian as to the Chinese concept of the border, the divergence between them not being very great. The Chinese then asserted that the "Naga of Mordo" lay west of Spanggur Lake—thus attempting to disprove the Indian contention that the boundary cut across the eastern portion of the lake. But they were unable to provide specific coordinates for the "Naga of Mordo" or identify it with any natural feature or place name when pressed to do so.

In contrast to the comparatively meager historical materials submitted for the disputed areas around the Pangong and Spanggur lakes, the Indians cited a large number of references to support their contention that the Sino-Indian border in the Chang Chenmo valley lay at the Lanak Pass rather than at the Kongka Pass. These citations included reports of journeys by Carey, Bower, Wellby, Deasy, Lydekker, and Kennion,[17] all of which specifically identified the Lanak Pass as the border between Ladakh and Tibet. The Chinese, for their part, were unable to refer to a single nonofficial or historical document that said the Kongka Pass was the border. They limited their comments on the accounts cited by the Indians to an allegation that "these people themselves admitted their having travelled beyond Indian territory into China. This can be seen from the titles of the books referred to by the Indian side which have the words 'Tibet,' 'Turkestan,' etc."[18] The Indians replied that "authors gave general and epigrammatic names to books and no conclusion could be drawn from such names."[19] The importance of many of these accounts lies in the fact that they specifically identified the boundary and mentioned when and where they had crossed it going from Ladakh into Tibet or Sinkiang. All of them stated that the Lanak Pass defined the border.

Proof that the disputed areas on the Ladakh-Tibet border had been "customarily" within their respective boundary alignments centered on demonstration that these territories had been used for economic purposes (primarily grazing) and hunting parties. The Indian report stated that the inhabitants of Tanktse district had used the pasture lands of the Chang Chenmo valley as far as the Lanak Pass for grazing their goats and sheep as well as those further south above Pangong Lake. They also claimed that the pastures in the Spanggur area had been "the close preserve" of the inhabitants of Chusul, while the Ladakhis in Hanle and Rupshu had always used the pastures south of Chumar on either side of the Pare River. The Indians emphasized that hunting parties (usually, but not always, British) had gone into certain of these areas regularly. The Chinese countered that these were merely further examples of imperialist intrusions into Chinese territory by Westerners. Whatever the character of the hunting parties might have been, the Indians replied, the fact that their right to hunt in this area had never been challenged previously by the Tibetan or Chinese Governments proved that there was no substance to the Chinese claim that they had always exercised effective jurisdiction over these areas.

In direct contradiction to the claims of the Indian Government, the Chinese contended that the pastures in the vicinity of the Kongka Pass, around Pangong Lake, and near Demchok had always been used by the "Tibetan people of China," and that Tibetan herdsmen had customarily guarded the boundaries in this area for more than a hundred years under the authority of the local officials at Gartok. They also asserted that guards had been posted at Demchok and Khurnak. However, the Chinese submitted no documents—official or unofficial—to substantiate this claim, nor were they able to produce records of any kind detailing revenues collected for the use of the disputed pasture lands, as the Indians did for several of these areas.

The Government of India submitted a comprehensive selection of official records to support their assertion that the Kashmir Government had exercised effective administrative jurisdiction over Demchok for many years. Included among these documents were:

1) A sketch map drawn by a Kashmiri official about 1865 that showed Demchok as the boundary of the state.

2) A tour report by Faqir Chand, the Governor of Ladakh, in 1904–5, who said that "I visited Demchok on the boundary with Lhasa. . . . A nullah falls into the Indus River from the southwest and it [Demchok] is situated at the junction of the river. Across is the boundary of Lhasa. . . . In between at the mouth of the nullah stands a big minaret of stones. In it is fixed a wood which looks like a flag. This is the boundary line."[20]

3) Consolidated Revenue Register of Ladakh Tehsil giving a consolidated statement of revenues due and collected from Demchok from 1901–40.

4) The Settlement Report of 1908, section on Demchok.

5) The Census Report of 1921, section on Demchok.

6) Demchok Revenue records for 1947–48.

The Chinese representatives refused to admit that these documents were relevant, alleging that inconsistencies in some of them discredited their reliability. They pointed out specifically that one document in the 1901 revenue records showed 28 rupees as the Demchok revenue, while another showed a total revenue of 297 rupees for the same year. They also argued that two other documents were inconsistent, one stating that there was "no permanent habitation" at Demchok while the other said there were four inhabitants. The Chinese concluded:

> The circumstances described in the evidence of the Indian side are absolutely inconsistent with the facts. The evidence cited by the Chinese side, on the other hand, shows that Demchok has always been a [sic] inhabited point of Chinese inhabitants of Tibetan nationality, and not a place where there are no or few permanent inhabitants as alleged by the Indian side.[21]

In reply, the Indian representatives noted that the Chinese were ignoring most of the documents submitted and could not cast doubts on their authenticity. They then denied that there was any inconsistency in the records. In the first instance, one of the revenue records was for the revenue year 1900–01 and showed total revenue collected, while the other was for the calendar year 1901 and showed revenue collected only under certain categories. As for the supposed inconsistency in the records on the number of inhabitants in Demchok, the Indians pointed out that the document stating there were no permanent inhabitants was dated 1908, while the one giving four inhabitants was the 1921 census report. It was not unreasonable, they contended, to believe that there could have been a change in population between 1908 and 1921.

In contrast to the mass of official documents submitted by the Indian delegation, the Chinese cited only one document referring to Demchok. This was an official registrar of the two highest Tibetan officials in Gartok district, dated Iron-Sheep year (the Western calendar date was not indicated, but possibly it was 1820) that records:

> According to the items listed in the books and documents in the charge of the two Garpons of Ari, the annual income is now recorded item by item according to the old practice in the following: Tashigong Demchok Gzhigkha, according to the receipt of the produce of the manorial estate this year, besides the seeds there are some good chingko (grain), 568 ruka and 3 dze; and manching (a kind of food), 8 ruka 1 dze, and so on.[22]

The Chinese stated that a "Gzhigkha" was an administrative unit and that it could be seen from this document that "Demchok Gzhigkha" was administered directly by the Tibetan officials at Gartok. The Indian representatives noted that this "solitary reference" cited by the Chinese was no evidence of administrative jurisdiction over Demchok since a "shika" ("Gzhigkha") was a private estate and not a public domain. The most the Tibetan document proved was ownership of a private estate in Demchok, but not sovereign or administrative control over the whole area. The Chinese rejected this argument as an "arbitrary" conclusion running counter "to facts and common sense."

The official records submitted by India as proof of jurisdiction over the pasture lands near the Spanggur and Pangong lakes included:

1) The report and map prepared by Captain Henry Strachey who surveyed the eastern border area in 1847–48;
2) Captain Godwin-Austen's survey of the Pangong Lake area in 1863;
3) The 1902 Revenue Assessment Report of the Kashmiri Government, which included Chushul in a list of Ladakhi villages;
4) The 1908 Settlement Report regarding revenue in kind, which showed the amount of revenue collected at Khurnak; and
5) The Jammu and Kashmir Game Preservation Act of 1941, which classified Khurnak and Chushul as "game reserves."

*In toto*, the documents cited by the Indian officials applied only to part of the disputed border lands around the Spanggur and Pangong lakes. But the Chinese were in an even more embarrassing position, for they were unable to cite any official documents. The only governmental record they referred to was a directive issued by the *Kashag* (cabinet) of the Tibetan Government in the Wood-Tiger year (the Western date was not indicated but from internal evidence it is probable that it was 1846) stipulating that "after the mountain route is opened, those foreigners who come without permission should . . . be strictly stopped."[23] To prove that this order had been carried out, the Chinese cited Wellby's account of 1898, where he reported that Tibetan border guards had barred him from entering Tibet via the Pangong Lake route. The Indians replied that this had little to do with the alignment on the Ladakh-Tibet border. Moreover, Wellby stated explicitly that the Tibetan guards were located at a point between the two halves of Pangong Lake—in other words, along the alignment claimed by the Indian Government.[24]

Kashmiri Government records were more substantial for the area of the Chang Chenmo valley between the Lanak and Kongka passes than they had been for the section of the border directly to the south. In addition to the revenue records, 1908 Ladakh Settlement Report, reports of several survey teams, the Jammu and Kashmir Game Preservation Act of 1951, they included Kashmiri documents relating to the construction and maintenance of trade routes, rest houses, and storehouses in the Chang Chenmo valley. All of them placed the entire valley up to the Lanak Pass within Ladakh. Once again, the Chinese could not cite an official document either from the Tibetan or Sinkiang records supporting their contention that the border lay at the Kongka Pass. They did attempt to dispute the applicability of the documents submitted by the Indian Government to the eastern area of the Chang Chenmo valley, claiming that they referred only to the area west of the Kongka Pass, which China recognized as part of India. But this was easily refuted, since the documents specifically referred to the Lanak Pass as the eastern border of Chang Chenmo valley.

Directly connected with the question of administrative jurisdiction over the disputed areas along the Ladakh-Tibet border was the disagreement over developments there since 1950. The Indian position was that these areas had been under effective Indian control—exerted by the periodic dispatch of reconnaissance forces—until 1959, when Chinese forces moved into most of the area now claimed by China with the exception of Demchok, which remained under Indian control. The Chinese took the contrary position that Chinese units had maintained effective control over the entire area with the exception of Demchok—which, they charged, had only recently been invaded and occupied by Indian troops.

To refute the Chinese, the Indian representatives submitted detailed information on patrols carried out by Indian army and police units up to the Lanak Pass in 1952, 1954, 1956, and 1959. The Indian patrol that entered eastern Chang Chenmo in June, 1959, found no trace of Chinese personnel there at that time. It was only when another Indian patrol attempted to cross the Kongka Pass into eastern Chang Chenmo in October, 1959, that a clash occurred with entrenched Chinese units. The Chinese asked how the Chinese could have crossed the Aksai Chin in 1950 and later constructed a road through it, if that were the case. Their question could only have been an attempt to confuse the record for those without adequate maps of the area, for as the Indians knew and any detailed map showed, the 1956–57 road did not go through the Lanak Pass nor was it near the Chang Chenmo valley.

THE LADAKH-SINKIANG BORDER. Far more complex than the Ladakh-Tibet border dispute and much less susceptible to a negotiated settlement is the disagreement over the boundary between Ladakh and Sinkiang—involving the Aksai Chin, Lingzi Tang and, in the Chinese viewpoint, the easternmost section of the Chang Chenmo valley. The extent of territory in dispute is much greater, approximately 12,000 square miles. Moreover, the strategic value of these districts has been greatly enhanced by the construction of two roads across the Aksai Chin since 1957, linking the western sections of Sinkiang and Tibet. Because of these and other considerations, both China and India devoted a large proportion of their reports on the western sector of the Sino-Indian boundary to this region. Yet, while more extensive, the documents cited were, on the whole, less conclusive than for Ladakh's eastern boundary.

Published sources of a nonofficial or semiofficial character were given considerable attention by both sides. The Chinese delegation cited three Chinese sources to verify their claim that Sinkiang's borders extended below the Kunlun mountains to the Kongka Pass. The first was the *Chin-Ting Huang-Yu Hsi-Yu T'u-Chih* (*Geographical Records of the Western Regions of China*), an "authoritative and comprehensive work" sanctioned by the Ch'ing Emperor Ch'ien-lung. The section on southern Sinkiang in the 1782 edition states: "Hotien is a sound derivative from Yutien and is an abode of Muslims in the western regions. . . . Yutien is a component part of our territory and, according to old historical records, here lie the river sources."[25] The second reference was to the *Chia-Ch'ing Chung-Hsiu Ta-Ch'ing i T'ung-Chih* (*Official Annals of the Empire of the Great Ch'ing Dynasty*) (1820), which includes this passage: "Nimangyi Mountains are in the south of Hotien. There are two mountains in the east and west and the Hotien River springs therefrom."[26] The last document was the *Hsin-Chiang T'u-Chih* (*Geographical Records of Sinkiang*), compiled and edited by the Governor of Sinkiang in 1911, describing the southern boundary of Sinkiang as "passing Kanjut, it turns in an east-west direction, reaches the sources of the Karakash River in the Nimangyi Mountains and terminates at the Tibetan border."[27]

According to the Chinese delegation, these statements prove that the sources of the Qara Qash River lie in Hotien (Sinkiang) in the Nimangyi Mountains, which, the Chinese maintained, were to be identified with the Karakoram Mountains. The Chinese were unclear as to whether the Nimangyi Mountains were the same range as the Tsungling Mountains, which they had elsewhere attempted to identify with the Karakoram range.

The Indian representatives characterized these references as too vague and general to be authoritative. They noted that the 1762 edition of the work sanctioned by Emperor Ch'ien-lung stated clearly that the "Ho't'ien (Qara Qash) River rises from the Nan Shan (Kunlun)" range. They also cited a map in the earlier edition which showed Sinkiang's southern border at Sanjutagh, sixty miles *north* of the Kunlun Mountains. The Indians also commented that the second work cited by the Chinese showed the Nimangyi Mountains directly to the south of Khotan—which would identify them with the Kunlun rather than the Karakoram range.

The *Hsin-Chiang T'u-Chih* compiled by the Governor of Sinkiang appears to be even more damaging to the Chinese position. His description of the border as turning in an east-west direction beyond Kanjut was consonant with the Indian alignment along the Kunlun range rather than the Chinese alignment along the Karakorams. The Indian officials also noted that in another section of the book, the Governor inaccurately described Shahidulla as part of Kashmir, thus indicating that as late as 1911, Chinese authority had not even been extended as far as the Kunlun range. The remarkable ignorance of what lay south of the Kunlun range displayed in this twentieth-century work by the highest Chinese official in Sinkiang is convincing proof that the Chinese did not exercise jurisdiction over these territories at that time.

The Chinese also cited a number of British sources which, they claimed, proved that the Karakoram Mountains formed the northern border of Ladakh. The first of these was a posthumously published note of William Moorcroft that said: "The Rivers of Khoten—The Karakash, Kara Dereas or Black River (*Kara* meaning *black* in Toorkee, and *Kash, river*) proceeds from the mountains of Khoten."[28]

Cunningham was also cited, stating that "on the north it [Ladakh] is divided by the Karakoram Mountains from the Chinese."[29] And G. W. Hayward, who traversed this area several times in the 1860's, asserted that:

> The natural boundary of Eastern Turkistan to the south is the main chain of the Karakoram; and the line extending along the east of this range, from the Muztagh to the Karakoram, and from the Karakoram to the Chang Chenmo Passes, may be definitely fixed in its geographical and political bearing as constituting the limit of the Maharajah of Kashmir's dominions to the north.[30]

The Chinese also cited a book by Colonel S. G. Burrard, saying that the Survey of India had never been able "to survey the eastern limits of the Depsang Basin beyond the Ladakh border,"[31] and the following statement of R. C. F. Schomberg in 1936:

> The Karakorams form the northern frontier of the present State of Kashmir. They stretch southeast from the tangle of great ranges where China, Russia, Afghanistan and the Indian Empire meet, through parts of Baltistan and Ladakh to the confines of Tibet.[32]

The relevance of the first three Western sources was questioned by the Indians, who noted that the first two had never visited the northern areas of Ladakh, while the third had surveyed only the western extremity of the Aksai Chin and could not speak with authority on the eastern sector. The excerpt from Burrard distorted the real significance of the original passage. Burrard actually defined the Depsang Basin as the area between the main Karakoram range and the Karakoram watershed range lying approximately twenty miles north of the crest. He further stated that both these ranges extended far beyond the Ladakh boundary into central Tibet. Thus, the reference to "the eastern limits of the Depsang Basin beyond the Ladakh border" can only signify that area of the Basin within Tibet. Any possible doubt as to the meaning of the Burrard passage disappears when his statement is taken in context. After stating that British surveys of the Depsang Basin had not extended beyond the Ladakh border, Burrard goes on to cite the conclusions of the well-known Tibetan explorer, Sven Hedin, concerning the continuation of this basin into Tibet. The sentence excerpted by the Chinese may appear somewhat obscure, but if Burrard's use of terminology is given careful attention, there is no reason for confusion.

With regard to the Hayward passage, the Indians correctly pointed out that the author was merely recommending that, for geographical and political reasons, the border of Kashmir state should be placed at the Karakorams, but was not describing the existing situation. It is important to note that Hayward states that the Karakorams are the "natural border" of Sinkiang, but describes the Kunlun mountains as the actual southern border of that province.[33] Thus he excludes the entire region between the Karakoram and Kunlun ranges from the jurisdiction of either the Sinkiang or Kashmir governments.

The Schomberg passage cited by the Chinese, if quoted in context, again supports the Indian rather than the Chinese concept of the border. Schomberg's exploration of the Karakorams was limited to the area west of the Karakoram Pass, and his comment that the range formed the northern border of Kashmir is relevant only to the westernmost section of the boundary. Moreover, in referring to the more easterly sections of the Karakorams he noted that this range runs "*through* parts of Baltistan and Ladakh to the confines of Tibet."[34] This is precisely in accord with Indian Government claims.

The Indians cited the travel accounts of a number of British survey teams and hunting parties that had traversed the Aksai Chin and Lingzi Tang on numerous occasions after 1860. The most interesting of these was the report from W. H. Johnson to the Government of India dated April 22, 1866, concerning his trip into Khotan in southern Sinkiang. Johnson informed Calcutta that he had been invited by the Khotan ruler (who had expelled the Chinese authorities earlier) to visit his capital. The Khan wrote Johnson "that he had dispatched his Wazier, Saifulla Khoja to meet me at Brinjga, the first encampment beyond the Ladakh boundary for the purpose of escorting me thence to Ilchi." Brinjga is a few miles southeast of Karanghtagh; thus the Khotan ruler accepted the Kunlun range as the southern boundary of his dominion. Johnson also noted that the Qara Qash valley was "within the territory of the Maharaja of Kashmir."[35] Another British official who served in Ladakh, Frederick Drew, also classified the Aksai Chin and Lingzi Tang as Kashmiri territory.[36] The Chinese representatives made no effort to counter this evidence except to charge that they merely described "occasional intrusions . . . into China's Sinkiang and Tibet, but their mere presence there cannot turn these places into Indian territory."[37]

Both the Chinese and Indian governments claimed that their nationals had customarily used the Aksai Chin and Lingzi Tang for salt-mining and grazing since the eighteenth century. Peking claimed that Kirghiz and Uighur inhabitants of Sinkiang regularly visited the area and that there still remain "many stone houses, stone sheep enclosures and other constructions built by them."[38] The Indian officials merely commented that the Chinese had submitted no documentary proof from either Sinkiang archives or contemporary records and accounts to support this contention. For their part, they claimed that Ladakhis from Phobrang and Man had collected salt and used pasture lands in the Aksai Chin and Lingzi Tang, and submitted a number of Kashmiri Government documents to prove it. The Chinese denied that Ladakhis had customarily used the area and argued that when they did, it was a case of "trans-border salt-mining by inhabitants of a neighbouring country." They claimed that the documents concerned only the western portion of Chang Chenmo and not the Aksai Chin and Lingzi Tang. The Indians then pointed out that these records referred specifically to the Gunto Lunpa and Skydpo Lungpa pastures in the Aksai Chin, which were used regularly by Ladakhi herdsmen.

A rather curious argument over the origin of the place names in the disputed area preoccupied the two deputations for some time. The Chinese claimed that many of the place names here are of Turki origin and that this constituted proof that Turki-speaking people from Sinkiang used the areas. They specifically noted "Karakoram," or "heap of black stones"; "Karakash Daria," or "river of black jade"; and "Sariq Jilganany Kol," or "lake in a valley of yellow mountains." In addition, incidentally, they translated "Aksai Chin" as "Chin's desert of white stone," attempting to create the impression that the name itself substantiates China's territorial claims. The correct translation of Aksai Chin is merely "desert of white stone," however—there is no relation between "Chin" and China. The Indians contended that the origin of place names was irrelevant, but pointed out how dangerous it was to the Chinese position to proceed with such an argument. Not only are many place names in the disputed area originally Ladakhi, but many place names in Tibet and Sinkiang are Sanskrit or Prakrit. "Khotan," for example, is derived from the Sanskrit "Kustana."

The customary use of trade routes, the maintenance of roads, and the construction and maintenance of rest houses and storehouses by the Kashmir Government right up to what the Indians claimed as the border was cited as further proof that the disputed territories were Indian. There were two main caravan routes through these districts, both originating from Pamzal, on the Chang Chenmo River. The first and more easterly was the route via Nischu, Lingzi Tang, Lak Tsung, Thaldat, Khitai Pass, Haji Langar, and then along the Qara Qash valley to Shahidulla. The other main route ran through Shamal Lungpa and Samzung Ling to Dehra Gompa, along the upper valley of the Qara Qash River to Qizil Jilga and Chungtosh, through the Qara Tagh Pass and the Chibra valley to Malikshah and Shahidulla. That both these routes skirted the western extremity of the area in dispute was noted by the Chinese representatives who argued, furthermore, that in any case these routes were in Chinese territory: It was inconceivable that Kashmir had title to the territory simply because Ladakhi traders were permitted to use them. The Indians replied that at no time prior to 1950 had Indian traders contacted Chinese or Sinkiang authorities south of the Kunlun range or sought their permission to use the trade routes.

In earlier correspondence with the Government of India, China had asserted that a Chinese route, which the road constructed in 1957 through the Aksai Chin roughly followed, had long been the customary trade route between Sinkiang and Tibet. It had fallen into disuse in the nineteenth century, the Chinese stated, as a measure to bar British "encroachers" from the area.[39] It is true that for several centuries there was an alternative route used by traders in Sinkiang's commerce with Ladakh, Tibet, and northern India, via the various Himalayan passes east of Kashmir, but the route did not cross the desolate Aksai Chin as the Chinese claimed. Chinese and Western sources agree that the ancient road between Sinkiang and Tibet lay to the east in undisputed Chinese territory, through the Polu and Keria valleys.* The Chinese citation itself places the road "in the Pulo mountain." The route followed by the newly constructed road across the Aksai Chin may have been a seasonal one used by nomads, but there is no indication that it was ever a major trade route maintained and supervised by Chinese officials.

Each side presented widely differing and conflicting views on the question of administrative jurisdiction over the Aksai Chin and Lingzi Tang. The Indians cited Kashmir state records that classified them as part of the *ilaqa* (subdistrict) of Tanktse in Ladakh Tehsil (district). Revenue records were submitted showing that regular assessments and settlements of revenue were made from time to time and revenue collected from all inhabited places up to the Indian boundary alignment. Moreover, the large stretches of uninhabited territory in this area were shown in Kashmir revenue maps, and control was maintained through the levy of duties on flocks and pastures, in the maintenance

* See, for instance, the description in *Wei-Tsang T'ung-Chih* (*Topography of Wei and Tsang Provinces*), compiled toward the end of the Ch'ien-lung period (1795). The author is unknown, but it was possibly Ho-lin, Assistant Resident-Envoy at Lhasa from 1792 to 1795. Another early nineteenth-century Chinese work, *Hsi-Yu Shui-Tao Chi* (*Annotations about the Watercourses of the Western Regions*) by Hsu Sung and published in 1824, describes this route in some detail. There are many Western sources describing the Polu-Keria route, including the Wellby and Deasy articles already cited, and Sven Hedin, *Southern Tibet* [*Trans-himalaya*, Vol. III], (Stockholm: Lithographic Institute of the Central Staff of the Swedish Army, 1916–22), pp. 38–39, 58–61.

of caravan routes and rest houses, and supervision over trading parties. Documents the Indians cited included:

1) A Kashmir Government map of 1865 showing the location of police check-posts in the vicinity of the Yangi Pass in the northern Aksai Chin;
2) The Gazetteer of Kashmir and Ladakh, 1890, regarding use of the Aksai Chin and Lingzi Tang for collection of fuel and fodder;
3) The Preliminary Report of the 1908 Ladakh Settlement, which included the Aksai Chin and Lingzi Tang in Ladakh;
4) A map of Ladakh Tehsil (*ca.* 1913) showing that Tanktse *ilaqa* included the Aksai Chin and Lingzi Tang; and
5) A Kashmir Government Record of 1950 regarding salt collections by Ladakhis from the Amtogar lake region of the Aksai Chin.

The Chinese officials took exception to the Indians' claim of administrative jurisdiction over the disputed areas and to the documentary materials they submitted. They argued that such a "small village" as Tanktse could not possibly "administer such a big area of more than 27,000 square kilometers."[40] The Indians replied that the dimensions of an *ilaqa* were not determined by the extent of the territory, but on the population and the amount of revenue collected. Moreover, the Aksai Chin and Lingzi Tang were no further from Tanktse than from Shahidulla (in which district the Chinese claimed they belong), nor was the latter any larger than the former.

The Chinese then charged that the documentary materials submitted by the Indians failed to prove Ladakh's jurisdiction over the disputed area. The authenticity of the 1865 police check-post map was challenged, and the Chinese cited in rebuttal the 1908 edition of the Imperial Gazetteer of India which stated that "no police force is maintained [in Ladakh], but a small garrison of State troops is quartered in the fort at Leh."[41] The other documents and maps were too imprecise, the Chinese asserted, and did not show the confines or limits of Tanktse *ilaqa*. The Indians retorted that, with regard to the police-post question, the 1908 Imperial Gazetteer was authoritative only for the period of its publication and certainly not for 1865 or 1960. The police check-post map had been submitted as proof that as early as 1865 Kashmir had exercised effective jurisdiction over the Aksai Chin and not that police posts had functioned continuously there ever since.

No directly relevant documents were submitted by the Chinese officials to support their contention that the Aksai Chin and Lingzi Tang were part of the Shahidulla district in Sinkiang. The only record they produced was a petition from Yang Tsung-hsin, Governor of Sinkiang, who proposed in 1927 that Shahidulla be made a *Sheh-Chih-Chu* (bureau of administration). The Chinese translation of this document states in part:

> With reference to Shahidulla, which lies in the south-east of the area under the jurisdiction of Ghuma Bazar County now belonging to Hotien Tao, it is a district which on the southern side extends to Kalahulumu Tapan [Karakoram Pass], borders on British Tiaopaiti [Ladakh] and is an important place through which Chinese and Indian traders and people travel to and from India. On the eastern side it extends to Changchiliman Tapan of Hotien, where there is also a small route leading to India and also links with Houtsang [Tibet]. . . . Taking into account both the internal and external aspects of the matter and considering repeatedly the various facts concerning the history, alien affairs, geography and administration of that place, I see that the setting up of an administrative unit there really brooks no further delay.[42]

The following year the proposal was approved by the Chinese Government, though there is no evidence that the administrative post was ever set up.

The exact location of some of the places named in Yang Tsung-hsin's petition is a subject of dispute between the Chinese and Indians, since they did not appear in any of the Chinese or Western maps referred to by either side. The most crucial was that concerning "Changchiliman Tapan," on the "eastern side" of Shahidulla. The Chinese first maintained that Changchiliman Tapan was the Kongka Pass. When this was shown to contradict other evidence they submitted and the directions specified in the 1927 petition itself, the Chinese revised the identification to Changlung Barma "and its vicinity, which is very close to the Kongka Pass."

The Indian delegation found this Chinese document interesting for a variety of reasons. In the first place, they were surprised that the Chinese would admit that it was not until 1928 that Shahidulla had been set up as an administrative unit—in view of their repeated assertions elsewhere that Chinese officials had exercised effective jurisdiction in the area since 1759. They interpreted this as substantiating their view that Chinese jurisdiction had not even extended down to the Kunluns—much less further south—before the 1930's. Furthermore, even if the Chinese identification of Changchiliman Tapan with Changlung Barma was correct and Shahidulla district extended up to this point, this did not conform with the current Chinese alignment—which showed Shahidulla district as extending to the Kongka Pass, some distance south of Changlung Barma.

Lastly, there is no reason to believe that Changchiliman Tapan and Changlung Barma are one and the same. The Sinkiang Governor described the former as east of Shahidulla, while the latter is actually almost directly south of it. The Indians contended that Changchiliman Tapan probably referred to the Khangili Mountains east of Shahidulla in the Kunlun range. Thus, the description of the boundary in Yang Tsung-hsin's petition would conform with the Indian alignment. The Chinese rejected this Indian interpretation, and asserted that no proof had been submitted to identify Changchiliman Tapan with the Khangili Mountains and that it was "futile" for India to deny that "the area of Changlung Barma" was part of Shahidulla district. The traditional Chinese method of describing the extent of a place, they maintained, was to point out only its four principal limits to the east, west, south, and north. This does not explain why a place largely south of Shahidulla was said to be on the eastern limit of that district, however.

Despite the evidence the Chinese themselves submitted which indicated that their administrative jurisdiction had not been extended even to the Kunluns until 1928, they claimed that Chinese guards had patrolled the Aksai Chin since "early in the middle of the eighteenth century." A number of documents were cited that allegedly supported this view. The earliest was a report from Pan Chen, Commissioner of Hotien, dated May 23, 1898, which stated: "To the south-west of the Polu Mountain there is a road leading to Tiaopaiti (Ladakh) of Britain. This mountain road is rugged and has long been severed and closed. And sentinels have been dispatched to guard it."[43] Also in 1898, the Chinese stated, the English traveler, Captain H. H. Deasy, was denied permission to journey from Tibet to Sinkiang via the Polu route by the Chinese official in that area. Deasy reported that: "The Amban of Keria, who several times informed me that the Aksai Chin is part of the province of Sinchiang and under his jurisdiction, refused to allow me to use the Polu route."[44] Finally, the Chinese cited an incident in 1941 when eleven Ladakhis were arrested "in the area of Aksai Chin Lake," according to the protest submitted to the British Consul General at Kashgar by the Sinkiang authorities. These were positive proof, the Chinese claimed, that they had exercised effective jurisdiction over the Aksai Chin.

The first two references cited are not relevant, for they refer to Sinkiang-Tibet routes via the Polu and Keria valleys that India concedes to be Chinese territory. Deasy's account, in particular, makes it quite clear that this was the route he was referring to and not the one across the Aksai Chin followed by the new Chinese road.[45] Deasy's reference to the Amban of Keria's statement that Aksai Chin was under his jurisdiction also diminishes in importance when placed in its proper context. The term Aksai Chin applies also to areas beyond the boundary claimed by India. That Deasy used the term in this manner is shown by the map illustrating his travels,[46] in which Aksai Chin was also written across the territory east of the Indian boundary. Furthermore, Deasy knew clearly and reported correctly the boundary in this sector. Since he had been careful to note the existence of a boundary dispute with Sinkiang in the Hunza section of the boundary, it is unlikely that he would have let the Amban of Keria's comment go unnoticed if he thought it constituted a claim to the Indian section of the Aksai Chin.

The Indian representatives also denied any significance in the arrest of eleven Ladakhis near the "Aksai Lake" by Sinkiang border guards in 1941. There is no lake called "Aksai Lake" in the Indian section of the Aksai Chin, they pointed out. Numerous lakes dotted the area on both sides of the Indian border alignment, and the arrest of the Ladakhis must have taken place east of the boundary in Chinese territory. The "imperialist" British Consul General at Kashgar would scarcely have accepted a protest from the Chinese authorities in Sinkiang over the arrest of British nationals in territory considered part of the British Indian empire. The Chinese insisted that the arrest of the eleven Ladakhis occurred at Lake Amtogar within the territory currently in dispute, but no evidence was submitted to support this claim.

If the reports of survey teams submitted by both sides are completely accurate, there is little justification for describing the Aksai Chin as a "little-known region of the world." The Indian officials cited a number of surveys conducted in this area under the auspices of the Government of India in the nineteenth and twentieth centuries. Most of the earlier expeditions were connected with the Great Trigonometrical Survey, extended to northern Kashmir around 1860, or with the Muslim revolt in Eastern Turkestan from 1860 to 1877, or both. During this latter period, the British were interested in developing road communications between their possessions and that of the local ruler in Turkestan. A number of survey teams, including Johnson (1862), Godwin-Austen (1862), Ryall (1862–63), Cayley (1870), Montgomerie (1871), and Trotter (1873)—traversed this entire area on several occasions. Later surveys, such as Stein's in 1908 and De Filippi's in 1913–14, were more purely scientific.

The Government of India claimed that Indian officials, survey parties, and patrols had "constantly visited" the area up to the Indian alignment from 1911 to 1949, and that this constituted proof of Indian administrative jurisdiction. The Indians noted that the Chinese Government had never protested these activities, some of which were well-publicized and must have come to the attention of Chinese authorities. To the Indians, this constituted positive evidence that the Chinese claim to the Aksai Chin was recent. The Chinese representatives denied it strongly, and once again denounced the British expeditions as "illegal explorations and surveys" in Chinese territory.[47] They were part of the British plot to detach Sinkiang from China and join it to the British Indian empire, they contended, and under no circumstances could the surveys be conceived as a basis for claiming British administrative jurisdiction. Moreover, British survey teams had surveyed other parts of China (Sinkiang, Kansu, etc.). "It is of course absurd to regard whatever places where the British and Indian personnel went or surveyed as under British administrative jurisdiction."[48] This last argument is completely spurious as a glance at the records of British survey teams clearly indicates. In every instance, the teams carefully distinguished between operations carried out within British India and those conducted on foreign soil. The current Indian territorial claims have been strictly limited to those areas that were classified as part of the Indian empire by the survey teams. Furthermore, the instructions to these teams make it clear that British interest was in defining Kashmir's boundary with Sinkiang, not in detaching Sinkiang from China, which would have further complicated Anglo-Russian relations in Central Asia.

To prove that Chinese administrative jurisdiction had extended south of the Kunlun range, the Chinese representatives referred to two Chinese expeditions that supposedly surveyed the Aksai Chin–Lingzi Tang area. The first of these occurred in 1891, when two Chinese officials, Hai Yin and Li Yuan-ping, were ordered "to go separately to the southwestern and northwestern borders for inspection and survey." According to the report from the Governor of Sinkiang in 1894, "these officials went deep into these places and conducted surveys again and again."[49] The Chinese representatives stated that Hai Yin had surveyed the Pamir area while Li Yuan-ping had traveled along the Karakoram Mountains down to the Kongka Pass. A map of the Pamirs prepared by Hai Yin and an itinerary of Li Yuan-ping's journey were submitted.

The Indian officials commented on several aspects of these surveys. In the first place, the orders issued by the Chinese authorities specified surveys on Sinkiang's northwestern and southwestern borders. The Aksai Chin, however, is on Sinkiang's southern border and nowhere in their report is it stated that this area was included. The document on Li Yuan-ping's travels gives no indication that he surveyed the Karakorams, and even his itinerary—as the Chinese interpret it—does not show that he went as far as the Kongka Pass. The Indians said that

Li was an "ill-informed" traveler who "intruded into Kashmir." In any event, Li nowhere stated that the places he visited were within Sinkiang. The Chinese made no attempt to answer these arguments, and merely noted that the orders issued by the Chinese authorities had explicitly stated that the surveys should be conducted on the "southwest 'borders of those extensive lands under Britain,'" which, in the Chinese view, included Ladakh.[50]

The second survey cited by the Chinese was conducted in 1940–41 with the assistance of experts from the Soviet Union (the virtually autonomous Sinkiang Government was under strong Russian influence at that time), and Shahidulla district was included, the Chinese asserted. The official document submitted, however, only concerned the Sino-Russian border, and did not indicate that a detailed survey had extended down to the Karakorams—as the Chinese claimed. If it were the case, the Indian officials asked, then why had the Chinese denied a detailed knowledge of the alignment in the Karakorams under *item 1* of the agenda? The Indian officials requested further documentation before they would be prepared to accept Chinese claims in this respect.

The Chinese then asserted that a detailed map on the scale of 1:200,000 had been prepared on the basis of the 1941 survey. They produced a photostat of a map, but the Indians charged that it "appeared only to be an enlargement of a small-scale map, and did not contain even that amount of information given in maps published by 1940 or available to the Chinese Government at that time."[51] The Indians obviously questioned the authenticity of the map, though they politely refrained from expressing their doubts in precise terms. The Chinese denied that it was a small-scale map blown up in the photostat to large-scale proportions. The photostat map included "detailed terrain features," they asserted, and "cannot possibly be of small scale."[52]

There seems to be ample justification for the suspicion that this was just one more instance of Chinese officials busily manufacturing evidence. If a large-scale map actually existed, why was a photostat of it submitted rather than the map itself—especially when the Indians had expressed skepticism about the authenticity of the photostat? The border talks were being conducted in Peking at that point, so there could not have been any difficulties involved in producing the map, nor any justifiable apprehension over its security. Moreover, if it had been prepared by a Chinese survey team in 1941, why was it that there is so much divergence among the various Chinese maps published after that? There appears to be only one possible answer here—and it scarcely enhances the reputation of the Chinese Communist Government.

As further evidence of administrative jurisdiction, both the Chinese and Indians referred to military patrol activity conducted in the Aksai Chin since 1950. The Indians mentioned the dispatch of a force to the Aksai Chin and Lingzi Tang in 1951; a reconnaissance party's journey up to the Qara Tagh Pass in 1957; and visits to the Sarigh Jilganany and Lake Amtogar, Haji Langar, and Qara Tagh Pass areas by three patrol parties in 1958. The Chinese referred to the crossing of the Aksai Chin by Chinese army units in 1950; reconnaissance activities by Chinese frontier guards in 1954–55; and the survey of the area by teams seeking the best route for the road that was then constructed across the Aksai Chin in 1956–57. Both governments classified the activities of the other as "illegal intrusions," not to be construed as constituting a legal basis for a claim to jurisdiction.

Not directly related but an issue contended in these discussions nevertheless, was the exact status of Minsar, a village located near Mount Kailash in West Tibet. Minsar had long been a Ladakhi enclave in Tibetan territory—a status first defined in the 1684 treaty between Ladakh and Tibet. Just why Ladakh retained sovereign rights in the village when it surrendered its rights to the rest of West Tibet has never been made entirely clear, but appears to be connected with the Ladakhi trade caravans that traveled over the Indus-Tsangpo route from Leh to Ladakh since the inhabitants of Minsar were obliged to perform *ula* (free porterage) services for these caravans.* To assure the enforcement of this right, the Lhasa authorities may have conceded rights of sovereignty in this area to the Ladakh Government in 1684. Whatever the explanation, the Government of India contends that the Ladakh (later Kashmir) Government has held and exercised "full sovereignty" in Minsar since 1684 and that India inherited these rights when Kashmir became part of the Republic.

In 1959, after the Tibetan revolt had spread into the western region, the Chinese seized Minsar. In notes exchanged between India and China since then, and also in the 1960 border talks, China consistently refused to recognize Indian rights in Minsar, which is described as "situated deep within China" and "indisputably part of

* The Bhutan Government also held enclaves in the same area, granted to them by Ladakhi authorities. Whether this occurred before or after the 1681–83 Ladakh-Tibet war is not indicated in published sources, but it seems probable that it took place while Ladakh still controlled West Tibet. The reasons for establishing the grant are unclear. Perhaps trade or religious connections were involved. The seizure of the Bhutani enclaves is also an issue in post-1959 Sino-Indian correspondence.

Chinese territory." The Chinese quoted the report of a Kashmiri official who, in 1908, described Minsar as "situated within the territory of Lhasa." They argued that Minsar's sole obligation to Ladakh was the performance of *ula* services, the result of the "former historical relations of Ladakh being subordinate to Tibet." Under no circumstances can this be construed to provide the basis for a territorial claim, they contended.[53]

The Indian representatives did not deny that Minsar was an enclave deep in Tibetan territory, and they disavowed any intention of claiming the intervening land. They simply stated that Ladakhi authorities had exercised full sovereign rights in Minsar, and submitted documentary evidence to support their view. The report of the Kashmiri official cited by the Chinese was quoted in context—to show that what he had actually said was that Minsar was a state village of Ladakh situated within the territory of Lhasa. The Indians denied that Minsar's sole obligation to Ladakh was in the performance of *ula* services. Kashmiri revenue documents were submitted to show that Minsar had paid revenue to the Kashmir Government at least from the middle of the nineteenth century—that is, from the time of the Dogra conquest of Ladakh. The Chinese attempted to discredit the authenticity of these records by charging that there were inconsistencies in the revenues listed for Minsar in two of them. The Indians denied any inconsistency, and showed that these records were for different periods and for different forms of revenue. As was always the case in the discussions on the western sector of the boundary, the Chinese submitted no official documentary evidence of Tibetan jurisdiction over Minsar.

This concludes the summarization of the various proofs and documentation submitted by the governments of India and China in support of their respective concepts of the borders of Ladakh with Tibet and Sinkiang. The most striking contrast in the two reports is the basic difference in their approach. The Indian Government was both thorough and careful in presenting its case, and attempted to fulfill the stated purpose of the talks—to examine in detail the differences between the two governments on the border question. On the other hand, the Chinese Government showed no interest in the substance of the talks, as their astonishingly careless presentation amply demonstrated. The maze of internal inconsistencies, quotations out of context, and even blatant and easily discernible falsehoods—easily discernible, that is, to those *with access to the materials cited*—make it obvious that China had paid little or no attention to the preparation of their case.

In view of the confused historical background of this area and the intricate and complex character of the relevant ethnic, cultural, and geographic factors, it should have been possible for the Chinese to advance a more plausible case had they chosen to do so. Certainly they could have made a less discreditable presentation. Why, then, did the Chinese insist on holding the border talks, when they could scarcely have hoped for a satisfactory settlement on the basis of discussions for which they were so ill-prepared? Possibly they wished to gain time. Perhaps they wished to examine the Indian evidence. Perhaps the reason lay in internal developments within China or the world Communist movement. It has even been suggested that the Chinese wished to avoid putting the Indian Communist Party in an embarrassing position. It is more likely, however, that the Chinese felt a need to counter the unfavorable publicity throughout Asia that had accompanied their brutal suppression of the revolt in Tibet and their deliberate incitement of a border dispute with India. By advocating border talks, they could play the role of a party most anxiously seeking peacefully to settle the dispute, while at the same time they could approach the talks in a manner that precluded any actual settlement. In any event, they clearly expected—as subsequent developments have demonstrated—to use the report of the talks (which they may have assumed would not be published) as the basis for a propaganda campaign which would make it appear that they had presented a well-documented case whereas the Indians had been forced to rely on nothing but a legacy from British imperialism. They may have counted on the length and complexity of the report—together with the unfamiliarity of the place names involved—to prevent an exposure of their shoddy "documentation." At worst, they could count on sowing confusion and doubt among those with no opportunity to check the sources cited, and those who would not easily believe that a government would sponsor *demonstrably* false assertions.

The impact of the Chinese propaganda campaign on the rest of Asia was lessened by the Government of India's prompt publication of both the Chinese and Indian reports, which exposed the hollowness of the Chinese claims. Nevertheless, China's evident readiness to hold talks was not without effect—for it did appear to relieve the acute apprehensions that arose in parts of South and Southeast Asia in 1959 concerning China's ultimate intentions. As far as India was concerned, however, the experience was scarcely reassuring. There the demand of the government and the general public alike was for a tangible expression of good will rather than a hollow, and on the whole contemptuous, gesture from China.

Yet the talks did have one positive result as far as India was concerned. Most of India's leaders had received their baptism by fire in the struggle for independence from Western imperialism; even though they were aware that Chinese claims were no less "imperial," they were vulnerable to the charges that British imperialism had determined the establishment of the boundaries between the British Indian and Chinese empires. This sensitivity had been reflected in more than one official Indian statement in the early phases of the border dispute. Once the documents were assembled, however, it was clear that the Indian case was not only far stronger than the Chinese, but also possessed a solid basis quite apart from any questions of "British imperialism," and any tendency to be apologetic about the Indian position has completely disappeared.

In this connection it is interesting to note that J. S. Bains, whose book *India's International Disputes* had tentatively suggested that China could make out a case concerning the Aksai Chin area on the basis of effective occupation, changed his views after studying additional material made available to him, saying:

> In the last few weeks some recent publications of the Government of India and other material, especially the editorial comment by Dr. K. Krishna Rao on "Title to Territory" dealing with my comments in this context which is published in the latest issue of the *Indian Journal of International Law*, have been made available to me, and after studying them I have found that there is irrefutable evidence to show that even in the western sector [of Ladakh] India had continued to exercise jurisdiction in one form or the other and that the kind of *corpus occupandi* and *animus occupandi* possible in such a terrain was present. In view of this, I believe that India's rights even in the Ladakh area are well established in international law and that the Chinese have occupied the area illegally. I shall, therefore, make the necessary revisions in the new edition of my book.[54]

It is possible, however, that the Indians, in their pleasure over the contrast between their own case and the near absence of genuine historical or legal documentation offered by the Chinese, lost sight of some of the major implications of the way in which the Chinese handled the border talks. The very fact that the Chinese could scarcely have intended to convince the Indians of the justice of their case, constituted in itself a barely veiled threat of no mean proportions.

# XII

## *RECENT DEVELOPMENTS AND EMERGING TRENDS*

The immediate effect of the 1960 border talks was to dispel any hope in India that a basis could be found for negotiating the border dispute with Communist China. The Chinese, confident in the superiority of their military position, had been arrogant not only in their obvious disdain for genuine documentary justification of their claims, but also in the subtle variation of Hitlerian technique by which they advanced these claims. China had offered nothing so straightforward as a series of "final" demands. Their method was a nibbling process, which began by denying the existence of any but the most trivial and easily settled differences, and continued with a series of contradictory assertions evidently designed to keep the adversary off-balance, uncertain of China's ultimate intentions, and therefore prey to alternating hopes and fears.

Such was the history of the Chinese advance in Ladakh. Under cover of their denial that differences of any importance existed with respect to the border, chunks of territory claimed by India were secretly seized in 1956–57 and a new map issued. China then gave assurances several times that this map accurately represented the official Chinese concept of the traditional border. Nevertheless, at the border talk at Peking on June 27, 1960, the Chinese casually produced a map incorporating an additional 2,000 square miles of Ladakh.* This new map altered the boundary previously shown between Ladakh and Sinkiang in the important Karakoram Pass area, and the boundary between Ladakh and Tibet in the vicinity of Pangong and Spanggur lakes. The 1956 border near the Karakoram Pass area had followed the

* See map of Ladakh and Surrounding Areas.

watershed between the Shyok and Qara Qash rivers; the 1960 alignment cut the Upper Shyok (Chip Chap) River southeast of the Karakoram Pass and continued due south and then southeast, incorporating a large segment of the Depsang Plain. On the Ladakh-Tibet border, the 1960 line cut across the western arm of Pangong Lake and took in all of Spanggur Lake, in contrast to the 1956 map, which had bisected it.

When the Chinese officials were taxed with enlarging their claims, they first tried to dismiss the differences in the maps as trivial, and then took the position that the boundaries on the two maps were *equally valid.* This remarkable statement was made in December, 1961, by no less than the Chinese Foreign Minister Ch'en Yi:

> The sector of the Sino-Indian traditional customary boundary is most clear and definite. It is the boundary marked on the 1956 Chinese map which was mentioned in Premier Chou En-lai's letter of December 17, 1959; it is also the boundary marked on the maps handed over to the Indian side by the Chinese officials during the meeting of Chinese and Indian officials in 1960.[1]

Since the two maps are demonstrably different, there would appear to be only one interpretation that could make such a statement meaningful: neither map represents anything more than a stage in a campaign the ultimate aims of which Peking has no intention of revealing.

Circumstances had greatly favored the Chinese in the early phases of the Ladakh dispute. As Prime Minister Nehru himself conceded, his government's early frontier policy had rested in part upon a basic miscalculation.* Preparations for the security of the northern border had been largely concentrated on its eastern sector, on the assumption that any serious Chinese threat to India would develop in the northeast frontier region. With the lessons of World War II in mind, India had striven to bring these tribal areas under effective administrative control—a task the British had never carried to completion. The far western section, guarded by the lofty and difficult Karakoram Pass, was considered relatively secure and therefore in no need of high priority in the allocation of India's limited resources. Consequently, India was not prepared for immediate and effective countermeasures against Chinese encroachment when the Ladakh dispute came into the open in 1958. China, spurred on by the Tibetan uprising and the flight of the Dalai Lama, had succeeded by the end of 1959 in establishing control over most of the parts of Ladakh they had claimed

* See Nehru's remarks during parliamentary debate, November 28, 1961. (*Lok Sabha Debates* (Fifteenth Session), second series, Vol. LIX, No. 7, col. 1853.)

on the 1956 map, with the exception of the Demchok area. This Indian frontier post on the Indus trade route lacked natural defenses and Indian military posts had been established there, forestalling the Chinese.

India had no alternative but to accept the challenge, severe though the economic burden would be. Various countermeasures were pushed, with high priority on developing an effective communications system. A road from the Kashmir valley via the Zoji Pass and Kargil to Leh was completed, and the construction of other roads was undertaken to provide access from Leh to vital sectors of the frontier area and to obviate the need for continued reliance on air transport. The effort to make up for a late start could not have been immediately successful, but by the end of 1961 Nehru was able to make a cautiously optimistic appraisal of Indian prospects.[2]

Indian military strength in the immediate vicinity of the frontier was progressively augmented as the communications system was improved. By mid-1962, forty-three new Indian posts were established within the border area. Most of them were located within territory claimed by China on the 1960 map, and they blunted Chinese efforts to consolidate control without resorting to armed attack. Moreover, the effectiveness of the posts was considerably enhanced by the establishment of year-round barracks near the border. Until the winter of 1961–62, both Chinese and Indian forces had withdrawn from advanced positions during the winter months because of supply and maintenance difficulties. This procedure had given the Chinese an advantage, since geographic and climatic factors had in general permitted their forces to remain longer in winter and return earlier in the spring. The Indian army's ability to maintain limited year-round operations on the border somewhat reduced this advantage, but did not completely eliminate it.

The earlier situation, in which forward posts were separated from each other by a no man's land, was also greatly changed by the beginning of 1962. The new Indian posts "leapfrogged" Chinese posts in an effort aimed not only at blocking potential lines of advance, but also at forcing the withdrawal of Chinese forward posts by interspersing Indian posts and patrol activities between them, cutting supply lines where possible. As a result of these tactics, Nehru reported in August, 1962, control had been regained over nearly 2,500 square miles of the 12,000 square miles previously lost to the Chinese.[3]

At that point, both China and India appeared to operate on the assumption that the adversary was either unable or unwilling directly to challenge established military positions in Ladakh. But as their rival posts came closer together, competing for control over surrounding areas, and as patrol activities were extended more widely into the disputed areas, the likelihood of resort to violence increased. In July, 1962, just after an Indian post had been established to cut the supply line to a new forward Chinese post on the Galwan River, a numerically superior Chinese force virtually encircled the Indian post, hoping to intimidate the Indians into withdrawing through a gap the Chinese had left open for this purpose. When the Indians stood their ground, the Chinese soldiers advanced to within fifteen yards of the post, halting when the Indians threatened to open fire if they came any closer. The situation remained tense for several days of continued siege while notes were exchanged between the two governments. India stood firm in the face of threats from Peking, and the Chinese eventually retired, presumably on orders from their government.

At the time, this incident appeared to mark a critical point in the Ladakh border controversy, and later events confirmed this view. The Chinese were put on notice that mere display of superior force would not of itself permit them to consolidate control of the Aksai Chin. The incident suggested not only that further significant Chinese intrusions in the Ladakh area were unlikely to succeed without resort to arms, but also that maintenance of the Chinese position would soon require armed action. A prior order that had prohibited Indian forces from firing until they had first been fired upon was rescinded, leaving the Indians free to fire first in their own defense if the situation warranted. This must have removed any lingering illusion the Chinese may have had that their objectives could be achieved by threat of force alone. New policies were obviously called for and they were not long in coming.

What direction the new policy would take was not at once discernible. However hostile relations had become, economic considerations appeared burdensome enough to provide a real impetus to search for a negotiated solution. A protracted contest over their common frontier imposes serious economic burdens on both India and China, whether or not the contest develops into a full-scale shooting war. The initial Chinese advantages—including their possession of high ground and the relative ease with which they can build roads—are obvious. Indian difficulties in developing a strong defense posture along the extended Himalayan border are staggering, and have diverted popular attention in both India and the West from the fact that the difficulties faced by the Chinese are also formidable, particularly from a long-range viewpoint. Virtually all items of supply, including fuel, have to be brought into Tibet from distant bases in China. Once, supplies could be obtained through India, but the ban on the export of "strategic goods" into Tibet imposed by New Delhi in 1959, greatly reduced the volume of trade between Tibet and India. And the quantities of equipment and other resources that have to be diverted from China in order to maintain a large military establishment in Tibet must place a considerable burden on the already over-strained Chinese economy.

The 1960 talks not only failed to provide a basis for negotiation but also had made it obvious that the Chinese had no genuine interest in negotiating. Relations between the two countries deteriorated following the talks to the point of an almost complete breakdown in normal communications. Two episodes occurred, however, which deserve more than cursory attention: the visit to Peking in July, 1961, of R. K. Nehru, Secretary General of the External Affairs Ministry, and the lapse of the 1954 Sino-Indian trade agreement on Tibet.

R. K. Nehru's visit to Peking was the subject of much critical comment in the Indian press, leading Prime Minister Nehru to explain that the Secretary General had taken advantage of a trip to Moscow and Outer Mongolia to stop off at Peking on his return home "to find out the trend of Chinese thinking on the official report on the border dispute." He was not, the Prime Minister emphasized, entrusted with any mission to conduct negotiations with the Chinese Government.[4] No further official clarification of the objectives of his visit or the exact nature of his talks has been made public, but it is known that he had considerable opportunity to appraise the trend of thinking in Peking. He was met upon arrival by Keng Piao, the Vice Foreign Minister, and was taken directly to meet Liu Shao-chi, President of the Chinese People's Republic. Later he journeyed to Shanghai, where he held a six-hour interview with Chou En-lai and Foreign Minister Ch'en Yi, during which the entire scope of Sino-Indian relations was said to have come under review.[5] In general, Indian observers thought that India had gained nothing by his stopover in China and might even have lost a little ground. His visit, in any case, appeared to reinforce the Indian Government's conviction that a completely new atmosphere would have to be created before further negotiations with Peking would be possible.

December 2, 1961, was a significant date in the calendar of Sino-Indian relations, marking the deadline for any request to extend their 1954 trade agreement. Without an extension, the agreement was due to expire on June 2, 1962, eight years after ratification. December 2 came and went under the watchful eyes of the Indian press with no request for an extension by either signatory. On December 4, however, a Chinese note was received in New Delhi suggesting that the two powers consider terms of a *new* trade treaty. What China hoped to gain from this procedure is far from clear. India was prepared neither to renew a treaty whose provisions had been consistently dishonored, nor to negotiate a new one unless the Chinese were ready to prove good faith by withdrawing their forces from Ladakh.

The Chinese attempted to make political capital out of the Indian rejection by repeatedly pressing for trade talks to be conducted without reference to border issues, and then by trying to convince the Tibetans that the recent drastic deterioration in their standard of living was the result of India's trade policy. India was warned that continuation of that policy would aggravate "the unrest along the border and even augment the danger of clashes."[6] The Chinese also took the astounding position that the "peaceful coexistence" principles of the 1954 treaty applied only to "questions relating to trade, cultural relations and friendly intercourse" but not to "all the questions" existing between the two countries, and "did not even touch on the boundary question."[7]

In replying to the various Chinese notes, the Indian Government consistently maintained that a new trade treaty could not be separated from border issues and that talks on it could not be held until China abandoned aggressive policies and respected the boundary between the two states. On June 3, 1962, the 1954 treaty officially expired, to the accompaniment of full-scale denunciation of India in the Chinese press. China then demanded that the Indian trade agencies in Tibet be removed by July 3, despite previous assurances that "reasonable" facilities would be guaranteed. The Indian Government withdrew the agencies within two weeks. From then on, Nehru commented, trade and intercourse with Tibet would be regulated by the national laws and regulations of the countries concerned. Under prevailing conditions, this could only mean a virtual cessation of the steadily dwindling trade with Tibet. The tone and content of the notes exchanged between the two governments suggest that India viewed this probable outcome with much more equanimity than China did.

When relations between India and China reached this new low point—following the expiration of the 1954 agreement and the Galwan valley incident in Ladakh—the question of finding a new basis for negotiations inevitably came once again to the fore. The question of the preconditions for entering into negotiation found the two countries far apart. The Chinese continued to insist that there should be no preconditions, although they seemed ready to abandon their earlier opposition to basing new talks on the reports that had emerged from the 1960 discussions. The earlier Indian proposals (of November, 1959) for the mutual withdrawal of forces in Ladakh behind the frontier claimed by the other (with the proviso that the Chinese would be permitted to use the Aksai Chin road for civilian purposes) were unacceptable to the Chinese. In practical terms, these proposals implied acceptance of Indian sovereignty over the Aksai Chin, and would have prevented the military use of a road whose purpose is largely military, stripping the Chinese of most of their present advantages. Yet these were the only terms upon which India was prepared to renew negotiations. Nehru continued to insist on a "situation which will be free from tension and will involve withdrawals," although he was willing to agree to preliminary talks limited strictly to the issue of how such a situation was to be created. Talks exploring this limited objective had been agreed on and were scheduled to begin in a matter of days when it suddenly became clear that the Chinese had worked out a different solution to force the Indian Government to accept a "negotiated" settlement on their terms. Simultaneous blitz attacks were launched along the extremities of the long frontier.

The full extent of Chinese aims may not be known for some time, but it is clear that one major objective has remained unchanged since at least 1956—unchallenged possession of the vital Aksai Chin link between Sinkiang and Tibet. After obtaining control of the Aksai Chin by stealth in 1956, the Chinese attempted in a variety of ways to obtain Indian acquiescence in Chinese claims to it: by force; by threat of greater force; and by offering to renounce claims in the northeast frontier area in return for India's cession of Aksai Chin. At the same time they steadily expanded their military control in Ladakh.

The Chinese position, although militarily formidable, suffered from two important defects: growing Indian military pressure in Ladakh, and the obvious relevance of the Indian argument that no dispute existed on the eastern frontier since the McMahon Line was the *de facto* as well as *de jure* boundary there. The Chinese must have felt it necessary to answer the latter argument by creating a dispute by force of arms, particularly since it is doubtful that Chinese objectives in Ladakh could be attained, at least without heavy cost, in a campaign limited to Ladakh itself.

For political reasons, the Chinese were anxious to make it appear that their aggression—obviously under preparation for several months at least—had been provoked by Indian attacks on Chinese forces on their own side of the border. So a Chinese detachment was sent across the McMahon Line and established close to an Indian post at Dhola, two miles south of the border. The Indian Government's order to eject the intruders was then called "an attack upon China." One can safely assume that if no firing had occurred at Dhola, the Chinese would have sought provocations elsewhere until they had an incident to "justify" the "self-defense" operations that immediately swept them deep within Indian territory. The success of the Chinese "defensive" action is reminiscent of similar successful "defensive" actions taken by the North Koreans at the beginning of the Korean War.

After occupying those areas of the northeast frontier area that could be seized without coming up against India's main defense positions, as well as territory in Ladakh up to and even beyond their 1960 claims, the Chinese called for negotiations on the basis of the existing situation. New Delhi remained firm in rejecting any cease-fire proposal without the prior withdrawal of Chinese forces to the positions held on September 8, the date of Chinese intrusion south of the McMahon Line in the Dhola area.

Having failed to achieve what must have been their primary objective—the cession of the Aksai Chin area—a further display of China's military prowess was undertaken after a two-week lull, in a second massive offensive in the northeast frontier area. The badly outnumbered Indian forces at Tse La and Walong were outflanked and forced to withdraw. Chinese forces advanced deeply into the western (Kameng division) extremity of the northeast frontier area and threatened to erupt onto the plains of Assam.

After having dealt the Indian army a staggering defeat, the Chinese again moved dramatically, this time on the diplomatic front. Peking suddenly announced on November 21 that it was unilaterally imposing a cease-fire as of midnight, November 22, and that, starting on December 1, Chinese troops in both Ladakh and the northeast frontier area would withdraw twenty kilometers to the north and east of what was termed "the line of actual control" as of November 7, 1959. India was warned to withdraw its forces an equal distance to the south and west of this 1959 line under threat of the renewal of hostilities. The Chinese announced that they would retain "civil police" posts at points along the "line of actual control" in order "to insure the normal movement of the inhabitants in the Chinese-Indian border area, forestall the activities of saboteurs and maintain order there."[8]

The Chinese choice of the date for fixing a withdrawal line is interesting in itself. Why November 7, 1959, when the Indians were suggesting a return to the line of September 8, 1962? At first glance, it might appear that the Chinese were offering to give up the fruits of three years of penetration into territory claimed by India. Actually, prior to the Chinese break-through in the fall of 1962, the Indian military position had improved considerably from what it had been in 1959. And it was on November 7 of that year that Chou En-lai had written to Nehru suggesting that:

> In order to maintain effectively the *status quo* of the border between the two countries, to ensure the tranquillity of the border regions and to create a favourable atmosphere for a friendly settlement of the boundary question, the Chinese Government proposes that the armed forces of China and India each withdraw 20 kilometers at once from the so-called McMahon line in the east, and from the line up to which each side exercises actual control in the west, and that the two sides undertake to refrain from sending their armed personnel to be stationed in and patrol the zones from which they have evacuated their armed forces, but still maintain civil administrative personnel and unarmed police there for the performance of administrative duties and maintenance of order.[9]

Nehru's rejection of this proposal had been swift. On November 16, he replied, pointing out that outside of Ladakh, Chinese forces had occupied no point south of the Indian border except at Longju—where border clashes could be avoided if the Chinese would withdraw, since the Indians would agree not to reoccupy it. As for Ladakh, Nehru pointed out that the Indian Government unfortunately did not know with any precision where the Chinese considered the frontier line to lie, as the maps published in China were not only small-scale but inconsistent from one to the next. He rejected Chinese contentions of jurisdiction over this frontier area, stating:

> It is obvious that there is complete disagreement between the two Governments even about the facts of possession. An agreement about the observance of the *status quo* would, therefore, be meaningless as the facts concerning the *status quo* are themselves disputed. As we are at present discussing a short term interim measure to avoid border clashes, it is essential that we do not get involved in interminable discussions on the *status quo* at this stage.[10]

If this correspondence is kept in mind, the reasons for the choice of the November, 1959, date become clearer. If the "line of actual control" would have been the subject of "interminable discussion" even in 1959, it could only be a definite line in 1962 if the Indians completely capitulated to Chinese claims. In fact, the Chinese claim that their 1956 and 1960 maps were "equally valid" was soon used to define the 1959 "line of actual control" as essentially the border shown on the 1960 map—thus incorporating several thousand additional square miles, some of which had not been seized until after the hostilities had broken out in October, 1962. Under these deceptively worded proposals,[11] the Indians would have been forced to give the Chinese everything needed for a secure military grip on the part of Ladakh where their roads were constructed, and would have lost—among other important positions—their airfield at Chusul, the major pass between Chusul and Leh, the frontier posts at Demchok, and control of the Karakoram Pass itself. In the eastern part of the frontier, the Indians would have had to accept the Chinese version of the McMahon Line as the "line of actual control"—which was not only far from the actual situation of 1959, but would also, in effect, surrender Assam (and Bhutan) to Chinese control. In the middle section of the border, the Indian military position would have been equally hopeless; and Sikkim and Nepal would have become totally exposed in the event of a renewal of Chinese aggression. (It should be noted that the Chinese have always described their large military concentrations along the frontier as "border guards," and one can only assume that the "civil police" would likewise not be exactly what the term usually implies.)

Although the Indian Government was prepared not to break the cease-fire for the time being, only total military disaster would have induced it to accept the Chinese *diktat,* which would completely undermine India's security. On December 1, Nehru wrote to Chou En-lai in effect rejecting Peking's terms and once again calling for a withdrawal of the forces of both countries behind the September 8, 1962, line. Thus, the conditions under which there was *de facto* cessation of hostilities—for the time being at least—did not provide the basis for new negotiations between the two powers. As of mid-December, 1962, neither Peking nor New Delhi showed any great degree of flexibility in their respective stands. Nehru firmly expressed his belief that negotiations with China were useless under present conditions since India can place no reliance on the trustworthiness of the Chinese. China, on the other hand, showed interest in obtaining all the political advantages it could from offers to negotiate, but no interest in actual negotiations unless they were based on India's unconditional acceptance of its terms.

The question of negotiations has implications extending far beyond the relations of the two governments most intimately involved. In a wider context, the border dispute has become inextricably entangled with the most serious political problems facing the world today. Adding immeasurably to the complexity of the Sino-Indian dispute is the fact that the vital interests of a third power, Pakistan, are directly concerned, not only because of its long-standing dispute with India over Kashmir but also because of Chinese claims to sections of Kashmir on both sides of the cease-fire line.

The precise extent of Chinese claims west of the Karakoram Pass cannot be determined from the small-scale maps so far published in Peking, but the discrepancy between Chinese and Pakistani maps may be as much as 6,000 square miles.* There are, therefore, three governments with three different concepts of the disputed border. And at present, there is no prospect whatever that tripartite negotiations could be arranged, nor that an agreement between two of the powers, supposing it could be achieved, would be acceptable to the third.†

Immediately following the outbreak of the revolt in Tibet, it seemed as if India's relations with Pakistan stood a chance of fundamental improvement. In the face of the Chinese threat, responsible quarters in both Pakistan and India stressed the necessity for cooperation in the defense of the subcontinent. In Pakistan, this took the form of a joint defense policy proposed as early as April, 1959, by President Ayub Khan. India preferred a more informal arrangement, including a "no war declaration" as far as their mutual dispute over Kashmir was concerned, combined with a tacit understanding that both governments would evolve similar policies toward Chinese aggression. For India, the joint defense proposal suffered from a number of glaring defects. Probably of greatest importance was the effect it would have upon a basic feature of India's foreign policy, nonalignment. On several occasions, Pakistani officials—including the President and the Foreign Minister—sought to reassure India on this point, arguing that a joint defense system could be evolved quite apart from the general foreign policy principles followed by the two powers. This argument was unconvincing to the Indian authorities. For them, a joint defense policy with Pakistan would be tantamount to India's adherence to Western military pacts unless, of course, Pakistan withdrew from SEATO and CENTO. Indian skepticism increased when President Ayub declared in October, 1959, that a joint defense system would be directed as much against Afghanistan and the Soviet Union as against China[12]—a factor that became even more crucial to India in view of Pakistan's then deteriorating relations with Afghanistan over the Pakhtunistan issue, and the importance to India of friendly relations with the Soviet Union to counter the Chinese threat.

Pakistan's insistence on the settlement of the Kashmir question—

* The latest Survey of Pakistan map, not yet available in the West, is said to show the northern boundary as "undefined," but to draw a tentative border that includes all of Hunza and Nagar, as well as the Taghdumbash Pamir and the Raskam valley (over which the Mir of Hunza claims grazing rights) as part of Kashmir. (*The Hindu Weekly Review*, February 1, 1961, 1:2.) The Survey of India maps, on the other hand, include only a small section of the Taghdumbash Pamir and none of the Raskam valley within Kashmir. Chinese maps include within Sinkiang province all the Taghdumbash Pamir and the Raskam valley as well as a slice of Hunza and Nagar.

† The Nationalist Chinese Government has already rejected in advance any agreement that might ensue from the Sino-Pakistani negotiations.

presumably along lines favorable to Pakistan—prior to the implementation of a military alliance[13] was another major obstacle to the conclusion of a joint defense treaty. Many Indians were convinced that Pakistan intended to use India's difficulties with China to force basic concessions on the Kashmir issue, and questioned the Pakistan Government's sincerity in proposing a joint defense system. These sentiments were reinforced when, in December, 1959—a particularly critical period in the Sino-Indian dispute over Ladakh—Pakistan decided to revive the Kashmir issue in the United Nations Security Council. Possibly, Pakistan feared that China and India would reach an agreement on the border dispute that ignored Pakistan's interests in Kashmir, and hoped the Security Council would provide an effective forum for the expression of Pakistan's views. Nevertheless, the main effect of the maneuver was to exacerbate the tension between Pakistan and India, making even more unlikely any form of mutual accommodation between them.

The failure of this approach to the Security Council apparently caused the Pakistani Government to reappraise its policy on the Sino-Indian dispute. Early in 1960, Pakistan first approached China to suggest negotiations on the Kashmir-Sinkiang boundary west of the Karakoram Pass.* Talks with China held certain advantages for Pakistan. In the first place, China's agreement to have the talks would constitute tacit recognition of Pakistan's sovereign rights on the western side of the cease-fire line. Furthermore, there was increasing awareness in Pakistan that adherence to SEATO and CENTO had not brought all of the advantages originally hoped for, but had instead complicated Pakistan's relations with a large part of the Afro-Asian world. At this stage, an outright withdrawal from the pacts was unfeasible, but the approach to China would allow wider flexibility within the overall framework of Pakistan's foreign policy.

Moreover, Pakistan's proposal to Peking was made at the very time that border talks were beginning between China and India. There was little Pakistan could do directly in these circumstances except alert China to the possible advantages of an arrangement with Pakistan should India prove intransigent. When it became apparent that India and China were unlikely to reach agreement, an understanding with China may have appeared even more attractive. It was obvious that China's primary goal was possession of the vital route between Sinkiang and Tibet across the Aksai Chin. There was some basis for assuming that China would agree to concessions west of the Karakoram

* The exact date of this overture and the manner in which it was done have not been made public. The first official reference to it was made by the Foreign Minister on January 15, 1961; he did not go into detail but merely mentioned that communications had been sent to China.

Pass if, in the process, its position in the much more important Aksai Chin were strengthened.

China's initial reaction to Pakistan's proposal was one of extreme caution. Its position on the boundary question at that time explicitly recognized India's right to negotiate for the sections of the Kashmir boundary under Indian control but was noncommital about the boundary west of the Karakoram Pass. China awaited the results of the border talks with India before considering Pakistan's proposal, for only in January, 1961—less than a month after the end of the Sino-Indian border talks—did China agree "in principle" to negotiate with Pakistan.

An agreement to negotiate "in principle," however, was not quite the same as an agreement to negotiate. For more than a year, Pakistan and China sparred with one another, and talks between them were indefinitely postponed. If their public statements are taken at face value, neither government was even prepared to admit that there was anything in dispute. On several occasions, officials in Rawalpindi denied that China had laid claim to Pakistani territory, attributing such reports to hostile quarters in India interested in creating bad blood between China and Pakistan. In like manner, China carefully refrained from any mention of the western Karakoram boundary, despite numerous statements asserting the validity of Chinese claims elsewhere in Kashmir. It was not until the spring of 1962 that an official Pakistani publication confirmed reports that Chinese maps showed 4–6,000 square miles of Pakistani-controlled territory as part of China.[14] According to the article, Pakistan had approached Peking and been told that the maps (used as the basis for Chinese claims against Ladakh incidentally) had been prepared by the Chinese Nationalist Government and that a survey since undertaken by the Communists was not yet completed. The Pakistani officials could scarcely have missed the similarity between this Chinese response and those given to India a decade earlier on the same question. It had become obvious that there was more to be negotiated between Pakistan and China than the demarcation of a generally accepted boundary.

Originally, the initiative for border talks had come from Pakistan and it was China that was reluctant to assent to them. Peking's hesitation may have arisen from a desire to avoid unnecessary territorial concessions to Pakistan, while at the same time to make as much political capital as possible out of closer Sino-Pakistani relations.* But by the spring of 1962, China was pressing eagerly for talks with

* For example, the Chinese Ambassador, in his interview with the press at Rawalpindi on December 7, 1961, stressed the connection between Chinese "reasonableness" on the border question and Pakistani "reasonableness" on the question of Communist China's admission to the U.N.

Pakistan—a move that presumably reflected the changed situation on the Aksai Chin border and the increasing pressure placed on China by the Indian military build-up there. Once it was clear that India was not only refusing to concede control of the Aksai Chin but was challenging the Chinese position there, Pakistan's overtures may well have appeared more attractive.

On May 3, 1962, China and Pakistan published simultaneously the text of an agreement calling for negotiations between the two powers on border questions.[15] It was agreed that the boundary between Sinkiang and Kashmir had "never been formally delimited and demarcated in history," and "that after the settlement of the dispute over Kashmir between Pakistan and India, the sovereign authorities concerned shall reopen negotiations with the Chinese Government regarding the boundary of Kashmir so as to sign a formal boundary treaty to replace the provisional agreement." Here, for the first time, China publicly refused to recognize Kashmir's accession to the Indian Union —a point it had previously been careful to obscure.

The existence of a real, if limited, community of interest with China encouraged some Pakistanis to argue that Pakistan's whole foreign policy should be re-examined. These sentiments received their clearest and most positive expression in the period immediately following India's move into Goa in December, 1961. Several papers pointed up the failure of NATO to come to Portugal's assistance in the Goa crisis and questioned whether SEATO and CENTO would be of any more value to Pakistan in similar circumstances. One influential daily argued that Pakistan should withdraw from the military pacts and seek closer relations with Communist China.[16]

The eruption of Sino-Indian hostilities in October, 1962, increased public support of this proposal. Virtually all of the Pakistani press, as well as numerous political leaders in the recently established National Assembly, spoke out, and broad hints of qualified support even came from some high officials. The Western powers were subjected to intensive and continuous criticism for their program of military assistance to India which, it was argued, threatened the security of Pakistan. The argument was, in essence, that Sino-Indian hostilities were merely localized border disturbances that did not seriously endanger the peace and did not require building up India's military strength. There were even suggestions that Pakistan should use the situation to force a solution of the Kashmir issue (by implication, in alliance with Communist China) even if this led to a break with its Western allies.

While proposals of this nature may be superficially attractive and not without emotional appeal, the practical disadvantages are obvious —and presumably decisive. Where, for instance, would Pakistan find a reliable replacement for the economic and military aid now furnished by the United States? There are also serious domestic complications. The Mir of Hunza and the "Azad Kashmir" government (the local authorities in that part of Kashmir under Pakistan's jurisdiction) have shown signs of restiveness over the present direction of Rawalpindi's policy toward China, since it is their territory that is in question. Finally, the Pakistan Government must be aware of its potential conflict of interest with China. It may have suited Pakistan's purposes to pretend to full faith in Communist China, but it is scarcely imaginable that the lessons of India's relations with Peking made no lasting impression in responsible quarters in Pakistan. Presumably Pakistan is interested in using the present situation to extract concessions from India over Kashmir, rather than to negotiate an alliance with China.

The Sino-Indian conflict has, indeed, raised hopes in some quarters that a solution of the Indo-Pakistani dispute over Kashmir may be forthcoming. It is conceivable, but the obstacles are still formidable. For one thing, the insertion of China into the Kashmir question throws grave doubts on the capacity of the United Nations to serve as an effective instrument for settling the Indo-Pakistani dispute. For another, the Security Council resolutions on Kashmir are—under existing conditions—inapplicable, for according to their terms, both Pakistan and India would have to withdraw the bulk of their forces from Kashmir, while China would be able to maintain its present position. The feasibility of a plebiscite is also open to question, even if Pakistan and India were prepared to assent to one.

What this situation does point up with dramatic clarity, however, is the great strategic importance of the mountainous regions of Kashmir to the security of both Pakistan and India. Neither of the governments can safely afford to allow Kashmir to come entirely under the control of the other. Gilgit and Baltistan are certainly vital to Pakistan, while the Indian defense system would be gravely weakened by the loss of Ladakh. The best—indeed only suitable—access routes to both Baltistan and Ladakh run through the Kashmir valley. No proposed solution ignoring these fundamental security considerations can possibly form the basis for agreement between Pakistan and India, or between either of them and China.

Another aspect of the current three-cornered dispute over Kashmir concerns the role played by the Soviet Union. Russia has explicitly recognized the validity of Kashmir's accession to the Indian Union and has consistently supported India's position in Security Council deliberations. Moreover, the Soviet Union gave India implicit support in the dispute with China through the extension of a form of military assistance specifically intended for use in the Himalayan areas. Most of the transport planes and helicopters used to supply advanced Indian posts in Ladakh, for instance, were purchased from the Soviet Union on favorable terms. Moreover, Russian instructors were sent to train Indian Air Force pilots in the use of these planes in mountain regions, a form of technical assistance of which the political implications could scarcely escape Peking. In 1962, when India was seeking late-model jet fighters, the Soviet Union expressed its readiness to sell to India a more advanced type than had been supplied to China, and again on favorable terms.

Speculation on Soviet motives can range far and wide, but one need not look beyond Russia's basic and long-standing interest in Central Asia—specifically, in strategic and mineral-rich Sinkiang—to find sufficient explanation for the Soviet Union's Indian policy. It was to Russia's interest to encourage developments diverting Chinese attention from the still unsettled Sino-Russian border and the competition for influence in Mongolia. A further consideration is the current ideological conflict within the Communist bloc, reflected in competition between the Soviet Union and China for influence with Asian and African Communist parties. The Indian Communist Party, battered and ineffectual as it may be internally, is vital to Russian plans—since it is the only major Asian Communist party to take an essentially pro-Soviet stand.

One of the considerations behind China's elaborate pretense that it acted in self-defense when fighting erupted October, 1962, was presumably the Sino-Soviet mutual defense pact. If the Soviet Union could be prevailed upon to accept the Chinese version of events, further Russian military and economic aid to India, at the very least, would be precluded. The dilemma this development presented to the Soviet Government is underscored by the silence of the Soviet press on the outbreak of hostilities. The first news given out by the Soviet Government emphasized the necessity for a cease-fire and called for negotiations, urgently required if Soviet policy toward India was not to become a major issue in Communist-bloc politics, if not another bone of contention between Khrushchev and his opposition within the Russian Communist Party. It is quite probable that broad considerations of this nature contributed to the Chinese decision to invade India. If so, Chinese policy appears to have failed, in so far as the Soviet Union and Eastern Europe—with the usual exception of Albania—are concerned. For after an initial hesitancy, the Soviet Union and Communist parties throughout Europe—again except for the Albanian party—became increasingly critical of China's "leftist deviationist" and "adventurist" foreign policy. Whether China can turn its militancy to better account in Asia, Africa, and Latin America remains to be seen.

Today, more than ever before, it is evident that India plays a vital role in the calculations of both the Soviet Union and the Western powers as China's only major Asian rival in an expanding area of operations that promises to assume great importance in the next decade. Prior to the Tibetan revolt in 1959, neither the Chinese nor the Indian governments spoke openly of a potential struggle for influence in Asia and Africa, but emphasized instead Sino-Indian friendship (the "Chini-Hindi bhai-bhai" phase) and "peaceful coexistence." These useful cliches did not completely obscure the preparations then under way on both sides for an eventual confrontation along the border, but they did help to set the framework within which the preparations were undertaken. Today, both governments not only act on the assumption of a wider power struggle but also speak more or less openly of the compulsions this situation forces on them. The area of open conflict is no longer confined to their common frontier but involves a competition for influence throughout the rest of Asia, with increasing repercussions in Africa. Certainly China's policy toward Burma, Nepal, Pakistan, and, less directly, Cambodia and Indonesia is not fully understood except in the context of Chinese objectives in its relations with India.

One major objective of Chinese foreign policy has clearly been for some time to demolish Indian prestige. This policy has taken many twists and turns. The initial Chinese probings of the Indian border —whatever other purposes were involved—were used to hold India up to contempt in the eyes of her Asian neighbors. When, at the "neutralist" conference in Belgrade in August, 1961, Nehru turned the attention of the conference from issues of colonialism (which, he argued, was a dying phenomenon) to more vital issues of war and peace, China launched a furious campaign of personal abuse against him intended to convince Asians and Africans alike that Nehru was an "imperialist stooge" and that India had forfeited all right to the leadership of nonaligned nations.* The Goa crisis of December, 1961, was linked in Chinese propaganda to charges of Indian "aggression" in Ladakh, in an attempt to arouse fear of India in neighboring states.

The minimum objective of China's military onslaught in the late fall of 1962 presumably was—as we have said—to tighten their grip on the Ladakhi corridor between Tibet and Sinkiang. Very little reliable information comes out of Sinkiang, but what is known about Sino-

* The Chinese press published a highly distorted version of the statement Nehru made at Belgrade. The Indian Embassy at Peking thereupon published the official version of Nehru's statement side-by-side with the Chinese one. This resulted in fresh anti-Indian outbreaks in Chinese journals and a new issue for the exchange of notes between the two governments. (See *Notes . . . Exchanged Between the Governments of India and China* [Government of India] Ministry of External Affairs, White Paper No. IV [New Delhi: November, 1961], pp. 146–47, 157–61.)

Soviet competition there in the past,[17] pieced together with the trickle of more recent reports of unrest,[18] provides a basis for speculation that this corridor, once essential for retaining Tibet, may now be equally essential for retaining Sinkiang.

In any event, one must assume that Chinese aims have by no means been fulfilled and that new Chinese initiatives can be expected before long, although it is hard to say what form these initiatives will take. To date, the Chinese Communists have shown a decided predilection for deception in the initial attempt to gain new strategic positions, and a diplomatic offensive of some sort may well precede any fresh outbreak of hostilities. It is virtually certain that one Chinese goal is the complete control of Southeast Asia, but it would be idle to speculate on how and when this aim is to be achieved. India would presumably have to be dealt with first, yet it is most improbable that the Chinese have in mind the military conquest of India. That they mean to hold the Ladakhi corridor is plain. Perhaps they also intend to detach oil-rich Assam. It is possible that the Chinese believe that Indian efforts to meet the military threat posed by Chinese control of the Himalayan bastion will so ruin the Indian economy that the country will be left a prey to Communism. If this is what they are counting on, they may be content merely to keep the threat very much alive, without burdening their own resources to the extent of renewing active hostilities. In any event, the desire to humiliate India appears very strong. Perhaps the Chinese Communists, as heirs to the Chinese empire, will not be content until they have dictated a humiliating "unequal treaty" to the Indian heirs of the British empire.

# NOTES

*Chapter II: Ladakh's Role in Central Asia:* A.D. *600–900*

1. G. Tucci, *Preliminary Report on Two Scientific Expeditions in Nepal* ("Materials for the Study of Nepalese History and Culture," Vol. I; "*Serie Orientale Roma*," Vol. X [Rome, 1956]), pp. 104–8.
2. Ma-twan-lin, "Thien-chu–India," trans., James Burgess, *Indian Antiquary*, IX (1880), 21.
3. U. N. Mukerjee, "Chronology of the Karkota Naga Dynasty of Kashmir . . . ," *Uttara Bharati*, IV, No. 2 (March, 1958), 49.
4. Pandit Daya Ram Sahni, "References to the Bhottas or Bhauttas in the Rajatarangini of Kashmir" (Notes from Tibetan sources by A. H. Francke), *Indian Antiquary*, XXXVII (July, 1908), 181–92.
5. See H. Goetz, "The Antiquities of Chamba State: An Art-Historical Outline," *Journal of the Uttar Pradesh Historical Society*, New Series, I (1953), 92.
6. E. H. Parker, "How the Tibetans Grew," *Asiatic Quarterly Review*, Series 3, XVIII (1904), 244.
7. A. H. Francke, "Antiquities of Indian Tibet," *Archaeological Survey of India*, II, 88.

*Chapter III: Ladakh's Emergence as an Independent State*

1. A. H. Francke, "Antiquities of Indian Tibet," *Archaeological Survey of India*, II, 94.
2. L. Petech, "A Study on the Chronicles of Ladakh, Indian Tibet," *Indian Historical Quarterly*, XV, No. 4, Supplement (December, 1939), 108; and Francke, *op. cit.* (The Kings of Gu-ge), p. 168.
3. Francke, *op. cit.* (Registrar of the Vassal-Kings of Bzan-la in Zans-dkar), p. 94.
4. *Ibid.*, pp. 91, 93.
5. Francke, *A History of Western Tibet, One of the Unknown Empires* (London: S. W. Partridge, 1907), p. 62.
6. Petech, *op. cit.*, pp. 108–9.
7. G. Tucci, *Indo-Tibetica* (Rome: Reale Accademia d'Italia, 1937), II, Part II, 17–21.
8. *Report of the Officials of the Government of India and the People's Republic of China on the Boundary Question* (New Delhi: [Government of India] Ministry of External Affairs, 1961), p. CR-57.

9. *Ibid.*, p. 57.
10. *Loc. cit.*
11. *Loc. cit.*
12. Petech, *op. cit.*, p. 104
13. *Annual Report of the Archaeological Survey of India*, 1905–6, p. 165.
14. *Hudud al-'Alam* (*The Regions of the World*), trans., V. Minorsky (London: Luzac, 1913), p. 93.
15. G. Tucci, *Nepal: The Discovery of the Malla*, trans., Lovett Edwards (New York: Dutton, 1962), p. 60.
16. Francke, "Antiquities of Indian Tibet," p. 96.
17. Sarat Chandra Das, "Tibet Under the Tartar Emperors of China in the 13th Century," *Journal of the Asiatic Society of Bengal*, LXXIII, Part I (1904, Extra Number), 99.

*Chapter IV: Conflicting Pressures on Ladakh:* A.D. *1300–1600*

1. A. H. Francke, "The Rock Inscription at Mulbhe," *Indian Antiquary*, XXXV (1906), 75–76.
2. Mirza Muhammed Haider Dughlāt, *Tarikh-i-Rashidi* (*A History of the Moghuls of Central Asia*), trans., E. D. Ross; ed., N. Elias (London: Low, Marston, 1895), 423.
3. Prem Nath Bazaz, *The History of Struggle for Freedom in Kashmir*, (New Delhi: Kashmir Publishing Company, 1954), pp. 66–67.
4. Francke, "Antiquities of Indian Tibet," *Archaeological Survey of India*, II, 105.
5. *Ibid.*, p. 106.

*Chapter V: Ladakh's Relations with Tibet and India in the Seventeenth Century*

1. L. Petech, "The Tibetan-Ladakhi-Mogul War of 1681–83," *Indian Historical Quarterly*, XXIII, No. 3 (September, 1947), 171–8.
2. Francke erroneously places the war in 1650. (A. H. Francke, "Antiquities of Indian Tibet," *Archaeological Survey of India*, II, 118.)
3. Petech, *op. cit.*, p. 178.
4. *Ibid.*, p. 161.
5. Francke, *op. cit.*, pp. 116–17.
6. *Ibid.*, p. 115.
7. *Report of the Officials of the Government of India and the People's Republic of China on the Boundary Question* (New Delhi: [Government of India] Ministry of External Affairs, 1961), p. 59.

*Chapter VI: The Dogra Conquest of Ladakh*

1. L. Petech, "Notes on Ladakhi History," *Indian Historical Quarterly*, XXIV, No. 3 (September, 1948), 222.
2. *Ibid.*, p. 223.
3. National Archives of India (New Delhi), *Political Consultations*, February 14, 1838, Nos. 57–58; Wade to Macnaghten, January 1, 1838.
4. *Ibid.*
5. National Archives of India (New Delhi), *Political Proceedings*, No. 26; Wade to Government of India.

*Chapter VII: The Dogra-Tibetan War of 1841–42*

1. India Office Library (London), *Enclosures to Secret Letters from India,* Vol. 79, 1841; Thomason to Lushington, September, 1841.
2. National Archives of India (New Delhi), *Political Proceedings,* June 12, 1837, No. 41; Wade to Chief Secretary, Fort William.
3. National Archives of India (New Delhi), *Secret Consultations,* October 11, 1841, Nos. 46–51; Minute by Lt. Gov. T. C. Robertson, September 28, 1941.
4. Leo E. Rose, *The Role of Nepal and Tibet in Sino-Indian Relations* (Ph.D. dissertation, University of California, 1960).
5. *Enclosures* . . . , Vol. 79, 1841; Thomason to Lushington, September 1, 1841.
6. *Ibid.*, Vol. 77, 1841; Hodgson to Maddock, May 3, 1841.
7. *Ibid.*, Vol. 80, 1841; Hodgson to Maddock, September 19, 1841.
8. *Ibid.*, Vol. 81, 1841; Edwards to Maddock, December 1, 1841.
9. *Ibid.*, Vol. 82, 1841; Nepal Political Diary, December 15–17, 1841.
10. *Secret Consultations,* November, 1841, Nos. 35–37; Lushington to Assistant Secretary, Secret and Political Department, Northwest Province, October 9, 1841.
11. *Ibid.*, November 8, 1841, No. 45; Clerk to Cunningham, October 20, 1841.
12. Meng Pao to Emperor, November 8, 1841, in Meng Pao, *Hsi-Tsang Tsou-Shu* (*Tibetan Memorials and Reports*). (See Appendix.)
13. *Secret Consultations,* July 6, 1842, Nos. 40–44; Gumbo to Cunningham, April 18, 1842.
14. *Ibid.*, Cunningham to Gumbo, May 3, 1842.
15. *Enclosures* . . . , Vol. 89, 1849; Nepal Political Diary, September 1, 1842.
16. *Secret Consultations,* August 3, 1842, No. 22; Gyalpo to Cunningham, May 27, 1842.
17. *Ibid.*; Gyalpo to Sher Singh, June 13, 1842.
18. *Report of the Officials of the Government of India and the People's Republic of China on the Boundary Question* (New Delhi: [Government of India] Ministry of External Affairs, 1961), p. 266.
19. *Ibid.*, pp. CR-14–15.
20. *Loc. cit.*
21. *Ibid.*, p. 53.
22. Emperor to Meng Pao, January 15, 1843, in Meng Pao, *op. cit.* (See Appendix.)

*Chapter VIII: Ladakh and Great Power Rivalry: 1845–1950*

1. Article 1, Treaty of Amritsar. See C. U. Aitchison, A *Collection of Treaties, Engagements and Sanads Relating to India and Neighbouring Countries,* XII, 21–22.
2. Sir Alexander Cunningham, *Ladak,* . . . (London: W. H. Allen, 1854), p. 18.
3. National Archives of India (New Delhi), *Secret Consultations,* December 26, 1846, Nos. 1331–43; Hardinge to Lhasa, August 4, 1846.
4. Cunningham, *op. cit.*, p. 13.
5. India Office Library, *Foreign Department, Secret,* No. 33, August 14, 1846; Enclosure 28, H. M. Lawrence to P. A. Vans Agnew.
6. *Ibid.*, No. 33; Lawrence to Capt. A. Cunningham, July 23, 1846.

7. *Ibid.*, No. 35, May 25, 1847; J. F. Davis, H. M. Plenipotentiary, Hong Kong, to H. E. K'e-ying, High Imperial Commissioner, Canton, December 18, 1846.

8. *Ibid.*, No. 35; Enclosure 3, J. F. Davis, Hong Kong, to Hardinge, January 28, 1847.

9. *Ibid.*, No. 35; K'e-ying to Davis, January 13, 1847.

10. *Ibid.*, No. 35; Enclosure 4, K'e-ying to Davis, in a letter from Davis to Hardinge, January 30, 1847.

11. *Ibid.*, No. 36, May 2, 1848; Enclosure 6, Davis to Hardinge, August 12, 1847.

12. *Ibid.*, No. 36; Enclosure 9, H. Lawrence to H. M. Elliot, September 14, 1847.

13. *Atlas of the Northern Frontier of India* (New Delhi: [Government of India] Ministry of External Affairs, 1960), Maps 11 and 12, prepared by Lt. Henry Strachey in 1847 and 1848.

14. For English translation of the text of this agreement, see K. M. Panikkar, *The Founding of the Kashmir State*, . . . (London: Allen and Unwin, 1953), pp. 146–48.

15. India Office Library, *Foreign Department, Political*, No. 195, December 8, 1866.

16. *Ibid.*, No. 167, May 27, 1869.

17. *Foreign Department, Secret*, No. 330, October 11, 1869.

18. *Ibid.*, No. 25, May 17, 1870; Enclosure 14, Secretary to the Punjab Government to Government of India, April 21, 1870.

19. *Foreign Department, Political*, No. 212, October 4, 1870; Enclosure 5, Cayley to Secretary, Government of the Punjab, July 30, 1870.

20. T. E. Gordon, *A Varied Life* . . . 1849–1902 (London: John Murray, 1906), p. 97.

21. *Ibid.*, pp. 136–37.

22. *Proceedings of the Royal Geographic Society*, XI (1867), 165.

23. A. Durand, *The Making of a Frontier* (London: John Murray, 1900), p. 120.

24. *Ibid.*, p. 115.

25. *Ibid.*, p. 2.

26. *Ibid.*, p. 119.

27. See *The Autobiography of H. R. H. Mohamed Jamal Khan, Mir of Hunza* (unpublished, in library of University of California), p. 30.

28. H. Deasy, *In Tibet and Chinese Turkestan* . . . (London: T. Fisher Unwin, 1901), pp. 243–44.

29. India Office Library, *Foreign Department, Secret Frontier*, No. 2, January 6, 1897; "Memo of Information Regarding the Course of Affairs Beyond the Northwestern Frontier."

30. *Loc. cit.*

31. *Ibid.*, No. 170, December 23, 1897.

32. *Ibid.*, No. 198, October 27, 1898.

33. *Loc. cit.*

34. [Great Britain] Foreign Office, 17/1373; MacDonald to Prince Ch'ing, March 14, 1899.

35. *Report of the Officials of the Government of India and the People's Republic of China on the Boundary Question* (New Delhi: [Government of India] Ministry of External Affairs), pp. 63 and CR-16–17.

36. *Ibid.*, p. 155.

37. D. S. Fraser, *The Marches of Hindustan* . . . (Edinburgh, London: Blackwood, 1907), p. 158.

38. See Alastair Lamb, "Some Notes on Russian Intrigue in Tibet," *Journal of the Royal Central Asian Society*, XLVI, Part I (January, 1949), 46–65.
39. Mr. Max Miller to Sir Edward Grey, Peking, March 6, 1910, in [Great Britain] House of Commons, *Further Papers Relating to Tibet* (Command Paper No. 5240), No. 334, p. 203.
40. *Loc. cit.*
41. See R. Rahul, "Three-Point Agreement Between the Chinese and Tibetans, 12 August, 1912," *International Studies*, II (April, 1961), 420–24.
42. Sir Eric Teichman, *Travels of a Consular Official in Eastern Tibet* (Cambridge: Cambridge University Press, 1922), p. 40.
43. Sir Charles Bell, *Tibet Past and Present* (London: The Clarendon Press, 1924), pp. 15–52.
44. Quoted in letter from the Government of India to the Chinese People's Republic, February 12, 1960, in *Notes . . . Exchanged Between the Governments of India and China* (White Paper No. III [New Delhi: (Government of India) Ministry of External Affairs, February 29, 1960]), p. 93.
45. *Report of the Officials*, p. 55.
46. A. S. Whiting and General Sheng Shih-ts'ai, *Sinkiang: Pawn or Pivot?* (East Lansing, Michigan: State University Press, 1958), p. 117.
47. Satyanarayan Sinha, *The Chinese Aggression . . .* (New Delhi: Rama Krishna and Sons, 1961), pp. 42–47.
48. *Report of the Officials*, pp. 157, CR-81–82.

*Chapter IX: The Chinese Communist Conquest of Tibet and its Impact on Ladakh*

1. Statement made during debate in Parliament on November 25, 1961. [Jawaharlal Nehru], *Prime Minister on Sino-Indian Relations*, Vol. I, *In Parliament* ([Government of India] Ministry of External Affairs, External Publicity Division, 1961), p. 184.
2. See Letter from the Prime Minister of India to the Prime Minister of China, September 26, 1959, in *Notes . . . Exchanged Between the Governments of India and China* (White Paper No. II [New Delhi: (Government of India) Ministry of External Affairs, November 4, 1959]), p. 37.
3. *Asian Recorder* (New Delhi), VI, No. 19, p. 3301, col. 3.
4. *Ibid.*, p. 3302, col. 1.
5. *Ibid.*, p. 3302, cols, 2–3.
6. [Government of India] Lok Sabha Secretariat, *Lok Sabha Debates* (10th Session), Series 2, XLIII, No. 57 (New Delhi: 1961), Tuesday, April 26, 1960, col. 13797.
7. *Ibid.*, col. 14839.
8. *Ibid.*, col. 13797.

*Chapter X: The Sino-Indian Border Talks*

1. *Asian Recorder* (New Delhi), VI, No. 19, p. 3302.
2. *Report of the Officials of the Government of India and the People's Republic of China on the Boundary Question* (New Delhi: [Government of India] Ministry of External Affairs, 1961), p. 6.
3. *Ibid.*, p. 11.
4. *Ibid.*, p. 236.
5. *Ibid.*, p. CR-177.
6. *Ibid.*, p. CR-4.

7. *Ibid.*, p. 38.
8. *Ibid.*, p. CR-4.

*Chapter XI: Analysis of Conflicting Border Claims*

1. *Report of the Officials of the Government of India and the People's Republic of China on the Boundary Question* (New Delhi: [Government of India] Ministry of External Affairs, 1961), p. 151.
2. *Ibid.*, p. CR-123.
3. *Notes . . . Exchanged Between the Governments of India and China* (White Paper No. III [New Delhi: (Government of India) Ministry of External Affairs, February 29, 1960]), p. 53.
4. *Report of the Officials*, p. 151.
5. *Ibid.*, p. 268.
6. Ippolito Desideri, *An Account of Tibet; . . . 1712–1727*, ed., Filippo de Filippi (Rev. ed., London: George Routledge and Sons, 1937), p. 81.
7. J. B. Fraser, *Journal of a Tour . . .* (London: Rodwell and Martin, 1820), p. 309.
8. H. Strachey, "On the Physical Geography of Western Tibet," *Journal of the Royal Geographical Society*, XXIII, (1853), 38.
9. Sir Alexander Cunningham, *Ladak . . .* (London: W. H. Allen, 1854), pp. 18, 329.
10. [Great Britain] Foreign Office, Historical Section, *Tibet* (London: 1920), p. 4; Sir Charles Bell, *Tibet Past and Present* (London: Clarendon Press, 1924), p. 7.
11. *Report of the Officials*, p. CR-38.
12. *Ibid.*, pp. 160–61, 263–64.
13. R. L. Kennion, *Sport and Life in the Further Himalaya* (Edinburgh, London: Blackwood & Sons, 1910), p. 298.
14. H. Trotter, "Account of the Pandit's Journey in Great Tibet from Leh in Ladakh to Lhasa, and of his Return to India via Assam," *Journal of the Royal Geographical Society*, XLVII [1877], 89; and M. S. Wellby, *Through Unknown Tibet* (Philadelphia: Lippincott, 1898), p. 73.
15. Kishen Singh, *Record, Survey of India*, VIII, Part I, 158.
16. *Report of the Officials*, p. CR-38.
17. A. D. Carey, "A Journey Round Chinese Turkistan and Along the Northern Frontier of Tibet," *Proceedings of the Royal Geographical Society*, New Series, IX (December, 1887), 732.
   H. Bower, "A Journey Across Tibet," *Geographical Journal*, I (May, 1893), 386.
   M. S. Wellby, "Through Tibet to China," *Geographical Journal*, XIII (1898), 264.
   H. Deasy, "Journals in Central Asia," *Geographical Journal*, XVI, Part I (August, 1900), 142.
   R. Lydekker, *The Game Animals of India, Burma, Malaya and Tibet* (London: Ward, 1907), p. 183.
   R. L. Kennion, *op. cit.*, p. 227.
18. *Report of the Officials*, pp. CR-55–56.
19. *Ibid.*, p. 67.
20. *Ibid.*, p. 138.
21. *Ibid.*, p. CR-111.
22. *Ibid.*, pp. CR-79–80.
23. *Ibid.*, p. CR-78.

24. M. S. Wellby, *op. cit.*, pp. 264–65.
25. *Ch'in-Ting Huang-Yu Hsi-Yu T'u-Chih* (*Geographical Records* . . .) 1782 ed., Chapter xix, 9.
26. *Chia-Ch'ing Chung-Hsiu Ta-Ch'ing i Tung-Chih* (*Official Annals of the Empire* [1820]), Vol. DXXVIII, 4.
27. *Hsin-Chiang T'u-Chih* (*Geographical Records of Sinkiang* [Tientsin, 1911]), V, 2.
28. W. Moorcroft, "Notice on Khoten," *Journal of the Royal Geographical Society*, I (1832), 244.
29. Cunningham, *op. cit.*, pp. 17–18.
30. G. W. Hayward, "Journey from Leh to Yarkand and Kashgar, and Exploration of the Sources of the Yarkand River," *Journal of the Royal Geographical Society*, XL (1870), 49.
31. S. G. Burrard and H. H. Hayden, *A Sketch of the Geography and Geology of the Himalaya Mountains and Tibet* (Delhi: Government of India, 1933–34), Part II, 121–22.
32. R. C. F. Schomberg, *Unknown Karakoram* (London: M. Hopkinson, 1936), p. 9.
33. Hayward, *op. cit.*, p. 125.
34. Schomberg, *op. cit.*, p. 9. [Italics supplied.]
35. *Report of the Officials*, pp. 145–46.
36. F. Drew, *The Jummoo and Kashmir Territories; A Geographical Account* (London: Edward Stanford, 1875). [See map at end of book.]
37. *Report of the Officials*, p. CR-55.
38. *Ibid.*, p. CR-35.
39. *Ibid.*, p. CR-77.
40. *Ibid.*, p. CR-112.
41. *Imperial Gazetteer of India* (1908), XVI, 94.
42. *Report of the Officials*, p. CR-76.
43. *Ibid.*, p. CR-77.
44. H. Deasy, "A Journey to Northern Tibet and Aksai Chin," *The Geographical Journal*, XIII (February, 1899), 155.
45. H. Deasy, *In Tibet and Chinese Turkestan* . . . (London: T. Fisher Unwin, 1901), pp. 163–64.
46. H. Deasy, "Journeys in Central Asia," p. 596.
47. *Report of the Officials*, p. CR-117.
48. *Ibid.*, p. CR-118.
49. *Ibid.*, p. CR-80.
50. *Ibid.*, p. CR-126.
51. *Ibid.*, p. 157.
52. *Ibid.*, p. CR-127.
53. *Ibid.*, p. CR-112.
54. *National Herald* (Lucknow), 1962, October 17, 1:1–2.

*Chapter XII: Recent Developments and Emerging Trends*

1. New China News Agency (English, Peking, December 6, 1961), *Survey of China Mainland Press*, No. 2637 [December 12, 1961], p. 27.
2. *India News* (Indian Embassy, Washington, D.C.), Vol. 6, No. 24 (December 15, 1961), 1.
3. *The Hindu Weekly Review*, August 27, 1962, p. 2.
4. *Ibid.*, August 21, 1961, 3:2.

5. Report of the press conference held by R. K. Nehru in New Delhi on July 20, 1961, *ibid.*, July 31, 1961, 3:1–2.
6. *Asian Recorder* (New Delhi), Vol. VIII, No. 19 (May 7–13, 1962), 4563.
7. "New Delhi Blocks Sino-Indian Trade and Intercourse," *Peking Review*, V, No. 20 (May 18, 1962), 12–13.
8. Text of Chinese statement as issued by the New China News Agency, in *New York Times*, November 21, 1962, 3:1–5.
9. *Notes . . . Exchanged Between the Governments of India and China* (White Paper No. III [New Delhi: (Government of India) Ministry of External Affairs, February 29, 1960]), pp. 45–46.
10. *Ibid.*, pp. 47–51.
11. For text of proposals as issued by the New China News Agency, see *New York Times*, November 21, 1962, 3:1–5.
12. *Asian Recorder* (New Delhi), V, No. 47 (November 21–27, 1959), 3011.
13. *Ibid.*, VI, No. 3 (January 16–22, 1960), 3107:1.
14. *Jamhuriat* (Dacca), May 12, 1962 (as quoted in *The Hindu Weekly Review*, May 21, 1962, p. 3).
15. "China and Pakistan Agree to Negotiate Boundary Question," *Peking Review*, V, No. 19 [May 11, 1962], 10.
16. *Dawn* (Karachi), December 20, 1961, 7:1.
17. See A. K. Wu, *China and the Soviet Union . . .* (New York: John Day, 1950); Owen Lattimore, *Pivot of Asia* (Boston: Little, Brown, 1950); and Allen S. Whiting and General Sheng Shih-ts'ai, *Sinkiang: Pawn or Pivot?* (East Lansing, Michigan: State University Press, 1958).
18. See Satyanarayan Sinha, *The Chinese Aggression: A First Hand Account from Central-Asia, Tibet and the High Himalayas* (New Delhi: Rama Krishna, 1961).

# APPENDIX

## THE ACTION AGAINST THE SHEN-PA

"Shen-pa" is literally "the Singh people," a term used by the Tibetans and Chinese to refer to both Sikhs and Dogras, whose names characteristically contain the word "Singh" ("lion"). Here the reference is to the Dogras, and the "action" is the Dogra-Tibetan War of 1841–42.

1. *Notes on the Chinese original*

*The Action Against the Shen-pa* is Volume I of a rare, privately printed Chinese compilation of official documents entitled *Hsi-Tsang Tsou-Shu* (*Tibetan Memorials and Reports*), the work of Meng Pao, Imperial Resident at Lhasa from 1839 to 1844, and containing the documents that either originated with him or passed through his hands during his tenure. These state papers were arranged according to subject matter, and the date of publication was around 1851. Because of the destruction by fire in 1850 of the archives of the Board of Colonial Affairs at Peking, this collection is the only known source of certain state papers dealing with Tibet, Nepal, Ladakh, etc., during the important period from 1839 to 1844.

The work was first brought to public notice in a brief description by William Frederick Mayers, British Consul at Canton.* Camille Clément Imbault-Huart saw the notice by Mayers, searched for the work, eventually finding a copy in Peking, and translated portions of the third volume under the title "Relations diplomatiques de la Chine avec le Népal."† Searching for the original Chinese documents, we were also fortunate enough to obtain a copy (now in the library of the University of California).

The work is in five volumes divided into 10 "chüan" with an Appendix:

Volume I, Chüan 1. The Action Against the Shen-pa [Dogras].
Volume II, Chüan 2. The Installation of the New Dalai Lama.

* *Notes and Queries on China and Japan* (Hong Kong), I, No. 1 [January 31, 1867], 6.

† *Revue de l'Extreme-Orient*, III (1887), 1–23.

Volume III, Chüan 3. Correspondence with the King of the Gurkhas [Nepal].

Volume IV, Chüan 4. The Affairs of the Cha-ya Tribe [Tibetan Draya, located in eastern Tibet].

Chüan 5. The Training of Tibetan Garrisons.

Chüan 6. Judicial Affairs in Tibet.

Volume V, Chüan 7. Tibet's Annual Tribute.

Chüan 8. The Visit to Tibet of the Raja of Sikkim.

Chüan 9. The Appointment of Manchu and Chinese Officials in Tibet.

Chüan 10. The Appointment of Tibetans for Religious and Temporal Functions.

Volume VI, Appendix [historical inscriptions on tablets erected in Tibet from the T'ang dynasty to the Ch'ing period, and a number of poetic recitals by the Emperor Kao-tsung and others commemorating the conquest of Tibet].

2. *Selected Memorials and Reports from* The Action Against the Shen-pa

These documents, translated for the first time into any western language, so far as we have been able to find out, are extremely repetitive. In this type of correspondence it was customary to summarize the contents of the letter or report being answered. We have accordingly selected those portions of the various memorials that carry on the chronicle of events, and have omitted repetitious and unimportant detail. Written Chinese does not have any convention to show direct quotation, but where it was obviously indicated that a Tibetan report was being quoted, we have indicated it so. The first time a personal name or geographic term is used, the Chinese syllabification is given, with the more familiar English equivalent in parentheses; thereafter the English term only is used. The page references are to the Chinese original.

1. Tao Kuang, 21st year, 7th month, 17th day [September 2, 1841]

*Memorial:* Meng Pao to the Emperor: reporting that as the chief of Ladakh, in league with the Shen-pa aborigines, had occupied certain areas of Tangut [Tibet], Tibetan officers had to be sent with troops to deal with the situation:

A communication received from Silon Samadipakhshih of the Shang-shang* reported that beyond the northwestern border of Tibet is the

* Nag-dban-Jam-dpal-ts'ul-k'rims, Abbot of Tsomoling monastery. He had been appointed Regent of the tenth Dalai Lama in 1822, and was in charge of the Dalai Lama's treasury. He is hereafter referred to as the Regent. Silon is a title given to Councillors of State.

Ladakhi tribe whose border is adjacent to T'ui-ko-erh-pen [Gartok] in Tibet. In the 4th month of this year [May 21–June 19], the military post official at Gartok reported that he had ascertained that the Ladakhi chief was in league with the aborigines of the Shen-pa tribe. This official had received a message [from the Shen-pa leader] saying that their combined force, numbering over 400 men, mounted and on foot, was advancing toward the Tibetan border on a pilgrimage to the Hsüeh shan ["Snow Mountain," here Mount Kailash]. However, with a force this large, the official feared that some incident might occur, and he therefore requested that the officer in charge of Frontier Affairs be sent to look into the situation.

Upon receipt of the above report, Tai-pon [General] Pi-hsi* of central Tibet [the officer in charge of Frontier Affairs] was immediately ordered to hurry there and take steps at once to prevent the entry of this aboriginal force. He departed and his report was received from the scene on the 29th day of the 6th month [August 15]:

> The area of Gartok is very vast with only five† military posts, none of which has ever been fortified. Over 3,000 Ladakhi barbarians and Shen-pa aborigines had already assembled there before my arrival. In ten days they had occupied the two Tibetan posts at Ru-t'u [Rudok] and Gartok. The invaders claim all the territory beyond [west of] Man-yü-na Shan [the Mayum Pass] that formerly belonged to Ladakh. The invaders intend to conquer all the territory up to the Mayum Pass and force the people there to dress in their fashion and lend them assistance. As things are, they will soon reach the Tibetan post at Pu-ren [Purang, better known as Taklakot]. The situation has become very serious.

General Pi-hsi has now gathered together 500 local troops and is encamped at Ka-erh-tung [Kardung]. He sent a petition requesting immediate reinforcements to cope with the emergency. The situation was studied and it was decided that reinforcements should be sent immediately. One thousand Tibetan soldiers from the military post at Gyantse in Ulterior Tibet, and 300 soldiers from central Tibet,‡ all skillful soldiers with bows and arrows or fowling-pieces were selected. An additional 1,000 local [Lhasa]

* General Pi-hsi appears in the Ladakhi chronicles as Pi-si-sakra [Sarkar]. A Tai-pon (sometimes written *depon,* literally, "Lord of the Arrows") is equivalent to a colonel or general, depending on the number of men under his command.

† These were Gartok, Rudok, Tsaparang [Chabrang], Daba, and Taklakot [Purang].

‡ During the Ch-ing dynasty (1644–1912), Ch-ien Tsang [central Tibet] was the name given to the area including both the western part of K'ang [Kham] and Wei [U], previously known as Chung Tsang [Middle Tibet], where the Dalai Lama was stationed.

Hou Tsang [Ulterior Tibet] included both Tsang, or K'a-chi, where the Panchen Lama was stationed, and Ngari [Ari; the area west of the Mayum pass], bordering on Kashmir and the P'un-che-pu [Punjab] region of India.

troops were sent. Ch'a-tien-tun-chieh* and Cho-mei-ch'a-wang-pa-chiu-erh,† two Kalons‡ who are familiar with the military situation, were also commissioned. They left on the 13th day of the 7th month [August 29] with the troops, and hurried off to different strategic points to prevent any further encroachment. They were ordered to cooperate with General Pi-hsi and carefully to guide him in making immediate arrangements, and were warned to avoid taking anything for granted and spoiling this affair through overconfidence in the large number of troops at their disposal. The Tibetan Treasurer's Office is responsible for providing foodstuffs and supplies. The Regent has been notified by urgent dispatch to make proper arrangements without fail. Any further reports from the two Kalons after their arrival will be submitted in future memorials. [1a-2b]

2. Tao Kuang, 21st year, 7th month, 17th day [September 2, 1841]

*Supplementary Memorial:* Meng Pao to the Emperor.

It has been learned that south of Ladakh there is a very large aboriginal tribe named Ren-chi-shen. Subordinate to this tribe are two smaller tribes—Sa-re-shen and Ko-lang-shen, who together are known as the Shen-pa.§ After the death of the Ladakhi ruler [Tshe-pal Nam-gyal], a certain Ladakhi chieftain had secret connections with the Shen-pa, who then occupied Ladakh. Now this Ladakhi chieftain is once again in league with the Shen-pa aborigines who have invaded Tibetan territory, occupied two of our military posts at Gartok and Rudok, and claimed the territory west of the Mayum Pass that had formerly belonged to Ladakh. Actually they intended to occupy more territory than this. However, according to our survey, the distance between the Mayum Pass and [the capital of] Central Tibet is more than 3,000 *li* and from the Mayum Pass to Ladakh is 1,700 *li*. Although the Shen-pa and Ladakhi tribes are comparatively close to Nepal there is still peace in that area.

(The Emperor's acknowledgement and approval was dated October 9, 1841.)

3. Tao Kuang, 21st year, 8th month, 6th day [September 20, 1841]

*Memorial:* Meng Pao to the Emperor reporting that more Tibetan troops were being sent to meet the Ladakhi and Shen-pa invasion, and that food supplies were also being provided:

* Known as Surkhang or Zurkhang in Indian and Ladakhi sources.

† Known as Ra-ga-sa in Ladakhi and Rakasa in Indian sources.

‡ Chinese *Kopanlan*, Tibetan *Ka-blon*, cabinet ministers of the third rank.

§ Ren-chi-shen is presumably Ranjit Singh; Sa-re-shen, Zorawar Singh; and Ko-lang-shen, Gulab Singh. These terms were probably obtained from Tibetan informants, and described with fair accuracy the relations between Sikhs and Dogras just before Ranjit Singh's death.

On the 17th day, 7th month of this year [September 2, 1841], it was reported that an army had been sent to meet the Ladakhi and Shen-pa invasion.

This report from General Pi-hsi was received on the first day of the 8th month [September 15]:

> The invaders took possession of Rudok and Gartok military posts, as no Tibetan border posts had been fortified. They then advanced toward Kardung which is under the jurisdiction of the Taklakot military post. On [my] arrival at Taklakot a force of only about 1,000 local troops could be mustered, which was divided and stationed as guards at different posts. A guard post was quickly established at a strategic pass near Taklakot to stop the invaders, but these local troops were not brave enough to fight off the Shen-pa and fled at the approach of the invaders. The distance between central Tibet and Taklakot is several thousand *li*. As the reinforcements of Tibetan troops had not yet arrived, the force of over 3,000 invaders was able to occupy successively the three military posts of Ta-pa-ko-erh [Daba], Tsa-ren [Tsaparang], and Taklakot, on the 6th and 7th days of the 7th month [August 22–23]. The fight took place against great odds, and both sides sustained some casualties. Because of the cowardice of the local troops, our forces had to withdraw to the foot of Tsa Mountain near the Mayum Pass. Reinforcements are essential in order to withstand these violent and unruly invaders.

Since the local troops were not sufficiently vigorous in resisting the invaders, it was necessary to arrange for the dispatch of Tibetan troops. In addition to the 1,300 Tibetan soldiers sent previously, there will be sent two Jupons [fifth rank officers], four Chiapons [sixth rank officers], and twenty Tingpons [seventh rank officers] together with 500 Tibetan soldiers from U and Tsang on the 13th day of the 8th month [September 27]. Also, by urgent dispatch, the two Kalons sent previously to command the troops were requested to speed their advance by day and night and commence attacking the invaders.

Moreover, there are high mountains along the Mayum Pass which are usually blocked by heavy winds and snow in the 9th and 10th months [October–December], thus making communications impossible. In addition to the local soldiers, over 2,000 Tibetan troops and officers have been sent from U and Tsang. We must hasten the transport of all necessary food supplies before the snows come. It would be of great concern if the food supplies failed to be transported or were delayed. The matter has, therefore, been taken up personally with the Regent and an estimate has been made of the grain stored in all the military post warehouses. This amounted to a total of 89,100 *k'e*, altogether 17,800 odd *piculs*,* constituting a nine-months' supply, which was ordered transported to the front.

* Five *k'e* make one *picul;* a *picul* equals 133.5 lbs.

Next spring when the snow melts, additional supplies can be sent in plenty of time. In case anything more is required it will be provided.

A great number of animals are needed for the transportation of such large quantities of food supplies. Delays might have resulted if we had allowed all the food to be carried by animals belonging to the merchants. Therefore a consultation was held with the Panchen Lama before his return to Ulterior Tibet, and he was asked to commission the Tashilhunpo monastery to help arrange the transportation of these provisions. A reply has since been received from the Panchen Lama stating Tashilhunpo's willingness to assist inasmuch as provisions are now so essential. It was also taken into consideration that some of the Tashilhunpo forced labor might be unable to support themselves. Therefore consultations were held with the Regent asking him to extend financial support to those in great need so that their work would be performed more efficiently and without delay. Also some faithful Tibetan officials have been selected to constantly supervise and expedite transport all along the route and to see that everything receives the best of care. It is estimated that all provisions will arrive at the military posts by the 9th month [October–November], before the passes are blocked by heavy snow, so that there will be no need to worry about food supplies. Very careful consideration will always be given to what should be done. [5a–7a]

(On October 27, 1841, the Emperor approved the measures taken and ordered that the affair should be managed with great care and be brought to a conclusion expeditiously.)

4. Tao Kuang, 21st year, 9th month, 25th day [November 8, 1841]

*Memorial:* Meng Pao to the Emperor: reporting the cause of the incident and the continuation of hostilities:

In the previous memorial dated September 20, 1841, it was reported that the Ladakhi barbarians and the Shen-pa aborigines occupied some Tibetan territory and that steps had been taken to repulse their invasion. A report has since been received from Kalon Surkhang which states:

> We arrived at Cho-hsü* on the 18th day of the 8th month [October 2], and investigated the true cause of the incident precipitated by the barbarians. It was learned that the Ladakhi tribe was formerly very friendly and had trade relations with Tibet. Recently the Ladakhi chieftains planned to occupy Gartok and some other places belonging to Tibet, where very coarse wool and gold are produced. They then made secret arrangements with the Shen-pa aborigines. They used the

* In Tibetan–Dro-shod or Gro-shad, in English–Dokthal, a district in Tsang province east of the Mayum Pass.

subterfuge of a pilgrimage to Mt. Kailash and crossed into Tibet without permission, robbing the people and occupying five military posts inside Tibet. The invaders took advantage of their successes to make further advances. General Pi-hsi led some local soldiers in an attempt to resist them. More than twenty of the enemy and two of their officers were killed. On the Tibetan side, fifteen local soldiers and one Tibetan officer named Ch'ung-ren-pa were lost. The invaders then withdrew a short distance.

Now the enemy are more than 3,000 strong and have occupied the military post at Taklakot. In each of the other four posts seized they have stationed 300–500 men and have strongly fortified their positions. Having heard of our arrival, the invaders submitted a peace proposal stating that they would withdraw if Tibet would promise to pay an indemnity. Now our troops are in position and the invaders will not be allowed to advance any further. But winter is at hand, and the passes will soon be blocked by snow storms, and any attack by our forces is out of the question.

The above report was studied, and the conclusion is that these barbarian invaders must be dealt with very severely. They first planned to occupy the places where gold is mined, then they dared to fight with us, mustering a large force. Finally, out of fear, they sued for peace, promising to withdraw on condition of a money payment from Tibet. These aborigines are so unruly and utterly abominable that should the other tribes follow their evil example there will be a succession of troubles without end. They must be severely punished by a strong force so that their greed will be diminished. But now the situation is that, as the Kalons reported, their force is unable to advance across the Mayum Pass in view of the approach of winter. At the same time, however, a long delay might hamper an attack by allowing the invaders to grow stronger. Therefore, consultations have repeatedly been held with the Regent and the geographic aspects of the situation closely examined. The Mayum Pass is the route normally used by the army. However, in view of the obstacles presented by snow conditions, it has been arranged that the army should be divided. Detachments must be stationed at the different strategic passes to hold the enemy back, while other troops must be sent toward Rudok via another route along the Ma-Tsang.* We would then attack the invaders from both front and rear and the morale of the enemy would thus be weakened. Should they then sue for peace out of fear, we will then reconsider our decision. Under no circumstances will indemnity be promised as that would deviate from all of our fundamental rules.

Twice the Kalons there have been advised to act as instructed. Also communications have frequently been sent them as to how to manage the attack in order to bring these troubles to the earliest possible conclusion. [9a–10b]

* See map of the Dogra War.

(On December 14, 1841, the Emperor approved what had been done to date and gave emphatic orders to put an end to these troubles as soon as possible.)

5. Tao Kuang, 21st year, 11th month, 4th day [December 16, 1841]

*Memorial* to the Emperor: reporting the victorious attack upon the Ladakhi and Shen-pa invaders and the recapture of Taklakot:

The Emperor's reply dated October 27, 1841, to our memorial dated September 20, 1841, has been received. The Emperor's advice that the affair be managed carefully with the hope of ending the troubles caused by the Ladakhi barbarians and the Shen-pa aborigines as soon as possible is gratefully received. The Kalons in the field have been repeatedly and strictly ordered to bring the task to a rapid conclusion.

On the 10th month, 28th day [December 10, 1841], a report was received from the Kalons, stating:

> The invaders had first occupied our military post at Taklakot and then pretended to talk peace with us. At the same time, however, they continued to advance and an attempt was made to stop them as ordered. Now they have withdrawn to Kardung, which is under the command of Taklakot, and have fortified a high place half-way up the pass to prevent our soldiers from advancing. The only way to reach this place is over a main road which is very steep and dangerous. They have been attacked from the front while, at the same time, our courageous troops were secretly sent up the mountain from the rear. The invaders were thus surrounded and attacked from all directions. Fighting began on the 9th month, 26th day [November 9, 1841], and lasted from 3 A.M. to 3 P.M. Ninety-five Shen-pa aborigines were killed and eighty-six captured, along with three turbaned Mohammedans of the Pa-ti [Balti] aboriginal tribe and one Ladakhi barbarian. The food supplies and munitions they had stored in the fort were all captured. On our side, thirteen Tibetan and local soldiers were killed, and seventeen wounded. An officer, Cho-ni-erh-ch'a-ta-erh-cheh, under our command, was lost, and Chia-pon Cha-hsi-lon-chia was wounded during the attack. Now all the strategic points at Kardung and Taklakot have been regained.
>
> Moreover, four Shen-pa spies have been captured. According to their information, the invaders have recently constructed a strong fortification at a place called Chi-t'ang, about 200 *li* east of Taklakot.* The fortifications consist of three-storied stone houses on four sides with embrasures above, while at the base they have dug trenches 10 *ch'ih*† in width and depth. There are about two large and eight or nine small cannon on each side of this stone fort, which is strongly guarded by a force of over

* About 65–70 miles. The distance of Chi-t'ang from Taklakot is correct, but not the direction. See map.

† *Ch'ih* = 10 Chinese inches, 14.1 English inches, or 0.3581 metres.

500 Ladakhi barbarians, Shen-pa aborigines, and turbaned Mohammedans. Also, it is learned that several thousand of the invaders are concentrated as reserves at Tang-la [Tirthapuri], where they set up a big camp and prepared for further hostilities. This place is in communication with Kardung and Taklakot. Therefore, Tibetan officers with 1,100 soldiers have been sent to guard the routes and to cut communications between the invaders and their reserves. Because of the division of our forces, an additional thousand or more troops and some large guns are requested in preparation for further attacks.

In view of the situation, it was feared that the force would be insufficient once the Kalons started to attack. Through consultation with the Regent in advance, arrangements were made for 1,250 Tibetan cavalry, famous for generations, who all arrived at Lhasa on the 15th day of the 10th month [November 27]. In response to the Kalons' request for reinforcements, it was arranged immediately to send the cavalry to the front on the 29th day of the 10th month [December 11]. In view of the report that the invaders' fort is lofty and strongly fortified, big guns are essential for the assault. The guns on the Po-ta-la, according to information received from the Regent, are too old and decayed for use. Therefore the two big guns kept in the Lhasa garrison were sent along with the cavalry.

The Kalons killed and captured over 180 invaders and regained our post at Taklakot in their recent attack. When the big guns arrive, the fortifications at Chi-t'ang, difficult though they are at present, will be easy to attack. Once again, by dispatch, the Kalons have been given strict instructions concerning the invaders, who have occupied the territory of Tibet to the extent of more than 1,700 *li*. Now that the Taklakot post has been regained, the remnants of our forces that were withdrawn from the four military posts lost earlier, should take the opportunity provided by our victory to make an immediate attack and recover all four posts, in order to win back all the lost territory. This work should be carried out soon, without hesitation and without any further delay.

Instructions will continue to be sent to them in compliance with the Emperor's orders. [15a–17b]

(On January 21, 1842, the Emperor approved this report and ordered that a settlement be obtained quickly.)

6. Tao Kuang, 21st year, 12th month, 17th day [January 27, 1842]

*Memorial* to the Emperor: reporting the beheading of the commander of the invaders and the capture of some other officers:

In the previous memorial dated December 16, 1841, encouraging news of the attack on the Ladakhi and Shen-pa invaders was reported. The situation has been studied, keeping in mind the fact that the invaders are very treacherous. They had carefully selected a place with rugged physical features at Chi-t'ang where they recently built a very strong stone fort. Their plan was not only to prevent our forces from advancing, but they also intended to make gradual encroachments upon our territory. Under such circumstances, it was decided to take advantage of the winter months to launch strong attacks against them at a time when their escape route through the mountains would be blocked by snowstorms. Had swift action of this sort not been taken, the invaders would have spread out and become extremely difficult to pursue and capture. Fearing that the Kalons would face difficulties in meeting the situation, our dispatches have repeatedly encouraged and advised them. Officers and soldiers have also been appointed to go there and make factual, on-the-spot studies in co-operation with the Kalons.

A report has now been received by messenger from Kalons Surkhang and Ragasa, and General Pi-hsi, on the 8th day, 12th month [January 18, 1842]:

> In accordance with your secret orders, the stone fort at Chi-t'ang was repeatedly attacked, but the firing of the enemy's big guns from the fort made a frontal assault impossible. On the 13th day, 10th month [November 25, 1841], we ascertained that Wo-se-erh [Wazir Zorawar Singh], the commander of the Shen-pa force, had come from Tirthapuri with over 3,000 invaders and camped at Kardung,* a place near Taklakot. On the 14th day [November 26], the commander secretly sent one of his officers named Mien-shen [Mian Singh] with his men to cut the road which our soldiers usually take to get water. Shih-ti-pa-ch'a-tien was then ordered to lead a force there and fight against them. Seven of the invaders were killed, including the officer, Mian Singh. The Wazir then sent another force to do battle and in this fight sixteen of the invaders were killed by our Tibetan soldiers. The rest of the enemy withdrew without being able to block the path to our water supply. On the 21st day [December 3], the invaders divided into five groups, and advanced in five waves against our lines. We killed thirty-six of the invaders while losing nine Tibetan soldiers. Because of their repeated defeats, the Wazir himself came with his troops from their new fort at Chi-t'ang, where he joined the force led by T'a-la Ma-ta-erh,† intending to occupy a place named Do-yo, in order to cut our supply line. On receipt of this information, troops were immediately sent that night to occupy Do-yo before the arrival of the enemy. General Pi-hsi was placed in command there as it had also been discovered that the enemy commander, the Wazir, had broken camp and was proceeding from Kardung. He sent two agents, Koh-lan-k'an,‡ a Ladakhi officer, and

* The Ladakh chronicle says that Zorawar Singh set up his camp a little below Do-yo, a few miles nearer Taklakot.

† Mehta Basti Ram.

‡ Presumably Ghulam Khan, the son-in-law of Rahim Khan, "a half-blood Musalman of Chuchot (Chu-s'od)," who had been responsible for the destruction of Buddhist monasteries during the invasion, and was tortured to death by the Tibetans. (Cunningham, *Ladak* . . . [London: W. H. Allen, 1854], p. 352.)

another Ladakhi named Shan-cho-t'e-pa-kung-pu, to Taklakot. They pretended to talk peace with us, but actually this was a trick to use them as spies. However, this deception was quickly seen through. Immediately after their arrival at our post they were arrested and interrogated. They confessed and gave evidence stating that they had been commissioned by the Wazir, the commander of the Shen-pa, to discover the size of the government [Tibetan] force. This Ghulam Khan is the rightful chief of Ladakh, who had made a secret alliance with the Shen-pas to foment the recent troubles. This Ladakhi chief is very tall, strong, and vigorous. For fear that he would escape, his shinbones were first broken and then he was put in prison while all of his attendants were executed.

On the 28th day of the 10th month [December 10, 1841], the Wazir moved to Kan-ru-mi-mu-na, a place near Do-yo. On the following day, the enemy advanced to Do-yo, and a battle took place. General Pi-hsi led his troops and killed sixty-two of the enemy, and captured one large cannon before the enemy withdrew. Five Tingpons and eight Tibetan soldiers were lost on our side, and eighteen wounded. However, the enemy were still very fierce and violent, and were determined to capture Do-yo.

During this period, there was a great snowstorm and snow accumulated to the depth of several feet. A well-disguised ambush was carefully laid, in which a road was left open through the middle of our lines up which the enemy could advance. The invaders marched on Do-yo from 7 A.M. to 9 A.M. on the second day, 11th month [December 14, 1841]. These forces included the troops stationed at their new fort at Chi-t'ang in addition to the force led by the Wazir, the Shen-pa commander. They advanced in three units with flags flying and drums beating. General Pi-hsi led his troops to resist their advance. The invaders fell into the ambush that had been prepared and their rearguard was cut off and could not maneuver. They were attacked by our forces from all sides. The Wazir, the commander of the Shen-pa, was wounded, yet he dared to run up and attack us with his sword. He was killed by our courageous soldiers (it was then noon time) and he was beheaded. Also, more than forty of their higher and lower officers, and 200 of their soldiers were killed. The rest, seeing their leaders slain, dispersed in a disorderly fashion in all directions. One large cannon together with its mount, one large iron cannon, and six flags were captured, along with numerous muskets, daggers, cane-shields, and the like.

Then there came a Ladakhi chief, called Pak-ku Ka-lung No-no Szu-lan,* who had previously accompanied the Wazir to fight, and the Khan of the Balti aboriginal tribe, A-mu-erh-sha [Ahmed Shah], and his son.† They surrendered their arms and were all imprisoned in the post at

* No-no-Bsod-nams in the Ladakh chronicles and Nono Sungnam in Cunningham's account.

† Ahmed Shah had been deposed by Zorawar Singh in 1839 and his son, Ali Mohammad, placed on the throne of Skardu. Both were forced to accompany the Dogras in the invasion of Tibet.

Taklakot. After thorough inquiry and investigation, a further report will be submitted soon. As for those invaders and their officers who fled towards their fort [Chi-t'ang], their pursuit and capture have been ordered. Now Peng-ts'o-tun-chieh (the son of Kalon Surkhang), a Supply officer of Kalon Ragasa, General Pi-hsi, and Ta-tsang-ko-chieh (an interpreter of our administrative office) have been appointed to forward the head of the Wazir under their escort to your [Meng Pao's] Office for examination.

It has been learned that the Wazir, the commander of the Shen-pa invaders, was the highest official of the Sa-re-shen aboriginal tribe.* He was always stealthily encroaching on the territory of others and the large and small aboriginal tribes beyond our frontier suffered greatly from his vexatious and poisonous oppressions. Even their great Khan† was afraid of his tyrannical actions. He then assembled a large army in order to occupy by force several of our Tibetan military posts. It was he who was in fact the leader of the invaders. After a close examination, his head was placed at a thoroughfare [in Lhasa] for the public to view as a manifestation of the power of the national law. All the aboriginal traders at Lhasa were very gratified by this.

As for Ghulam Khan, the Ladakhi chief who initiated this disturbance, Nono Sungnam, the Ladakhi chief who surrendered, and the Khan of the Balti aboriginal tribe, they, along with others, will all be taken in custody to Lhasa for trial. By special dispatch the Kalons and General Pi-hsi have also been instructed that as the strength of the invading forces at the four military posts in Tibet still in enemy possession has not yet been ascertained, the movements of our troops sent to attack these posts should be more carefully planned than ever before. They should never act heedlessly, even to the slightest degree, because of over-confidence following the recent victory. Moreover, the enemy should not be permitted a breathing spell in which they could prepare another attack. The Kalons will be continuously urged to settle the matter as quickly as possible in order to show the good intentions of the throne with respect to the pacification of the frontier. [19a-22b]

(On March 4, 1842, the Emperor gave orders for the capture and extermination of all the invaders, in order to leave no nucleus for later retaliatory action. Orders were given for a list to be made of officers and men deserving of Imperial favor. The Emperor wrote in vermilion ink on this edict: "All was very well managed.")

7. Tao Kuang, 22nd year, 3rd month, 8th day
[April 18, 1842]

*Memorial* from Meng Pao to the Emperor: reporting that the enemy fort

* Zorawar Singh.
† Ranjit Singh?

had been taken, the four military posts recaptured, and the security of the frontier restored:

In the memorial dated January 27, 1842, it was reported that the Wazir, the commander of the invaders, had been beheaded and that some other aboriginal chiefs had been captured. Although the leader of the invaders has been killed, the other invaders should not be allowed to flee. All must be exterminated so that they will not be able to cause trouble in the future. The fortification built at Chi-t'ang by the aboriginal invaders obstructing the main road along which our troops will advance, should be captured soon in order to bring these disturbances quickly to an end. The Kalons have been repeatedly ordered by dispatch to act quickly and carefully. A report from them was received on the second month, 29th day [April 9, 1842]:

> When the Wazir, the commander of the invaders, was killed, all the invaders dispersed in confusion in various directions. Our troops were ordered to pursue and capture them wherever they went. In addition to the invaders who were killed or fell off the cliffs, it was learned that a total of 836 had surrendered. Thirteen Shen-pa chiefs, including Re-i-shen [Rai Singh],* were captured and have been sent to Lhasa under an escort of our Tibetan officers. The invaders' new fort at Chi-t'ang was now isolated. The right opportunity was seized to encircle and attack it. The invaders, relying on the strength of their stone fortifications on all four sides of which large and small cannon had been mounted, refused to come out. They were repeatedly attacked, and our courageous soldiers were secretly sent by night to bypass the fort at Chi-t'ang. They were placed at various key points to cut the invaders' supply lines, and all the invaders engaged in transporting supplies were killed. It snowed for nine days and nights. The invaders, short of food, planned to flee towards a place called Chiang Nor. Just at this time the big guns that had been previously requested from the Lhasa garrison arrived at our camp. Our troops took advantage of this opportunity to encircle and assault Chi-t'ang Fort. The western corner of the stone fort immediately came under the fire of our big guns. The invaders in that section poured out in disorderly fashion, but resisted us to the death. More troops with guns had already been placed in position and they quickly rushed in and killed 300 or more of the aboriginal invaders. Chi-t'ang Fort was thus captured, and over 700 different types of weapons, such as cannon, cane-shields, daggers, etc., were seized. Chie-mai-pa, an officer of the Taklakot military post, was rescued. He had been captured by the invaders and buried in the ground up to his head, and he was now dug out by us. This officer told us that in the 7th month [August–September, 1841] when he had been assigned to guard Taklakot, he had been captured by the Shen-pa aborigines, who had bound him up. Every day he was flogged and questioned about the routes into central and Ulterior Tibet and the volume of gold and silver

* A Dogra officer, second in command to Zorawar Singh.

held in reserve in Tibet, but he dared not tell them the truth. In the 8th month [September–October], he was buried in the ground up to his head at Chi-t'ang Fort and was given only a little food and water each day. Fortunately, he was not yet dead, although very thin and emaciated. He is now recuperating at the military post.

The invaders who fled from Chi-t'ang Fort were pursued. Fifty-two of them were killed at Chiang Nor, and their heads or left ears were cut off, and were brought back to the camp as verification. Their horses and weapons were also captured. Kalon Ragasa and his troops searched for the invaders along the Tun-sa-lang Valley, and 148 of them were killed or captured. Now all the rebels around Chi-t'ang have been exterminated and their newly built fort has been destroyed.

Our troops then proceeded to Gartok, which had previously been the headquarters for all the military posts in this area. Kalon Surkhang was stationed here to supervise troop movements. The three posts of Daba, Tsaparang, and Rudok were placed under the command of General Pi-hsi and the Tibetan officer Ts'o-koh-kang-ch'ing-pa, and others. All the troops were dispatched to various places to search for and attack the invaders, who had established posts all along the route through which our forces advanced. All the Ladakhi and Balti invaders surrendered as if swayed by the wind, and only the Shen-pa aboriginal invaders continued to resist us. Finally, over 100 of the Shen-pa invaders were killed, and Gartok could then be recaptured. General Pi-hsi and our Tibetan officers also reported from their posts that they had discovered that the remaining invaders were concentrated at Minsar, where they had stored a reserve food supply. Our Tibetan officers led their troops through the snow and occupied this place, but the invaders had muddied all the food supplies, and burned all the furnishings in their accounting office there. The invaders fled, and our forces followed them until they reached the Chia-na-o mountain range, where an additional 197 of the invaders were killed. The three military posts at Daba, Tsaparang, and Rudok were then recovered. Further searches were conducted at a place called Hsiang-tsai to which some of the invaders had escaped. Seventeen were killed there and fifty-five captured, including their commanding officer named Mu-k'a-ta-mu,* all of whom were imprisoned. Thus, the four military posts [the three named above, plus Gartok], have been recaptured and no more invaders remain anywhere in Tibetan territory.

The Shen-pa aborigines, relying on their strength augmented by several thousand troops from three aboriginal tribes, invaded and occupied by force five Tibetan military posts. When the attack on the invaders began in the 8th month of last year [September], the post at Taklakot was quickly recovered. The Wazir, the commander of the Shen-pas, was also killed and four Ladakhis were taken prisoner, including Ghulam Khan,

* This may have been Singhe Mankotiah, who had been one of Zorawar Singh's officers in 1834.

the Ladakhi chief who incited the disturbance through a secret arrangement with the Shen-pas. Moreover, more than forty Shen-pa and Ladakhi officers of higher or lesser rank were killed, and 836 of the invaders surrendered. Within two months, Chi-t'ang had been recaptured and an area consisting of over 1,700 *li*, in which the remaining military posts were located, was completely regained.

By now everything has been completed successfully, and the frontiers are once again tranquil. All this has been the result of the far-reaching wisdom of the Imperial Majesty, and the comprehensiveness of the Imperial instructions which were followed so that a swift settlement of the recent event has been effected. Very grateful for this. Arrangements are now being made to contribute some silver medals, silk pongees, tea, etc., for distribution as rewards to those officers and soldiers who had made great effort on the front. Arrangements will also be made for those Tibetan officers and soldiers who died in battle, and for their families, in accordance with precedents established in the past.

The geographical area covered by the various military posts is very large and is adjacent to the territory of different aboriginal tribes beyond our frontiers. Because of the ravages committed by the invading soldiers and brigands, all the Tibetan inhabitants of this area [Ari, or West Tibet] have fled and scattered. In a dispatch, the Kalons have been ordered to pacify the area, and bring the residents back to their homes safely. As to the reconstruction work, after careful study of their topographic situation and living conditions, and after deliberation, some rules and regulations will be formulated and the throne will be memorialized for instructions. [24a–27b]

(On May 23, 1842, the Emperor praised Meng Pao and the Assistant Resident Hai P'o for their efficiency and ordered liberal awards for them. He also called for lists of Tibetan officers and men deserving of awards.)

8. Tao Kuang, 22nd year, 3rd month, 15th day [April 25, 1842]

*Memorial* from Meng Pao to the Emperor, submitting proposed regulations for the defense of the frontier:

Kalon Surkhang and others have forwarded a joint petition from the Ladakhi aborigines and the Balti Khan together with his people, which states:

> The tribal peoples of our countries have been disturbed by the Shen-pa aborigines who do not know the law, and who occupied the territory of different tribes, relying on their superior strength. Now that the Wazir, the Shen-pa commander, has been killed, our tribal peoples beyond the frontiers will hereafter be able to avoid his oppressions, for which they are truly grateful. We petition that the Chinese and Tibetan officials

be kind enough to allow our tribal peoples to pledge allegiance to the Tibetan "Shang-shang"* so that all the tribes beyond the frontiers would learn to respect the Imperial law and there would be no more trouble caused in the future. Should this petition be granted, our entire people would be saved.

We are willing to give a bond to guard our respective borders and cooperate with each other against any aggression.

[The Kalons commented:]
The Ladakhi tribe had previously been very friendly with Tibet. In the past, their Khans used to send representatives every year to Lhasa bearing gifts to the "Shang-shang," and for many years the two peoples traded with each other. Later, due to the occupation of their land by the Wazir, the Shen-pa commander, the intercourse between the two people was discontinued. Moreover, at the time of the rebellion of the Mohammedan, Chang-ke-erh, some rebels escaped to Ladakh from Chinese Turkestan. The Ladakhi Khan captured the rebels. For this, the Khan was graciously awarded the fifth official rank, with peacock plume worn on the hat, by the Imperial throne. It seems that this tribe is somewhat different from the other barbarians beyond our frontiers. If the two tribes of Ladakh and Baltistan are allowed to re-establish relations with the Tibetan "Shang-shang," they should be ordered to guard their respective borders and to engage in trade with us as in the past. When they have come to depend upon us for assistance, they will certainly be very cooperative in guarding their respective borders. If their petition is granted, we will secure pledges from the officers and people of Ladakh and Baltistan, who will be obligated to observe reverently the customs and laws and never willfully offend us.

The petition sent by the Kalons indicates that the Ladakhi aborigines and the Balti Khan and his people are sincere in their expressed desire to re-establish relations with Tibet, and to offer their allegiance. Should their request be rejected, at some later date they might have to submit to others.† Then more trouble might result and another of our enemies would be strengthened. Moreover, the aboriginal tribes beyond the Tibetan frontier are very numerous, while the boundary of Gartok is extensive and has no natural defense positions. Even if we sent troops to guard the border, it is over 2,000 *li* in length. With such an extensive territory and a limited number of troops, the border would be difficult to defend. Now that the Khan and others are willing to return to their allegiance to us, it is best to accede to their desires. They can be restrained under such circumstances and be used as a wall on our frontier. It is completely desirable in both respects. Since the Balti and Ladakhi tribes will now belong to Tibet, rules and regulations should be carefully drawn up to assure permanent peace. According to their custom, the aboriginal tribes are very apprehen-

* Here the reference is presumably to the Dalai Lama's treasurer, the Regent.
† Probably a reference to the British.

sive of any reduction in their rations and fodder, and also in demands for services or for taxes. Quite often hostilities arose out of such matters. After their return to allegiance, they should send gifts to the Tibetan "Shang-shang" annually, as the Ladakhi Khan did previously, as evidence of their allegiance. No demand for an increase in the amount of gifts should be allowed. This is to show them that we do not want to exact concessions from them and that we are not interested in their territory. Thus both parties can live together peacefully without giving rise to fresh complications. However, as the nature of barbarians is somewhat like that of dogs and sheep, other measures should be taken under consideration as a precaution against further disturbances.

After careful consideration, it appears that Gartok is the proper center for all our military posts. Moreover, there are gold mines in this area. Usually several hundred Tibetans gather together there to engage in gold mining. The number of such people is irregular and no one has ever exercised control over them. The plan would be to limit the number of Tibetans allowed to dig for gold there to five hundred. All should be strong and skillful, selected from the Tibetans of central and Ulterior Tibet. They would be sent as gold miners, and from among their number ten competent men would be selected and deputed to supervise the miners. Further, nine military officers of different ranks—one Taipon, two Jupons, two Chiapons, and four Tingpons—would be selected and deputed from central and Ulterior Tibet. They would be stationed there for a fixed period of time and provide military training for the gold miners. In case of need, this force would be available for immediate use without worry over the danger of their being too far away for us to control. The gold miners would thus retain their occupation, and be guaranteed that their position would not be taken by others. Hence, they would be enriched and our frontiers would be well defended by these local Tibetans and no additional expenditures would be required.

The military officers deputed to this area should remain there for a term of two years. If the area is found to be tranquil and the training efficient, they should be rewarded by the Resident Envoy in Tibet, but should be punished if anything goes wrong. These military officers should not be considered as permanent residents in this area as they are responsible for frontier defense throughout Tibet. After trying this experiment for three or four years, the Resident Envoy should consult with the Regent as to whether or not these military officers should be sent back to the home army. Should the situation permit the departure of these military officers, the military training of the gold miners can then be carried out by army officers at the camps in accordance with regulations. Seasonal reports on local conditions, and also on whether or not things are tranquil in the area should also be made by the camp officials for our review and examination. [33a–36a]

(On May 31, 1842, the Emperor approved Meng Pao's proposed regulations for the training of Tibetan gold miners.)

Several documents relating to the meritorious activities of various officers and men and the awards to be given them have been omitted here. No information relating to what was happening on the frontier was sent to the Emperor between Document 8 (of April 25, 1842) and Document 9 (of December 8, 1842). See Chapter VII, and note the careful language used by Meng Pao in his memorials of December 8, 1842.

9. Tao Kuang, 22nd year, 11th month, 7th day [December 8, 1842]

*Memorial* from Meng Pao to the Emperor: reporting that the Shen-pa aborigines, seeking revenge, had renewed hostilities. Their leader was killed. They withdrew and gave bond to keep the peace permanently:

On the 22nd day of the 9th month of this year [October 25, 1842], a report was received from Kalon Surkhang and others stating:

> The widow of the Wazir, the late commander of the Shen-pas, managed to obtain the support of Pa-chan, a Shen-pa officer, and of the turbaned Muslims from Kashmir. From Tun-k'u,* a place beyond [to the west of] the Ladakh border, a force over 4,000 strong has come with the announced intention of taking revenge upon us. A defense post was then set up at Lung-wu,† a place on the Tibetan frontier. On the 27th day of the 7th month [September 2, 1842], Pa-chan, the Shen-pa officer, led the barbarians in a frontal assault upon the Lung-wu camp. After several consecutive days of fighting, Pa-chan,‡ the Shen-pa officer, was killed, and more than 120 other Shen-pas as well. They then withdrew twenty *li* to a place where there is a great lake, which separated them from our camp. They secretly built a large dam at the upper end of the valley in order to flood out our camp, which was situated in the lower end of the valley. Our forces were then forced to retreat to a higher, more strategic spot, where it was possible to resist them.
>
> On the second day of the 8th month [September 6], Tieh-wa [Dewan],§ another Shen-pa chief, led several waves of the enemy in an attack upon our position. In these battles, Jupon Tun-chieh-ch'a-wang and Chiapon Chi-pu-pa, together with one more Chiapon and two Tingpons, were lost. In this stout resistance, over 230 of the enemy were killed and two of their officers, and they were prevented from crossing the Tibetan boundary. As a result of their frequent failures,

* According to the Ladakhi chronicles, the Dogra relief force under Dewan Hari Chand followed the route to Leh via Khalatse [Purig district], entering Ladakh from the Kashmir valley, although it was at that time governed by a Muslim feudatory of the Sikh state, and not yet a part of the Dogra domain.

† "Klun-gyog-ma" in the Ladakhi chronicles, an area between Rudok and Pangong Lake, probably just within the Tibetan border.

‡ The only officer the Ladakhi chronicles list as killed in these encounters was "Kumidar Maca-Sin," a relatively minor officer.

§ Dewan Hari Chand.

they sent Re-tang,* a minor officer, and Ah-mieh-cho, an interpreter, to our camp to request a peace settlement. Careful account of the situation was taken, and when it was found that the Shen-pas were actually afraid of us, a truce was agreed upon. On the 13th day of the 8th month [September 17, 1842], the Dewan and the other officers from the aboriginal tribes of Gulab Singh and Ranjit Singh and Kashmir repented, and came with statements of submission and also signed an agreement calling for permanent peace, and pledging never to start trouble again. Subsequently, all the enemy forces were disbanded by their chiefs.

Last year the Shen-pa aborigines planned to occupy certain places in Tibet. The Wazir, the commander, formed an unlawful association with the people of Ladakh and the Balti aboriginal tribe, and initiated the disturbance. After the Wazir, the Shen-pa commander, was killed, these two tribes surrendered and offered submission. Over 40 Shen-pa officers and 1,500 men were killed, and 830 were captured during that affair. The possibility that the Shen-pas would seek revenge aroused apprehension, and it was necessary to take precautions against this contingency. The termination of the military campaign was therefore delayed, even though all our posts had been recaptured by the first month of this year [February–March, 1842]. The Kalons were ordered to remain in the area both to supervise the reconstruction work and to keep a careful watch at all times over the frontier defenses. They were strictly warned not to bring the campaign to a close or shirk their duties until they had a firm control over the situation and were confident of the security of the frontier. Now it is evident that the Shen-pas returned in the 7th month [August–September, 1842] to avenge themselves on us, in unlawful association with the turbaned Muslims of Kashmir. After more than 350 of the enemy were killed in successive battles, the Shen-pas withdrew out of fear of our strong force, and signed an agreement promising never again to cause disturbances. According to the customs of the barbarians and aborigines, once they are willing to take an oath in signing an agreement, they can be relied upon to abide by their word. As the aboriginal Shen-pa and Kashmir officers have signed an agreement vowing permanent peace, things will now be safe for us.

With regard to the Ladakhi Khan, who is still very young, General Pi-hsi was previously sent to pacify the country, and make suitable arrangements with his advisers. The Khan and all of his chiefs have already signed an agreement in which they vowed to guard the frontier and maintain permanent peace. The reports from our military posts there have not been solely relied upon. Our own deputies have also been secretly sent to the area to study and investigate the actual situation. The report of these deputies was submitted on the third day of the 11th month [December 4], and it verified what the Kalons had reported.

Now it is time for all aboriginal and native troops to be withdrawn. Gartok can be guarded by the gold miners in accordance with the estab-

* Wazir Ratanu.

lished regulations as recommended in a previous memorial. Whether or not all the generals who were formerly sent to guard the frontier should be summoned back, can be decided according to the existing conditions a year or two from now. The peace agreement signed by the tribal officers of the Shen-pa and others, guaranteeing that no more trouble will be caused, and the proposal as stated above for the withdrawal of our expeditionary force to their home stations, are respectfully submitted to the Emperor and instructions are awaited, which will be carried out.

10. Tao Kuang, 22nd year, 12th month, 15th day [January 15, 1843]

*The Emperor's reply* to the memorial of December 8, 1842, was received [at Lhasa] on the 24th day of the first month, 23rd year, Tao Kuang [February 22, 1843], conveyed by Court Letter from the Grand Council:

The memorial of December 8th was received and understood. The most important thing for the safeguarding of the frontier is to bring peace and order through demonstrating good intentions. But if the aborigines and barbarians should cause frequent disturbances because of their insubordinate attitude, of course they should be punished and brought under control. It is my fear that the Kalons posted there took advantage of their fortunate victory to win Imperial awards and to make use of their position as a pretext for further action, with the result that the aborigines and barbarians were frequently offended. Consequently, they were given ground for complaint and therefore contemplated revenge, allying themselves with other barbarians and thus giving rise to fresh complications. All these considerations should be taken as a warning. Now that the peace agreement has already been signed by the tribes, they should be pacified with great care in the hope that this would ensure permanent security. The Kalons should be very strongly advised to keep a strict guard hereafter and never again allow the aborigines to encroach on our territory, but they should also handle this situation with great caution and never cause any further unfortunate incidents. After these strict instructions have been made known to them, if they should dare to presume on anything in order to earn merit without caring for the possibly disastrous consequences, we will grant them no more favors. The rest of the memorial is approved as proposed. [55a–b]

11. Tao Kuang, 22nd year, 11th* month, 7th day [December 8, 1842]

*Memorial:* Meng Pao to the Emperor, on the death of Kalon [Ragasa]:

A dispatch has been received from the Regent, enclosing the following report from Kalon Surkhang:

* The Chinese text reads 12th month, but this is an obvious mistake, as both the date of the deputies' report upon which this memorial was based and the date of the Emperor's reply indicate.

The attack of the Shen-pa enemy, led by the widow of the Wazir, and Pa-chan, an enemy officer, who was seeking revenge, caused us to hurry to Lung-wu with General Pi-hsi and our troops. While Kalon Ragasa was stationed at Lung-pa-re, he learned that the rebel force was strong and aggressive. He feared that we would be defeated by the enemy, and he therefore announced his intention to stand or fall with the rest of us. He then decided to march to Lung-wu to reinforce our troops. He traveled with his staff and troops day and night without rest.

The difficult journey over two consecutive mountain passes exhausted the Kalon who, moreover, was greatly anxious over the situation at the front. Spitting out blood, he died instantly.* It is really a very pitiful thing. It is therefore requested that your Excellencies will kindly recommend to the throne that his son, La-mu-chieh-wang-tui-tu-erh-chi, succeed to his father's position as Kalon, or be made a General entitled to wear a peacock plume on the hat. In so doing, not only will his son be very grateful, but all the Tibetan officers will exert themselves in carrying out their duty, in case of any incidents in the future.

Kalon Ragasa achieved considerable success in last year's military campaign against the Shen-pa barbarians, defeating the invaders and recapturing the lost posts. It had been recommended that he be favored with the honors of a second rank official with button on the hat. Now the news has come that he overexerted himself in carrying out his duty when he was very weak, had undertaken a difficult trip, and had died suddenly spitting blood. Although he was not killed in action, the cause and effect was the same.

Now it has been proposed that his son succeed him. However, the office of Kalon involves both civil and military duties in Tibet, too high a position for the son. It is recommended that General Pi-hsi be promoted to fill the vacancy of Kalon and, through the Emperor's extraordinary favor, the General's post be assigned to the son of the deceased, who would also be favored with the honor of wearing a peacock plume on the hat, in order to show the Imperial sympathy.

Respectfully this memorial is presented to the throne and Imperial instructions are awaited, to act accordingly. [56a–57b]

12. Tao Kuang, 22nd year, 12th month, 15th day [January 15, 1843]

*The Emperor's reply* to the memorial of December 8, 1842, dispatched through the Grand Secretariat:

It is very sad to learn of the Kalon's death in military service as reported. General Pi-hsi shall be promoted to fill the vacant post as Kalon. We will also show favor to La-mu-chieh-wang-tui-tu-erh-chi, the son of the deceased

* According to the Ladakhi chronicles and British sources, Kalon Ragasa surrendered to the Dogra commander and later committed suicide while in captivity.

Kalon, who shall be appointed to the post vacated by General Pi-hsi, and shall be permitted to wear the peacock plume as an award, in order to show sympathy.

Let the Office in question be so informed. [57b–58a]

13. Tao Kuang, 22nd year, 11th month, 7th day [December 8, 1842]

*Memorial* from Meng Pao to the Emperor, requesting Imperial favor for those who have performed meritorious service:

In compliance with the Imperial edict dated the 19th day of the fifth month this year [June 27, 1842], instructing us to prepare a list of officers and soldiers who had performed meritorious service in the last campaign, our supplementary memorial replied that this would be done when the Kalons in the field had concluded the campaign and satisfactorily completed the work of reconstruction. This was consented to by Your Imperial Majesty in the edict received on the sixth day of the eighth month of the same year [September 10, 1842]. The officers and soldiers were in the field more than a year, serving valorously and patriotically during the campaign against the Shen-pa barbarians. When, in the seventh month of this year [August–September, 1842], they were again attacked by the vengeful Shen-pa aborigines, whose officers were then killed by the Kalons, the Shen-pa and Kashmiri tribes signed an agreement promising never again to cause trouble. Everything has been well managed and the reconstruction work has also been progressing satisfactorily. They were truly faithful and vigorous in service from beginning to end. Those have been selected who performed the most meritorious services and a list is attached, so that they may be rewarded and encouraged. For those Tibetan officers and soldiers who were killed in action, the Regent will be consulted about compensation or posthumous awards to be granted after thorough investigation. [59a–b]

(On January 15, 1843, the Emperor approved a list of awards "for meritorious service in the last campaign against the barbarians and aborigines.")

# BIBLIOGRAPHY

*Books*


BAINS, J. S. *India's International Disputes*. Bombay: Asia Publishing House, 1962. vii, 219 pp.

BAZAZ, PREM NATH. *The History of Struggle for Freedom in Kashmir*. New Delhi: Kashmir Publishing Company, 1954. 744 pp.

BELL, SIR CHARLES ALFRED. *Tibet Past and Present*. London: The Clarendon Press, 1924. xiv, 326 pp.

BURRARD, COL. SIDNEY GERALD, and HAYDEN, H. H. *A Sketch of the Geography and Geology of the Himalaya Mountains and Tibet* ("The Principal Mountain Ranges of Asia," Part II). 4 vols. in 1. Delhi: Government of India, 1933–34.

CHAKRAVARTI, P. C. *India-China Relations*. Calcutta: Firma K. Mukhopadhyay, 1961. 195 pp., map.

CUNNINGHAM, SIR ALEXANDER. *Ladak, Physical, Statistical, and Historical: With Notices of the Surrounding Countries*. London: W. H. Allen, 1854. xii, 485 pp., 31 pls.

DALAI LAMA XIV. *My Land and My People*. New York: McGraw-Hill, 1962. 271 pp.

DEASY, CAPT. HENRY HUGH PETER. *In Tibet and Chinese Turkestan: Being the Record of Three Years' Exploration*. London: T. Fisher Unwin, 1901. xvi, 420 pp.

DEMIÉVILLE, PAUL. *Le Concile de Lhasa* ("*Bibliothèque de l'Institut des Hautes Etudes Chinoises*," VII), Vol. I. Paris, 1952. 22 pls.

DESIDERI, IPPOLITO. *An Account of Tibet: The Travels of Ippolito Desideri of Pistoia, S.J., 1712–1727*. Edited by FILIPPO DE FILIPPI, with an introduction by C. WESSELS, S.J. Rev. ed. London: George Routledge and Sons, 1937. xviii, 477 pp., 17 pls., folded map.

DREW, FREDERIC. *The Jummoo and Kashmir Territories: A Geographical Account*. London: Edward Stanford, 1875. xiii, 568 pp., pls., maps.

DURAND, ALGERNON G. A. *The Making of a Frontier*. London: John Murray, 1900. 298 pp., 2 maps.

FIRISHTAH, MUHAMMAD KĀSIM. *Tarikh-i-Firishta* (*History of the Rise of the Mahomedan Power in India*). Translated from the Persian by JOHN

Briggs. Calcutta: R. Cambray, 1908. London: Kegan Paul, Trench, Trubner, 1910.

Fisher, Margaret W., and Bondurant, Joan V. *Indian Views of Sino-Indian Relations* ("Indian Press Digests Monograph Series," No. 1). Berkeley: Institute of International Studies, University of California, 1956. xxiv, 163 pp.

Francke, August Hermann. *A History of Western Tibet, One of the Unknown Empires.* London: S. W. Partridge, 1907. xiv, 191 pp., 23 pls., maps.

Fraser, David Stewart. *The Marches of Hindustan: The Record of a Journey in Thibet, Trans-Himalayan India, Chinese Turkestan, Russian Turkestan, and Persia.* Edinburgh, London: Blackwood & Sons, 1907. xvi, 521 pp., pls., maps.

Fraser, James Baillie. *Journal of a Tour Through Part of the Snowy Range of the Himāla Mountains and to the Sources of the Rivers Jumma and Ganges.* London: Rodwell and Martin, 1820. xx, 548 pp., map.

Gordon, Gen. Sir Thomas Edward. *A Varied Life; A Record of Military and Civil Service, of Sport and of Travels in India, Central Asia, and Persia, 1849–1902.* London: John Murray, 1906. xvi, 357 pp., maps, illus.

Gould, Sir Basil John. *The Jewel in the Lotus: Recollections of an Indian Political.* Foreword by Sir Ernest Barker. London: Chatto and Windus, 1957. xiv, 252 pp., maps, illus.

Hedin, Sven Anders. *Southern Tibet.* 4 vols. Stockholm: Lithographic Institute of the General Staff of the Swedish Army, 1916–22.

*Hudud al-'Alam (The Regions of the World).* [A Persian geography of 372 A.H. (982 A.D.) translated into Russian and annotated by V. Minorsky, with a preface by V. V. Barthold. English edition translated from the Russian. Oxford University, "E. J. W. Gibb Memorial Series," xi.] London: Luzac, 1937. xx, 524 pp., maps.

Hunter, Sir William Wilson. *Life of Brian Houghton Hodgson.* London: John Murray, 1896. ix, 390 pp.

Huth, Georg (tr.). *Geschichte des Buddhismus in der Mongolei.* From the Tibetan of Jigs-med nam-mk'a. Strasbourg: Trubner, 1892–96. 2 vols in 1. 456 pp.

*Imperial Gazetteer of India.* New edition. Oxford: Clarendon Press, 1908–9. 26 vols.

Kalhana. *The Rajatarangini, Containing the Supplements to the Work of Jonaraja, Srivara and Prajyabhatta, I–III* ("Bombay Sanskrit Series," No. 54). Bombay: Government Central Book Depot, 1896. 1,091 pp.

——. *Rājataranginī: A Chronicle of the Kings of Kaśmīr.* Translated with introduction, commentary, and appendices by M. A. Stein. 2 vols. Delhi: Motilal Banarsidas, 1961.

Kaul, Gwasha Lal. *Kashmir Through the Ages, 5000 B.C. to 1954 A.D.: A Historical Survey.* Srinagar, Kashmir: Chronicle Publishing House, 1954. 287 pp., illus.

KENNION, MAJOR ROGER LLOYD. *Sport and Life in the Further Himalaya.* Edinburgh, London: Blackwood & Sons, 1910. xii, 330 pp.

KHAN, MOHAMED JAMAL. *The Autobiography of H.R.H. Mohamed Jamal Khan, Mir of Hunza.* Unpublished manuscript in the library of the University of California, Berkeley.

LAMB, ALASTAIR. *Britain and Chinese Central Asia: The Road to Lhasa, 1767 to 1905.* London: Routledge and Kegan Paul, 1960. xi, 388 pp., maps.

LATTIMORE, OWEN. *Pivot of Asia: Sinkiang and the Inner Asian Frontiers of China and Russia.* Boston: Little, Brown, 1950. xii, 288 pp., maps.

LYDEKKER, RICHARD. *The Game Animals of India, Burma, Malaya and Tibet.* London: R. Ward, 1907. xiii, 408 pp.

MILLER, ROBERT J. *Monasteries and Culture Change in Inner Mongolia.* (*Asiatische Forschungen; Monographienreihe zur Geschichte, Kultur und Sprache der Völker Ost- und Zentralasiens,* Vol. II.) Wiesbaden: Otto Harrassowitz, 1959. xi, 152 pp., diagrams, biblio.

MOORCROFT, WILLIAM, and TREBECK, G. *Travels in the Himalayan Provinces, etc.* 2 vols. London: John Murray, 1841.

MUHAMMAD, MIRZA HAIDER DUGHLĀT. *Tarikh-i-Rashidi* (*A History of the Moghuls of Central Asia*). Translated from the Persian by E. DENISON ROSS, and edited with commentary and notes by N. ELIAS. London: Low, Marston, 1895. xxiii, 128, 535 pp., map.

PANIKKAR, K. M. *The Founding of the Kashmir State: A Biography of Maharajah Gulab Singh, 1792–1858.* London: Allen & Unwin, 1953. 172 pp.

PETECH, LUCIANO. *China and Tibet in the Early Eighteenth Century; History of the Establishment of Chinese Protectorate in Tibet.* (*T'oung Pao,* Monograph I.) Leiden: Brill, 1950. x, 286 pp., map.

RICHARDSON, HUGH EDWARD. *A Short History of Tibet.* New York: Dutton, 1962. 308 pp.

ROSE, LEO E. *The Role of Nepal and Tibet in Sino-Indian Relations.* Ph.D. dissertation, University of California, Berkeley, 1960.

SANGHVI, RAMESH. *India's Northern Frontier and China.* Bombay: Contemporary Publishers, 1962. 158 pp., maps.

SAPRU, A. N. *The Building of the Kashmir State.* Lahore: Punjab Record Office, 1931. vi, 90, ix pp.

SCHOMBERG, COL. REGINALD CHARLES FRANCIS. *Between the Oxus and the Indus.* London: M. Hopkinson, 1935. 270 pp., map, illus.

——. *Unknown Karakoram.* London: M. Hopkinson, 1936. ix, 244 pp., maps.

SINHA, DR. SATYANARAYAN. *The Chinese Aggression: A First Hand Account from Central-Asia, Tibet and the High Himalayas.* Foreword by GENERAL K. S. THIMAYYA. New Delhi: Rama Krishna & Sons, 1961. 125 pp.

SNELLGROVE, DAVID. *Buddhist Himalaya.* Oxford: Cassirer, 1957. xii, 324 pp.

TEICHMAN, SIR ERIC. *Travels of a Consular Official in Eastern Tibet.* Cambridge: Cambridge University Press, 1922. 248 pp.

TUCCI, GIUSEPPE. *Indo-Tibetica.* Rome: Reale Accademia d'Italia, 1937. maps, illus., genealogical tables.

——. *Nepal: The Discovery of the Malla.* Translated by Lovett Edwards. New York: Dutton, 1962. 96 pp.

——. *Preliminary Report on Two Scientific Expeditions in Nepal* ("Materials for the Study of Nepalese History and Culture," Vol. I; "*Serie Orientale Roma,*" Vol. X). Rome: Istituto Italiano per il Medio ed Estremo Oriente, 1956. maps, illus.

——. *Tibetan Painted Scrolls.* Translated by Virginia Vacca. 2 vols. Rome: Libreria dello Stato, 1949. illus., 256 pls.

VIGNE, GODFREY THOMAS. *Travels in Kashmir, Ladak, Iskardo and the Countries Adjoining the Mountain-Course of the Indus, and the Himalaya North of the Panjab.* 2 vols. London: H. Colburn, 1842.

WELLBY, MONTAGU SINCLAIR. *Through Unknown Tibet.* Philadelphia: J. B. Lippincott, 1898. xiv, 440 pp., maps.

WESSELS, CORNELIUS. *Early Jesuit Travellers in Central Asia, 1607–1721.* The Hague: M. Nijoff, 1924. xvi, 344 pp., map.

WHITING, ALLEN SUESS, AND SHENG, GENERAL SHIH-TS'AI. *Sinkiang: Pawn or Pivot?* East Lansing, Michigan: State University Press, 1958. xii, 314 pp.

WU, AITCHEN K., *China and the Soviet Union: A Study of Sino-Soviet Relations.* New York: John Day, 1950. xvi, 434 pp.

*Articles*

AHMAD, ZAHIRUDDIN. "The Ancient Frontier of Ladakh," *The World Today,* XVI (July, 1960), 313–18.

BAREAU, ANDRÉ. "Indian and Ancient Chinese Buddhism: Institutions Analogous to the Jisa," *Comparative Studies in Society and History,* III (1961), 443–51.

BOWER, CAPT. HAMILTON. "A Journey Across Tibet," *Geographical Journal,* I (May, 1893), 385–408.

CAREY, A. D. "A Journey Round Chinese Turkistan and Along the Northern Frontier of Tibet," *Proceedings of the Royal Geographical Society,* New Series, IX (December, 1887), 731–52; map opp. p. 790.

DAS, SARAT CHANDRA. "Tibet Under the Tartar Emperors of China in the 13th Century," *Journal of the Asiatic Society of Bengal,* LXXIII, Part 1 (1904, Extra number), 94–102.

DEASY, CAPT. HENRY HUGH PETER. "A Journey to Northern Tibet and Aksai Chin," *Geographical Journal,* XIII (February, 1899), 155–59.

——, "Journeys in Central Asia," *Geographical Journal,* XVI, Part 1 (August, 1900), 141–64; Part 2 (November, 1900), 501–27.

FISHER, MARGARET W., and BONDURANT, JOAN V. "The Impact of Communist China on Visitors from India," *Far Eastern Quarterly,* XV (February, 1956), 249–65.

FISHER, MARGARET W., and ROSE, LEO E. "Ladakh and the Sino-Indian Border Crisis," *Asian Survey*, II (October, 1962), 27–37.

FRANCKE, AUGUST HERMANN (tr.). "Ladvags rGyalrabs; the Chronicles of Ladakh, According to Schlagintweits's MS," *Journal and Proceedings of the Asiatic Society of Bengal*, Series 2, VI (1910), 393–423.

——, "The Rock Inscription at Mulbhe," *Indian Antiquary*, XXXV (1906), 72.

GOETZ, HERMANN, "The Antiquities of Chamba State: An Art-Historical Outline," *Journal of the Uttar Pradesh Historical Society*, New Series, I (1953), 76–99.

HAYWARD, G. W. "Journey from Leh to Yarkand and Kashgar, and Exploration of the Sources of the Yarkand River," *Journal of the Royal Geographical Society*, XL (1870), 33–166.

KINGDON-WARD, FRANCIS. "Tibet as a Grazing Land," *Geographical Journal*, CX (1948), 60–75.

KUMAR, GIRJA, and TEWARI, B. C. "India and World Affairs: An Annual Bibliography, 1959," *International Studies*, II (January, 1961), 317–49.

LAMB, ALASTAIR, "Some Notes on Russian Intrigue in Tibet," *Journal of the Royal Central Asian Society*, XLVI, Part I (January, 1949), 46–65.

MA-TWAN-LIN. "Thien-chu–India," extract from Book 338, Folio 14, translated from the French of STANISLAS JULIEN (*Journal Asiatique*, Series 4, X [1847], 81–121) by JAMES BURGESS, and published with annotations, *Indian Antiquary*, IX (1880), 14–24.

MEINERTZHAGEN, COL. R. "Ladakh, With Special Reference to its Natural History," *Geographical Journal*, LXX (1927), 129–56 [discussion, pp. 156–63], maps.

MILLER, ROBERT J., "Buddhist Monastic Economy: The Jisa Mechanism," *Comparative Studies in Society and History*, III (1961), 427–38.

MOORCROFT, WILLIAM, "Notice on Khoten," *Journal of the Royal Geographical Society*, I (1832), 233–47.

MUKERJEE, U. N. "Chronology of the Karkota Nāga Dynasty of Kashmir, the Ancient Land of the Nāgas," *Uttara Bharati, Journal of Research of the Universities of Uttar Pradesh*, IV, No. 2 (March, 1958), 49–53.

PARKER, EDWARD HARPER. "How the Tibetans Grew," *Asiatic Quarterly Review*, Series 3, XVIII (1904), 238–56.

PETECH, LUCIANO. "A Study on the Chronicles of Ladakh, Indian Tibet," *Indian Historical Quarterly*, XV, No. 4, Supplement (December, 1939), 39–189.

——. "Notes on Ladakhi History," *Indian Historical Quarterly*, XXIV, No. 3 (September, 1948), 213–35.

——. "The Tibetan-Ladakhi-Mogul War of 1681–83," *Indian Historical Quarterly*. XXIII, No. 3 (September, 1947), 169–99.

RAHUL, R. "The Structure of the Government of Tibet: 1644–1911," *International Studies*, III (January, 1962), 263–98.

——. "Three-Point Agreement Between the Chinese and Tibetans, 12 August 1912," *International Studies*, II (April, 1961), 420–24.

RAO, DR. K. KRISHNA. "Title to Territory," *Indian Journal of International Law*, II, (April, 1962), 200–210.

RAWLINSON, SIR HENRY. "Remarks Upon the Paper by Capt. Sherard Osborn, 'Notes on Chinese Tartary,'" *Proceedings of the Royal Geographical Society*, XI (1867), 162–66.

RICHARDSON, HUGH EDWARD. "The Myth of 'Suzerainty,'" *United Asia*, XII (1960), 384.

SAHNI, PANDIT DAYA RAM. "References to the Bhottas or Bhauttas in the Rajatarangini of Kashmir" (Notes from Tibetan sources by A. H. FRANCKE), *Indian Antiquary*, XXXVII, (July, 1908), 181–92.

STRACHEY, CAPT. HENRY, "On the Physical Geography of Western Tibet," *Journal of the Royal Geographical Society*, XXIII (1853), 1–69.

TROTTER, CAPT. SIR HENRY, "Account of the Pundit's Journey in Great Tibet from Leh in Ladakh to Lhasa and of His Return to India Via Assam," *Journal of the Royal Geographical Society*, XLVII (1877), 86–136.

WELLBY, MONTAGU SINCLAIR, "Through Tibet to China," *Geographical Journal*, XII (1898), 262–80.

*Documents*

AITCHISON, C. U. *A Collection of Treaties, Engagements and Sanads Relating to India and Neighbouring Countries*. 5th ed. 14 vols. Calcutta: Government of India, Central Publication Branch, 1929–33.

CHINA, PEOPLE'S REPUBLIC. *The Sino-Indian Boundary Question*. Peking: Foreign Languages Press, 1962. Second (enlarged) Ed. Maps. (Both the first and second editions were issued in November, 1962.)

GREAT BRITAIN, FOREIGN OFFICE. *Papers Relating to Tibet and Further Papers* (Command Papers Nos. 1920, 2054, 2370). London: H.M. Stationery Office, 1904–5.

——, FOREIGN OFFICE, HISTORICAL SECTION. *Tibet* ("Peace Handbooks," Vol. XII [*China, Japan, Siam*], No. 70). London: H.M. Stationery Office, 1920. 74 pp.

——, HOUSE OF COMMONS. *Further Papers Relating to Tibet, 7 September 1904–17 May 1910*. ("Parliamentary Publications, 1910," Vol. LXVIII; "Accounts and Papers," Vol. X; Command Paper No. 5240.) London: H.M. Stationery Office, 1910, 229 pp.

INDIA. *Annual Report of the Archaeological Survey of India, 1905–06*. Calcutta: Superintendent of Government Printing.

——, LOK SABHA SECRETARIAT. *Lok Sabha Debates* (15th Session), Series 2, LIX, No. 7. New Delhi, 1961.

——, MINISTRY OF EXTERNAL AFFAIRS. *Atlas of the Northern Frontier of India*. New Delhi: 1959. 39 pls.

——, MINISTRY OF EXTERNAL AFFAIRS. *Notes, Memoranda and Letters*

*Exchanged and Agreements Signed Between the Governments of India and China* (White Paper No. I, September 8, 1959). *Notes, Memoranda and Letters Exchanged Between the Government of India and China* (White Papers No. II, November 4, 1959; No. III, February 29, 1960; No. IV, November 9, 1960; No. V, November 27, 1961; No. VI, July 28, 1962; No. VII, November 1, 1962). New Delhi.

——, MINISTRY OF EXTERNAL AFFAIRS. *Report of the Officials of the Government of India and the People's Republic of China on the Boundary Question*. New Delhi: February, 1961.

INDIA OFFICE LIBRARY (London). *Foreign Department, Secret Frontier; Enclosures to Secret Letters from India; Foreign Department, Secret; Foreign Department, Political.*

NATIONAL ARCHIVES OF INDIA (New Delhi). *Political Consultations; Political Proceedings; Secret Consultations.*

NEHRU, JAWAHARLAL. *India's Foreign Policy, Selected Speeches, September, 1946–April, 1961*. Delhi: [Government of India] Ministry of Information and Broadcasting, Publications Division, 1961. xviii, 612 pp.

[——]. *Prime Minister on Sino-Indian Relations:* Vol. I, *In Parliament;* Vol. II, *Press Conferences*. New Delhi: [Government of India] Ministry of External Affairs, External Publicity Division, 1961–62.

"A PEKINESE." *The Boundary Question Between China and Tibet:* A *Valuable Record of the Tripartite Conference Between China, Britain and Tibet Held in India, 1913–1914*. Peking, 1940. 150 pp.

UNITED STATES, CENTRAL INTELLIGENCE AGENCY. *China: Provisional Atlas of Communist Administrative Units*. Washington, D. C.: [U.S.] Department of Commerce, Office of Technical Services, 1959. 14 pp., 29 pls.

*Periodicals and Newspapers*

*Asian Recorder*, New Delhi.
*Dawn*, Karachi.
*The Hindu*, Madras.
*The Hindu Weekly Review*, Madras.
*Hindustan Times*, New Delhi.
*India News* (Indian Embassy, United States), Washington, D. C.
*National Herald*, Lucknow.
*New York Times*, New York, Los Angeles.
*Peking Review*, Peking.
*The Statesman*, New Delhi, Calcutta.
*The Statesman Overseas Weekly*, Calcutta.
*Survey of China Mainland Press* (U.S. Consulate), Hong Kong.

*Chinese-Language Sources*

*Chia-Ch'ing Chung-Hsiu Ta-Ch'ing i Tung-Chih* (*Official Annals of the Empire of the Great Chi'ng Dynasty, Revised During the Reign of Chia*

*Ch'ing*). Compiled by MOCHANG-A and others. Originally compiled in 1743, enlarged in 1784, revised, completed, and published in 1820. 560 chüan (vols.).

*Ch'ing-Chi Ch'ou-Tsang Tsou-Tu* (*Memorial and Correspondence Concerning the Arrangement of Tibetan Affairs During the Latter Part of the Ch'ing Period*). Compiled by WOO FENG-PEI. Peiping: National Academy, 1938.

*Chin-Ting Huang-Yu Hsi-Yu T'u-Chih* (*Geographical Records of the Western Regions of China*). Compiled by order of the Emperor Ch'ien-lung in 48 chüan (vols.) by FU HENG and others, completed and presented in the 27th year of Ch'ien-lung, 11th month, 29th day [1762]. Revised and enlarged by YIN LIEN and others, presented in the 47th year, 5th month, 10th day [1782]. 1782 ed.

*Hsin-Chiang T'u-Chih* (*Geographical Records of Sinkiang*). Begun by HSUAN T'UNG in 1909; revised, enlarged, and completed in 1911 by YUAN TA-HUA, Governor of Sinkiang, and others. Tientsin.

*Hsi-Tsang Tsou-Shu* (*Tibetan Memorials and Reports*). 10 chüan (6 vols.). Compiled by MENG PAO. Privately published, [1851?]. See Appendix.

*Hsi-Yu Shui-Tao Chi* (*Annotations About the Watercourses of the Western Regions*). Annotated by HSU SUNG, published in 1824. Section entitled "Hsi-Tsang Shih" ("Description of Tibet") referred to here, translated by KARL HIMLY as *Ein Chinesisches Werk über das Westliche Inner-Asien*. Berlin: [*ca.* 1890]. 77 pp.

*Ta Ch'ing i T'ung Chih* (*Gazetteer of the Whole Ch'ing Realm*). Compiled by CHIANG TING-HSI and others. Revised ed., 1849.

*Wei-Tsang T'ung Chih* (*Topography of Wei and Tsang Provinces*). Compiled toward the end of the Ch'ien-lung period (1795). Author unknown, but possibly HO-LIN, Assistant Resident Envoy at Lhasa, 1792–95. Published in 1895. 2nd ed. Shanghai: The Commercial Press, 1936.

*Ladakhi Sources*

FRANCKE, AUGUST HERMANN. "Antiquities of Indian Tibet," *Archaeological Survey of India*, New Imperial Series, XXXVIII, Part I; L, Part II (1914–1926).

# GEOGRAPHICAL SURVEY

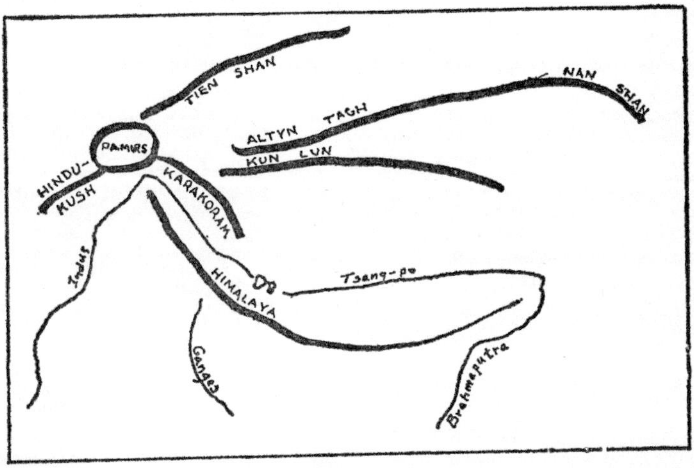


Aghil Mountains—*Aghil* refers to shepherds' camps. The Aghil chain lies close to and north of the Great Karakoram, in a roughly parallel line.

Aksai Chin—A "white stone" alkaline desert plateau, about 17,000 ft. above sea level, the northern extension of the Lingzi Tang. There is evidence it was once the bed of an extensive lake. Its present importance lies in its position in a gap between the glaciers of the Great Karakoram and the high peaks of the Kunlun range.

Ari (Tibetan: Mnga-ris)—Appears in English as Ari, Nari, and Ngari, and in official Chinese documents written in English as Ari or Ali. As used here, it is synonymous with West Tibet and refers to the area between the Mayum Pass on the east and the Ladakh border in the west, bounded on the north by the Chang Tang.

Badakshan—A frontier area in Afghanistan between the upper Amu Daria (Oxus) and the Hindu Kush. Ancient Bactria.

Baltistan—"Land of the Baltis," a rugged mountainous area in north-central Kashmir, on both sides of the cease-fire line. Skardu is the principal settlement.

Bara Lacha Pass—Elevation, about 16,200 ft. One of the principal passes in the Punjab Himalaya, separating the "Alpine" region of dense forest below the perpetual snow from the barren rocky region.

BASGO—One of the larger villages of Ladakh, some 20 miles below Leh, on the Indus.

BASHAHR—A former kingdom, later one of the Punjab hill states, now the part of Himachal Pradesh that shares a common border with Tibet.

BAZAR DARA—Situated in the Raskam (upper Yarkand) valley. A route ascending the Yarkand leads in a fairly direct line east through Bazar Dara to Shahidulla and Sugat Karaul. From Bazar Dara, as from several other points along the Raskam, routes lead north over transverse ridges to the Sinkiang plains. The most direct of them goes across the Yangi Pass to Karghalik and leaves the Raskam some distance upstream from Bazar Dara.

"BOLORIAN TIBET"—"Bolorian" may well mean "crystalline," i.e., "glacial," Tibet. The Pamirs are sometimes referred to in old accounts as the *Bolor* Mountains. *Belor Dagh* also occurs in reference to the Muztagh range and may be the Persian equivalent of the Turki *muztagh* (and Tibetan *Kang-ri*), "ice mountain."

BOZAI-GUMBAZ—Situated in the Wakhan valley in the Pamirs.

CHABRANG—A modern village close to the ruins of Tsaparang.

CHANG PASS (CHANG LA)—Important to the defense of Leh. Outward bound travelers have a choice of routes after crossing it: the Shyok valley route to the Karakoram Pass; the Chang Chenmo valley route to Pamzal, and thence to either the Lingzi Tang or the Lanak Pass; the Pangong Lake basin; or southeast to Chushul, whence the route branches to either Rudok by way of Spanggur Lake or Gartok by way of Demchok.

CHANG-AN—An important city in Shensi province. Among the other names by which it has been known are Hsien-yang, Siking, and Sian.

CHANG CHENMO—The "great northern" valley of Ladakh extending east from the junction of the Chang Chenmo and Shyok rivers to Lanak Pass.

CHANGCHILIMAN TAPAN—*Tapan* is the Chinese rendering of the Turki *dawan*, meaning "pass." It is at least possible that this pass is the Kilian Dawan, leading north from Shahidulla to the plains of Turkistan. The likelihood is the greater in that *chang* means north.

CHANG LANG PASS—Elevation, about 18,900 ft. A route crossing it connects the upper Qara Qash valley and the Lingzi Tang with the Chang Chenmo valley.

CHANG TANG—"Northern plains," the vast northern region of Tibet, with an average elevation of about 17,000 ft. It was formerly roamed only by wild herds and nomads, but recent reports indicate the Chinese are endeavoring to bring the region under control.

CHARDING PASS—Shown on the maps as 20–30 miles south and slightly west of Demchok.

CHENAB RIVER—The middle one of the "five rivers" of the Punjab.

CHIBRA—A camping place where two valleys cross, at the foot of the Sugat Pass on the south side.

CH'IEN TSANG—Central Tibet. *See* note, p. 157.

CHIP CHAP VALLEY—The Chip Chap River is a tributary of the Shyok in its upper reaches. The Chip Chap valley lies between the Depsang basin and the Karakoram Pass.

CHO-HSU—In Tibetan: *Dro-shod* or *Gro-shad*, anglicized as Dokthal. The district along the Tsang-po River just east of the Mayum Pass.

CHU—The Tibetan word for "stream."

CHUNG TSANG—*See* note, p. 157.

DARA—A Turki word meaning "valley."

DARIA (DARYA)—A Turki word meaning "river."

DAWAN (DABAN, TAPAN)—The Turki word for "pass."

DEPSANG—A Tibetan term meaning "an open elevated plain."
DEPSANG BASIN—A cup-shaped plateau in the upper Shyok valley, separated from the Karakoram Pass by the Chip Chap valley.
DRAS—A village in a basin of the same name, the first important stop after crossing the Zoji Pass en route to Leh. It is known for relatively heavy precipitation.
DYAP TSO—*Tso* is Tibetan for "lake." The Dyap Tso is a salt lake in a basin that drains the area east and south of the Lanak Pass.
DZONG—A Tibetan word designating the seat of an official.
GARTOK—Literally, "High Fort" in Tibetan. It was also referred to as Garo in early British records. There was some confusion about this administrative center of West Tibet for a time, until it was realized that there were two "Gars": *Gar Dzong*, or *Gar Gunsa*, the winter site, is about 40 miles down the Indus from *Gar Tok*, or *Gar Yarsa*, the summer site.
GILGIT—Strategically located on a tributary to the Indus, in the general area where that river turns Nanga Parbat. It commands the passes in several directions and was considered by the British to be vital to the defense of the lower Indus valley.
GORKHA—A former hill kingdom located in a valley west of Kathmandu, whose kings began the conquest of Nepal in the middle of the eighteenth century. The present King of Nepal belongs to this dynasty.
GUGE—An ancient kingdom the center of which was in the mountainous region of the upper Sutlej, in southwestern Tibet. Guge was famous for its capital, Tsaparang, and its royal temple and monastery at Toling. Its boundaries and political fortunes varied through the centuries, but its downfall came in the seventeenth century.
GYA—Situated on the Gya River, a tributary of the Indus. At the head of the Gya valley is the Taglung Pass, which gives access to the Rupshu plateau.
GYAMDA (GIAMDA)—About 60 miles east of Lhasa.
GYANTSE (GYANGTSE)—An important trading mart in Tibet, at the junction of several caravan routes. The first important stop in Tibet on the route from India via the Chumbi Pass.
HAJI LANGAR—The first Chinese road through the Aksai Chin runs through Haji Langar, which was also a stop on the easterly (Chang Chenmo) caravan route from Pamzal to Shahidulla.
HANLE—On the Hanle River, a tributary of the Indus. One of the principal stops on the route from Tsaparang to Leh.
HAZARA—A tribal area in the North-West Frontier Province, in northwestern Pakistan.
HINDU KUSH—One of the great Asian ranges, forming a watershed between the Kabul River on the south and the Amu Daria (Oxus) on the north.
HOTIEN—Chinese name for Khotan.
HUNZA—An isolated valley in Pakistan-held Kashmir, forming a mountain lair from which the inhabitants, known as Kanjuts (or Hunzakuts), once ambushed caravans plying the Pamir routes from Yarkand. The raiding expeditions, which utilized the Shimshal Pass and the Shaksgam valley, sometimes endangered caravans using the Karakoram Pass routes.
ILCHI—Turki name for Khotan.
INDUS RIVER—One of the three great rivers of the Indian sub-continent, some 1,800 miles long. It rises on the north slopes of the Kailash range in West Tibet and flows northwest for some 680 miles, after which it turns and flows southwest through Pakistan to the Arabian Sea. Most of the population of Ladakh inhabits one or another of three principal valleys—the Indus, the Nubra, or the Shyok—all part of the Indus system.

INNER TIBET—Refers only to the Sino-Tibetan border as proposed at the Simla Conference.

JAMMU—A former province occupying the upper Chenab valley in the southern part of the state known informally as Kashmir—formally Jammu and Kashmir.

JARA PASS—Crosses the Kailash range a little north and east of Demchok.

JILGA—Turki word for "deep valley" or "gorge."

JUMLA—A former kingdom, now a district in northwestern Nepal, from which several trade routes converge on Taklakot, just across the border in Nepal.

KAFIRISTAN—A mountainous district in the Afghan borderlands south of the Hindu Kush, inhabited by a small remnant of Kafirs (non-Muslims) of ancient Iranian origin.

KAILASH (KAILAS), MOUNT—A peak, covered with perpetual snow, in the center of the Kailash range, sacred to Hindus as the site of Shiva's paradise. The sacred lakes, Manasarowar and Rakas, lie close by. It is also known as *Kangri* in Tibetan.

KAILASH RANGE—A subsidiary parallel range just north of the main Himalaya.

KANGRI—A general Tibetan term meaning "ice mountain" or "snow peak," often applied specifically to Mount Kailash.

KARA—*See* Qara.

KARAKORAM PASS—Elevation, 18,290 ft. Gives its name to the principal caravan route between Leh and the plains of Sinkiang. It links the upper Indus system with the upper Yarkand system. The most used route north then crosses a spur of the western Kunlun range over the Sugat Pass and proceeds down the Qara Qash valley to the oasis towns of the Sinkiang plains.

KARAKORAM RANGE—One of the great ranges that appear to radiate from the central knot of the Pamirs. The name means "black gravel" and was applied by Turki traders to the Karakoram Pass only. The extension of the term by Europeans to the entire range, containing massive glaciers, a peak (K 2) second only to Everest, as well as many other mountain giants, was singularly inappropriate. Mason proposes that since Karakoram is too firmly established to be abandoned now, the term Karakoram Himalaya might be applied.

KARDUNG (KARDAM)—*See* Map of Dogra War.

KARGIL—A small village headquarters of Purig district, on the trade route from Kashmir valley to Leh. From it, branch routes lead northwest to Skardu and Gilgit.

KARPO—A Tibetan adjective meaning "white."

KARGHALIK (CHINESE: YEH-CH'ENG)—Between Khotan and Yarkand on the old southern caravan route—now a motor highway—from China through Sinkiang. The starting point for caravan routes to Leh, and also for the Yeh-ch'eng–Tibet highway built by the Chinese in 1956–57 that crossed a corner of the Aksai Chin.

KASHGARIA—A name referring to the southern section of Chinese Turkestan, separated from Dzungaria, the northern section, by the T'ien Shan range.

KASHGAR (CHINESE: SU-FU)—The westernmost of the chief towns of Sinkiang. Situated where highways converge near the gap in the mountains that separate Chinese from Russian Turkestan, it has always been of great commercial, political, and strategic importance.

KERIA (CHINESE: YUTIEN)—An oasis town in the Sinkiang plains, east of Khotan on the Keria River. A branch route ascends the Keria gorge to Polu (Polur), from which a route winds across the Kunlun range to the Tibetan Chang Tang and eventually to Leh by way of the Lanak Pass.

KERONG (KYIRONG)—District headquarters on the Tibetan side of the frontier with Nepal, on a major trade route leading north from Kathmandu by way of Nayakot.

KHALATSE (KALATSE)—A village on the Indus, in Purig district of Kashmir, famous for its iron bridge.

KHARBU (KARBU)—A settlement on the Srinagar-Leh route, in the hilly country between Kargil and the Indus valley.

KHOTAN (CHINESE: HOTIEN)—An important town on the southern branch of the China-Sinkiang caravan route, now a motor highway. Caravans from Leh to Khotan usually crossed both the Karakoram and Sugat passes and then followed the Qara Qash valley route.

KIZIL—*See* Qizil.

KOKO NOR (CHINESE: TSINGHAI OR CH'INGHAI)—"Blue Lake." Near Sining and not far from the famous Kumbum Monastery.

KHURNAK FORT—A ruined fort on the north side of Pangong Lake, close to the route that crosses between the two parts of the lake.

KISHTWAR—A mountain district situated in the Chenab valley in the Punjab Himalaya.

KONE PASS—The name means simply the "old" pass, and the maps show many passes with this designation. The pass in question here is on the Ladakh-Tibet frontier south of the Lanak Pass. The route into Tibet across it leads southeast.

KONGA PASS—Near the hot-spring area of the Chang Chenmo valley, midway between the Lanak Pass and the junction of the Chang Chenmo and Shyok rivers.

KULU—An ancient Rajput principality in the mountainous upper reaches of the Beas River. The chief town is Sultanpur.

KUMAUN (KUMAON)—The Kumaun Himalaya lies in India, just west of Nepal. The principal peak is Nanda Devi, elevation, 25,645 ft.

KUNAWAR (KANAWAR), UPPER—Situated in the Kumaun Himalaya.

KUNGRIBINGRI PASS—Elevation, 18,300 ft. On the route from Milam, in the Kumaun Himalaya, to the sacred lakes area in West Tibet.

KUNLUN (KUEN LUN) RANGE—Extends from the Pamirs and Karakoram range in the west into Central China, where it is known as the Nan Shan. For much of its length—together with its branch, the Altyn Tagh—it forms a barrier between the northern plains (Chang Tang) of Tibet and the desert area of Sinkiang. Beginning with the Aksai Chin, a number of significant gaps occur in the western Kunlun chain.

KUTI (NILAM OR NYA-LAM)—A trading center on the Tibetan side of the frontier with Nepal, situated on the Bhot Kosi ("Tibet river") on a trade route running northeast from Kathmandu.

LA—The Tibetan word for "pass."

LAHUL (LAHOUL)—A district in the Punjab Himalaya.

LANAK PASS—Elevation, 18,000 ft. On the Ladakh-Tibet frontier at the head of the Chang Chenmo valley.

LEH—Capital of Ladakh, a few miles from the banks of the Indus, at the junction of major east-west and north-south caravan routes. Elevation, 11,545 ft.

LEIGHTAN (LIGHTEN) LAKE—A large lake in the northwestern Chang Tang region of Tibet.

LINGZI TANG—A desert plain, in effect a southwestern extension of the Aksai Chin. A caravan route used seasonally between Leh and the Sinkiang plains passed through the Chang Chenmo valley and the western part of the Lingzi Tang.

LIPU LEKH PASS—One of the passes into Taklakot from Jumla, in northwestern Nepal. Elevation, 16,750 ft.

LONGJU—South of Migyitun in the border area of the Northeast Frontier Agency.

LUNGAR—A Turki word for a rest house.

MAN (MANG)—A village on the west side of Pangong Lake.

MANA PASS—Elevation, 18,400 ft. One of the principal border passes in the Kumaun Himalaya. It crosses the Zanskar crest on the route from Badrinath to Tsaparang (modern Chabrang) and the famous Toling Monastery.

MANALI—An outpost in the Punjab Himalaya from which a mule track traverses the Bara Lacha Pass and eventually reaches Leh.

MANASAROWAR, LAKE (TSO MA-PHAM)—One of the two sacred lakes in West Tibet, in the vicinity of Mount Kailash.

MANDI—One of the former Punjab hill states, now incorporated in Himachal Pradesh.

MA-TSANG RIVER—A Tsangpo tributary, the southern feeders of which were used by the Tibetans in the war against the Dogras during the winter of 1841–42 to circumvent the Mayum Pass, which was blocked by snow.

MAYUM PASS (MARYUM PASS, MARIAM-LA)—The dividing line between Tsang and West Tibet, elevation, 16,900 ft.

MINSAR (MISSAR) VILLAGE—A Ladakhi enclave in the sacred lakes area of West Tibet. The Dogras stored supplies here in the war of 1841–42.

MUZTAGH MOUNTAINS—*Muz* means "ice" in Turki, and *Muztagh* can refer to any mountain or mountain cluster whose crest is covered with ice or perpetual snow. The Muztagh referred to here (p. 68) is in a western spur of the Kunlun range, which forms the northern wall of the Raskam valley.

MUZTAGH PASS—Elevation, 19,030 ft, crossing the Karakoram range west of K 2.

NAGAR—A mountain valley in Pakistan-held Kashmir, near Hunza. The men of Nagar were sometimes the companions and sometimes the victims of Hunza raiders.

NISCHU—Elevation, 18,630 ft. A halting place on the Chang Chenmo valley route to the Linzi Tang.

NITI PASS—Elevation, 16,628 ft. At the head of the Alaknanda valley (in the Ganges system) leading across the Zanskar crest from the Kumaun Himalaya into Tibet.

NUBRA—The Nubra valley, one of three (with the Indus and lower Shyok) in which the population of Ladakh is largely concentrated, lies on the western route from Leh to the Karakoram Pass. The valley itself, with an elevation somewhat less than that of Leh, offers easy passage, but the pass from Leh into it (the Kardung Pass) and from it into the Karakoram Pass region (the Saser Pass) are both steep and impassible for several months in the year.

NYA-LAM—*See* Kuti.

NYINGPA—Tibetan word meaning "old." Following a place name, it can mean "old route to."

OUTER TIBET—Refers only to the Sino-Tibetan border as proposed at the Simla Conference.

PAMIR—A wide valley, above the timber line.

PAMIRS, THE—A central mountain knot, characterized by many wide valleys above the timber line and many peaks rising above 20,000 ft., the true "roof of the world" from which extend in various directions several of the great ranges. See sketch map for a simplified diagram of the basic interrelations of the major ranges with which this study is concerned—the Hindu Kush, Karakoram, Himalaya, Kunlun, Altyn Tagh, and Tien Shan ranges, and the Pamirs.

PAMZAL—A halting place (at about 15,400 ft.) in the Chang Chenmo valley, from which there are two routes to Shahidulla, both of which avoid the Karakoram Pass.

PANGONG LAKE—A spectacular lake at nearly 14,000 ft., in the Ladakh-Tibet borderland. The area of the lake has diminished below its former outlet, with the result that its waters, once fresh, are now salt.

PARE (PARA) RIVER—Rises in glaciers situated in the ridge between southeastern Ladakh and Spiti.

PHOBRANG (POBRANG)—A small settlement in Ladakh near the western end of Pangong Lake, between Tanktse and the Masimik Pass, which leads into the Chang Chenmo valley.

PITAK—Four miles below Leh on the Indus valley trade route.

POLU (POLUR)—A village at the head of the Keria gorge, from which a route winds south over the Kunlun Mountains and into the Tibetan Chang Tang. Deasy found that it was a gold-mining center.

PULO (POLU)—Literally, a "shelter hut," but sometimes used for selected camping places whether or not a hut exists.

PURANG—An ancient kingdom between the Mayum Pass and the Kailash range, now a district in West Tibet. Taklakot, on the Karnali River, is its most important center.

PURIG DISTRICT—An ancient kingdom, now a district of Kashmir, between Baltistan and Ladakh. District headquarters are at Kargil.

QARA (KARA)—The Turki word for "black," found in many place names in the Karakoram area.

QARA CHUKAR RIVER—In the Yarkand system, flowing east to a confluence with the Oprang (lower Shaksgam) River.

QARA QASH (KARAKASH) RIVER—Drains the northern slopes of the Karakoram area east of the Karakoram Pass. A route descending its valley leads to Khotan.

QIZIL (KIZIL)—The Turki word for "red."

QIZIL JILGA—"Red valley." The maps show more than one Qizil Jilga. The one referred to here is a stage on the route north to Shahidulla by the Lingzi Tang route, somewhat erratically named for two large red boulders beside the river.

RAKAS, LAKE (RAKAS TAL, LAGANG)—One of the two sacred lakes in the vicinity of holy Mount Kailash in West Tibet.

RASKAM RIVER (RASKAM DARIA)—The upper Yarkand River. The Raskam valley was part of an autumn caravan route between Yarkand and Leh, which veered due south at Karghalik, ascended the Tiznaf valley, and reached the Raskam by way of the Yangi Pass. The Chinese road of 1956–57, according to the map supplied by Peking in 1960, also uses the Raskam valley, although using a route west of the Tiznaf in the stretch between Karghalik (Yeh-ch'eng) and the Raskam valley. The 1956–57 road diverges considerably from all known caravan routes in passing through the Ladakh-Tibet borderland.

RUDOK—A frontier district in West Tibet with headquarters of the same name.

RUPSHU—A large upland plateau south of Leh, between the Himalaya and the upper valley of the Indus. Reached from Leh by ascending the Gya valley.

SACRED LAKES—Manasarowar and Rakas lakes, near Mount Kailash, in West Tibet.

SARIGH JILGANANG LAKE (SARIQ JILGANANY KOL)—A large turquoise lake in the Lingzi Tang, near the Ladakh-Tibet border. Reports vary as to whether it is a salt lake or brackish but drinkable.

SARPA—Tibetan word meaning "new." Following a place name, it can mean "new route to."

SHAHIDULLA—On the Qara Qash River, one stop north on the main caravan route after the Chinese border post at Sugat Karaul. It can also be reached from Leh via the Chang Chenmo valley and Lingzi Tang, without crossing the Karakoram and Sugat passes. From Shahidulla, there is also a route west to the Raskam valley and points beyond.

SHAKSGAM VALLEY—On the northern slope of the Karakoram range. It runs roughly parallel to the Raskam valley farther north but is separated from it for a considerable distance by the Aghil Mountains.

SHIGATSE—Tibet's second city, the capital of Tsang province, on the Tsangpo near Tashilhunpo, the seat of the Panchen Lama.

SHIPKI PASS—A major pass from the Punjab Himalaya into Tibet.

SHYOK (SHAYOK) RIVER—The most important tributary of the Indus, which it joins above Skardu. It takes its source in the great glaciers of the Karakoram range. It takes a great bend northeast of Leh, flowing west for a time parallel with the Indus but separated from it by the Ladakh Range. The upper Shyok is known as the Chip Chap.

SIKKIM—An Indian protectorate between Nepal and Bhutan. It owes its importance to the fact that one of the best routes crossing the Himalaya runs through it, from Kalimpong to the Chumbi valley in Tibet, by way of the Jelap Pass.

SILUNG BARMA RIVER—Flows south from the Lingzi Tang region to the Chang Chenmo River.

SKARDU—The principal settlement in Baltistan, on the Indus above the great gorge, and not far below the confluence of the Shyok and Indus. Elevation, about 7,300 ft.

SPANGGUR (PONGUR) LAKE—South of the Pangong Lake but in the same general area of the Ladakh-Tibet borderland.

SRINAGAR—The capital of Kashmir, a picturesque city on the Jhelum River in the "Vale of Kashmir," at an altitude of 5,250 ft.

SUGAT KARAUL—The Chinese frontier post and fort at the foot of the Sugat Pass on the north side. On the Qara Qash River.

SUGAT (SUGET) PASS—The "willow" pass, elevation, 17,610 ft. A major pass on a principal trade route between Leh and the oasis towns of the Sinkiang plains. It crosses the Ak Tagh ("White Ridge"), a spur of the Kunlun range that separates the upper Yarkand and Qara Qash valleys.

SUTLEJ RIVER—The easternmost of the "five rivers" of the Punjab.

SWAT—A former kingdom with an ancient past, in the valley of the Swat River, in the mountain area of Pakistan north and somewhat east of Peshawar.

TACHIENLU (TATSIENLU)—Modern Kangting. Capital of Sikang province, from which runs the major route west to Tibet, via Litang, Batang, and Chamdo.

TANG (THANG OR T'ANG)—The Tibetan word for "plain."

TANKSE (TANKTSE)—A village east of Leh from which several routes diverge into the Tibetan Chang Tang.

TASHIGONG—Site of a fort on the Indus, on the Tibetan side of the Ladakh border, on the Leh-Lhasa trade route.

TASHILHUNPO MONASTERY—Seat of the Panchen Lama, close to Shigatse, Tibet's second city.

THALDAT (TALDAT)—A halting place in the Aksai Chin marked by a spring.

TIRTHAPURI—*See* Map of the Dogra war.

TOLING (TOTLING, TULING)—A village on the Sutlej, site of Toling Monastery and the famed royal temple of Guge.

TSANG—That province of Tibet in which Shigatse is situated. Its size has recently been enlarged by the Chinese Communists at the expense of U province.

TSANGPO—The "great river" of Tibet. It rises in the Kailash range, flows east through southern Tibet, turns the Himalaya in a great bend around Namche Barwa, and flows southwest into the Bay of Bengal. Known in India as the Brahmaputra.

TSAPARANG (MODERN CHABRANG)—Once the cultural center of southwestern Tibet and the capital of the kingdom of Guge. It was destroyed in the seventeenth century and its ruins not identified until 1912. A Christian mission was established in Tsaparang in 1626, and Jesuit missionaries made regular visits to it from Agra, crossing the Himalaya by way of the Mana Pass.

TSO—A Tibetan word for "lake."

"TSUNGLING" RANGE—The "onion" range, variously identified by the Chinese Communist negotiators with the Karakoram or the Kunlun range. Older Chinese maps make it clear that the identification with the Karakoram range is untenable.

U PROVINCE (TIBETAN: DBUS; CHINESE: WEI)—That province of Tibet in which Lhasa is situated. Once large, it has been considerably reduced in size by the Chinese Communists.

ULTERIOR TIBET—The terms applying to Tibet in Chinese sources vary considerably with the period and the political relationship between China and Tibet. *See* note, p. 157.

URUMCHI (TIHWA)—Capital of Sinkiang, chief trade center of the Dsungaria region. The projected rail route between western China and Russia is known to have reached at least to Urumchi.

WEI—*See* U Province, and note, p. 157.

WU-JE—*See* Barahoti.

YANGI—A Turki word meaning "new."

YANGI PASS (YANGI DAWAN)—*Yangi Dawan* simply means "new pass" and the maps show several passes so named. One connects the upper Yarkand valley with the Tiznaf, on the preferred winter caravan route from Karghalik to Leh. Another is further east, permitting access from Khotan to the Aksai Chin and Lingzi Tang.

YARKAND (CHINESE: SO-CH'E)—Oasis and trade center on the great south caravan route (now a motor road) in southwest Sinkiang. Situated on the Yarkand River at the edge of the Takla Makan desert. Altitude, 3,900 ft.

YARKAND RIVER—The Yarkand and its tributaries drain the western portion of the Tarim basin. It rises from the same great glaciers from which tributaries of the Indus drain in the opposite direction. These two great river systems also share an almost imperceptible water parting at the rim of the Chip Chap valley, at a point somewhat northwest of the Karakoram Pass.

The upper Yarkand (once better known as the Raskam) flows first in a generally northwest direction, confined between the Aghil Mountains on the south and the Kunlun's western spurs on the north. Finally turning the Kunlun range, and augmented by various tributaries (among which the Shaksgam should be mentioned), it flows northeast through the plains of Sinkiang to Yarkand. It eventually joins with the Khotan to form the Tarim, which has given its name to the entire basin.

YARUNGKASH BASIN—East of the Qara Qash valley. The Yarungkash and Qara Qash rivers eventually join to form the Khotan.

YATUNG—Trade mart in southern Tibet in the Chumbi valley.

YUTIEN—The Chinese name for Keria.

YEHCHENG (YEH-CH'ENG)—The starting point of the Chinese road built in 1956–57 connecting Sinkiang with Tibet via the Aksai Chin. *See* Karghalik.

ZANSKAR—Occupies the Zanskar basin. The Zanskar River is the principal tributary on the left bank of the Indus.

ZAN ZUN—This Tibetan name appears to refer either to Guge or to a subdivision of it.

ZOJI PASS—Elevation, 11,570 ft. An important pass leading north from the Kashmir Valley, where the great Central Asian trade route to Leh and points north and east can be said to begin. The only Himalayan pass in the area, it also gives access to routes leading northwest to Skardu and Gilgit.

# INDEX